MIXED BLESSINGS FROM A CAMBRIDGE UNION

Elizabeth Nneka Anionwu

To Veta
Best wishes,
Elyabett N. A

Published by ELIZAN Publishing September 2016

www.elizabethanionwu.co.uk

British Library Cataloguing in Publication Data. A catalogue record for this book is available from the British Library.

ISBN: 978-0-9955268-0-8 (Paperback edition)
ISBN: 978-0-9955268-1-5 (E-book edition)

Edited by Catherine Gough, Fine Words Ltd

Cover design: www.emmagraves.co.uk

Typography: James Davis
Proofreader: Jacqueline Dias

This book is dedicated with love to my late mother and father, my daughter Azuka and granddaughter Rhianne.

About the Author

Elizabeth Nneka Anionwu
(David Gee *Nursing Standard*)

Elizabeth Nneka Anionwu CBE FRCN is an Emeritus Professor
of Nursing at the University of West London. She qualified as a
nurse, health visitor and community nurse tutor and has a PhD
in Health Education.

For more information please visit her website:
www.elizabethanionwu.co.uk

You can also follow her on Twitter via: @EAnionwu

Contents

Foreword

by Malorie Blackman OBE
– writer and past Children's Laureate

I have been lucky enough to know Elizabeth Anionwu for a number of years. From the moment I met her, her intelligence, compassion and warmth shone forth. I know her as a patron of the Sickle Cell Society, an eminent nurse and professor, and when she was vice-chair of the Mary Seacole Memorial Statue Appeal. I have long admired her and her achievements, so I was more than happy to read her memoirs, which provide a fascinating insight into her life and her dual heritage of Irish and Nigerian ancestry.

Elizabeth's memoirs explore her early years, from her time spent in children's homes, to living with her mother and then with her grandparents, and thereafter her life as an independent young woman. We are provided with an interesting insight into the social conventions and mores of the time when Elizabeth's mother was pregnant with her – the late 1940s – and the reactions of family and the church once Elizabeth, who is mixed-race, was born.

Throughout the memoir, Elizabeth's mother's love and determination are clearly evident. And Elizabeth's first meeting and subsequent relationship with her Nigerian barrister father make for riveting reading.

Elizabeth's memoirs illustrate her long and illustrious life, including her discovery and further research into the life of Mary Seacole, and her own efforts to improve the knowledge and treatment of Sickle Cell Disorder and Thalassaemia.

There are very many gems in Elizabeth's reminiscences, including her comment to His Royal Highness Prince Charles during her Investiture at Buckingham Palace where she received her CBE.

Mixed Blessings is interwoven with Elizabeth's usual humour and insightfulness and I very much enjoyed reading it.

Prologue

Letter from my mother, 18th April 1994.

My parents' reaction to the news of my pregnancy was sheer horror. They insisted that it must be kept secret, and I was virtually a prisoner in the house until I could be sent to a home for unmarried mothers, run by nuns in Birmingham. The official story was that I had had a nervous breakdown, and gone to stay with relatives in Ireland to recuperate.

In the spring of 1947 my mother Mary Furlong was twenty, single, and a student in her second year at Cambridge University. Her devout Catholic family lived in Stafford, where she had attended local convent schools before winning a scholarship to study Classics at Newnham College. It was on a visit home in the Lent term that my grandmother discovered her brilliant daughter was pregnant.

My aunt Pat describes how it happened:

Mum was making Mary a summer skirt, and when she went to try it on her it didn't fit around the waist. So mum asked her was she pregnant, and she said yes she was. Mum said when were you going to tell me about it, and she said that she wasn't. She was going to go and jump off a bridge.

This heartrending account sums up the desperation and shame that my mother must have felt. Everything had been going so incredibly well for her up until now. She was the first in her family to go to university. While at Cambridge she won the Goodhart Memorial Prize for Classics in 1945 and the Eleanor Purdie Prize for Greek in 1946, and she had gained a First in her Classics prelim exams. The Newnham College authorities later informed my grandfather that Mary had a very promising career ahead and was expected to obtain a First in Part 1 of her Tripos. Records I obtained from the college in 2013 noted that she was there for less than two academic years – 1945 until the Lent term of 1947 – and that she left due to illness.

- o – 0 – o -

The initial details my mother revealed about my father were simply that he was a fellow student at Cambridge. It was only after my birth that my grandparents saw I was brown-skinned. Their sense of stigma intensified, as did their fears for the future, as they now felt unable to look after me as their own child.

I am convinced that they would be pleasantly surprised at how my life turned out. Aged twenty-four, I found my father, and the missing piece of my identity. Over forty years later and in my retirement, I can reflect on having fulfilled my childhood dream of becoming a nurse.

I have experienced many upheavals, including being in care until the age of nine, physical abuse by my stepfather and having to leave school at sixteen. There has been immense pride, however, such as being at the forefront of successful campaigns 'from Sickle to Seacole'. In particular, setting up the first nurse-led centre in the UK to support families with sickle cell conditions and being Vice-Chairperson of the charity that raised the funds for Mary Seacole's Memorial Statue. I have also obtained a PhD, become a Professor of Nursing and been awarded a Fellowship of the Royal College of Nursing. In addition, I am a Commander of the British Empire. What an irony! 'Cool, Black & Exceptional' is how a friend wonderfully defined my CBE.

My grandparents were correct though in realising the negative impact that my arrival would have on my mother's future academic plans. On the brighter side, she was dearly loved by all five of her children, and she was happy that I came to know and love my father. Mixed blessings indeed!

FURLONG FAMILY TREE

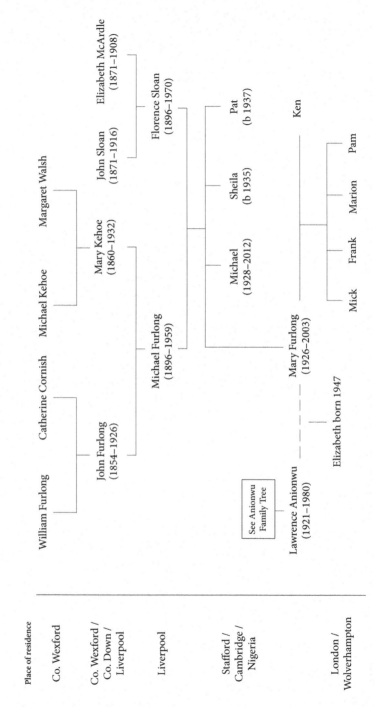

Place of residence

Co. Wexford

Co. Wexford /
Co. Down /
Liverpool

Liverpool

Stafford /
Cambridge /
Nigeria

London /
Wolverhampton

ANIONWU FAMILY TREE

Place of residence: Onitsha, Nigeria

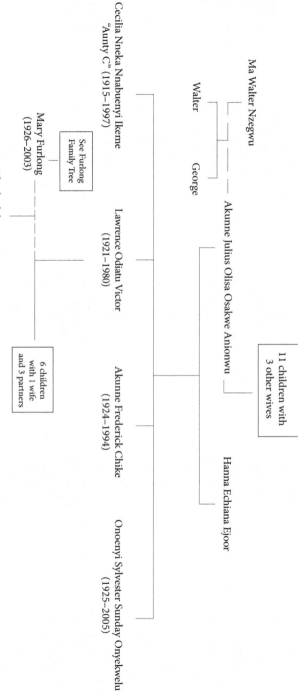

NEWNHAM COLLEGE TO
NAZARETH HOUSE

The Furlong family

What the f*** is a furlong?

*– one of the 'Unlikely things for a sports commentator to say',
according to comedian Rob Beckett on* Mock the Week, *BBC
Two, 1 October 2015.*[1]

Starting out in life as Elizabeth Mary Furlong, the origin of
my surname was for many years a mystery to me. It was
only in adolescence that I discovered it was my mother's maiden
name. All I knew until then was that a furlong is a measure of
one eighth of a mile. As a youngster I was thrilled to hear it
mentioned on the radio. It was the day of the Grand National
and the horseracing commentator excitedly screamed out something along the lines of: 'With just two furlongs to go, it's still
neck and neck!'

My mother was the first child of Michael Furlong and Florence
(née Sloan). Named Mary, she was born on 10th October 1926
at home in Lindsay Road, in the Walton district of Liverpool. As
her grandmother and aunt were also called Mary she was given
the pet name of Maureen, Gaelic for 'Little Mary'. There followed
a brother and two sisters born between 1928 and 1937. Uncle

Michael became a sea captain in the Merchant Navy, Aunt Sheila a nun and Aunt Pat an auditor.

Over the years I gradually learnt more about my maternal family history from my mother, Aunt Pat and cousin Anne (Uncle Michael's daughter). Anne had received a fascinating letter about the Furlong genealogy from our Great-Aunt Kate. Born in 1889, Kate was our grandfather's older sister. The letter revealed details going back to my Irish great-great grandparents and enabled professional genealogists to unearth my maternal family roots within the Irish diaspora. Starting out in County Wexford and County Down, my ancestors migrated from there to Liverpool as well as to Boston in the USA. It brought to mind the television series *Who do you think you are?*

My mother and her siblings were the second generation to be born in England. Their parents' birthplace was Liverpool in 1896 – my grandfather on 12th August and grandmother on 15th December. According to my mother they both grew up in the Irish Catholic dockland community, then jokingly referred to as the capital of Ireland. Both sets of her grandparents had emigrated from Ireland to Liverpool in the second half of the 19th century.

My great-grandfather John Furlong (1854–1926) came over from Wexford on the south-eastern coast of Ireland. The following account from the *Chronicles of Wexford*[2] sets out the origins of the Furlongs:

From the Report of the Commissioners appointed to inquire into the Forfeited Estates in Ireland in 1699, we learn that at that time alone there were 55,882 acres of land in this county confiscated. Bearing this in mind, is it not wonderful to find at the present day, that the descendants of the first Invaders are still located in the places of their first settlement — the Furlongs, Waddings, Prendergasts, Hays, Barrys, and Walshes.

John's parents were William Furlong and Catherine Corish, who were married in the parish of Wexford on 2nd September 1840. They had had a total of eight children between October 1841 and March 1863, with John being born on 22nd June 1854. His father and eldest brother Patrick were to drown in a sudden storm while out fishing in Wexford harbour. In addition, two older brothers and a sister appear to have died in childhood, leaving him with just three sisters. As a result, according to Great-Aunt Kate, 'John Furlong was an only boy in a house full of girls … The womenkind would not let John go near the harbour after that so he used to play truant from school to go to the boats and eventually, in his teens, he ran away to sea and made Liverpool his base.'

The first evidence of John's presence in Liverpool is found in the April 1881 census. He was living in Doncaster Street as a boarder with a family from Ireland named Corish (presumably relatives), and working as a fireman at sea, stoking the coal-fired furnaces on steamers.

It was in Liverpool that John Furlong would meet his wife Mary Kehoe (1860–1932) who hailed from Springwood, Wexford County. Her father, Michael Kehoe, was known as a hedge schoolmaster – that is, he gathered rural Catholic children together and taught them in out-of-the-way places, such as quiet roadsides or rooms in houses. One of the main characters in Brian Friel's play *Translations* is such a teacher. As this practice was illegal, there was always someone on the lookout to raise the alarm. According to Great-Aunt Kate, if he had been caught he could have been imprisoned, executed or transported – so he hid his teaching books on a shelf up the wide chimney. His Latin Primer book had been passed down to her, but 'it was browned and dried up and fell apart'. As hedge schoolmasters had no wages, only gifts, 'Michael Kehoe went into Wexford town and did the books for the English quarry owners to get money and did odd jobs at the Big House. His wife acted as sewing maid at

the same big house doing all the fine tucking on the men's shirts. Many a tale we were told of that life in Ireland.' The 'Big House' was in the townland of Tullycanna in the civil parish of Ambrosetown.

Mary Kehoe was born in about 1860 and was the youngest child. She probably moved to Liverpool between 1871 and 1875, living with her family in Latimer Street. The 1881 English census, taken six months before her marriage, shows her at O'Donovan's Terrace, Hook Street with her mother Margaret (née Welch) and elder siblings Annie (Anastasia) and Andrew. The latter two settled in Boston, USA, where sadly both were to die at an early age.

Great-Aunt Kate noted that Mary took up domestic work and 'had a great desire to have all her children properly educated'. Kate became an elementary school teacher, having studied at Liverpool's Notre Dame Training College. In the 1911 Census she is listed as Catherine Furlong, a student aged 21 years and living at Mount Pleasant, Liverpool. Political activism also ran in her veins as she was a member of the local Cumann na mBan (The Irishwomen's Council) and was once detained under DORA (1914 Defence of the Realm Act). According to the story handed down, she had stood on a crate inciting Liverpool dockers not to load arms destined for use in Ireland by the British against Irish nationalists. The teachers' union came to her rescue and charges were dropped.

My great grandparents were married in Liverpool's Saint Sylvester's Temporary Roman Catholic Church on 30th October 1881. The marriage certificate records John's occupation as a fireman (three decades later, the 1911 Census describes him as a 'Marine Fireman with a Steam Ship Company'). The couple rented a house in Lambeth Road in Kirkdale and had nine children, two of whom died in infancy. The youngest of the remaining seven was my grandfather Michael Furlong, born in 1896. I have a wonderful family photo taken when he was about 14 years old, very smartly dressed, kneeling in front of his parents and some of

his siblings. My mother recalled that Mary 'lived long enough to rear her children to adult years, and I remember seeing her once when I must have been very young – an upright, stern faced old lady in ankle length black clothes, who filled me with great awe'.

According to Pat, my grandfather was one of the first scholarship boys to attend the fee paying Catholic Institute (now St Edward's College) then located in Hope Street, Liverpool. Members of the Furlong and Kehoe families also lived at times in Fountains Road and Lamb Street. Michael Hill, author of *Liverpool's Irish Connection* described the area as populated by working class, mainly Irish Catholics with St John's Catholic Church as the centre of the community. My mother wrote of her father:

> *When the First World War broke out he enlisted in an Irish regiment, the Connaught Rangers, and spent the war years in the Middle East. We used to have a photograph on our living room wall that showed him seated on a camel beside the Sphinx, but he had a poor opinion of camels, and was unimpressed by the glories of the Orient … His regiment had a reputation for marksmanship and, inspired by this tradition, he became a crack shot. He regretted this later, when it led to his being selected for a firing squad, which had to execute cowards and deserters. On his return home after the war, he took a Civil Service examination which qualified him to enter the Customs & Excise. He then married my mother (Florence Sloan) who had been working as a bookkeeper.*

The Sloan family hailed from the Warrenpoint area of County Down, Ireland, which became part of Northern Ireland after partition of the country in 1920. My maternal great-grandfather was John Sloan (1871–1916) and his father (also named John) was a farmer. At the age of 21 he married Elizabeth McArdle

(1871–1908) on 19th October 1892 at the Roman Catholic Chapel of Warrenpoint. The marriage certificate recorded his occupation as a sailor and that he was residing in Moygannon, near Warrenpoint. Lizzie (as his wife was known) had been living in Warrenpoint, and her father Patrick McArdle's profession was listed as 'smith', which ties in with the family tradition that he was a farrier.

The 1911 England census records John and his children living in Flinders Street in the Kirkdale district of Liverpool and that he had had eleven children, of whom four had died. The two eldest, Elizabeth (Lily) and Mary Catherine, were born in County Down, but the next child – my grandmother Florence – was born in Liverpool on 15th December 1896. She was baptised at St Alphonsus Church the next day, as her mother was gravely ill. These dates point to the Sloan family arriving from Ireland sometime during an 18-month period from mid-1895 to late 1896, settling initially in Lemon Street. John Sloan worked as a Liverpool docks gateman, and I have a photo of him proudly wearing his uniform. Sadly, Lizzie died in childbirth at home in Flinders Street on 24th April 1908, aged just 37 years.

Another major tragedy would strike the family during the First World War. By now they had moved to Great Mersey Street and in 1916 John, aged 45 and accompanied by his eldest daughter Lily, travelled to Ireland following the death of his brother Peter. During the return sea crossing on 3rd November they drowned in a collision that caused the loss of 94 people. Their steamer *Connemara* had just left Greenore in Ireland heading for Holyhead. There was a severe gale and it crashed into the coal-carrying ship *SS Retriever*, both had dimmed lights for fear of U-boats:

> *One of the passengers on the 'Connemara', John Sloan from Rostrevor was returning with his young daughter to Liverpool, having been home for his brother's funeral.*[3]

8

My mother recalled in a letter to me that 'some of my mother's family were lost at sea while they were still young. The second sister took over the bringing up of the family, with help from relatives in Ireland.'

- o – 0 – o -

My Aunt Pat informed me that due to Lizzie's ill health, my grandmother Florence was sent to live with relatives in Rostrevor shortly after her birth in 1896. As a result she only saw her family once a year when they came to Ireland on holiday. However, she returned to Liverpool at the age of five to start school. Pat feels it must have been quite a shock to go from rural Ireland to living off the busy Scotland Road. According to Michael Hill, during this period the area was occupied predominantly by refugees from the 1840s potato famine, joined by smaller numbers of Italians in the 1890s, some of whom married into the Irish community.

There is a humorous story about my grandfather when he was an altar boy. One Sunday afternoon he failed to return home immediately after performing his duties at the Benediction. His mother went out looking for him and was incensed to find him in an Italian ice cream parlour. She hauled him out by the ear, as (apart from attending church services) Sunday was strictly a day of rest! The impact of Catholicism on the Furlong family passed down to the next generation, as a sister and cousin of my mother would become nuns.

My grandparents wed in Liverpool on 3rd September 1924 at St Alphonsus Catholic Church. One witness was granddad's older brother Bill Furlong who was married to my grandmother's older sister, Mary Sloan. There must have been great craic at this reception with so many relatives from both sides of the family!

My mother described how in the early stages of her parents' marriage, her father

was moved from one temporary post to another, and he and my mother travelled about the country, staying in boarding houses. I was born during this period, and travelled about with them. When I was two my father was given a permanent post in Stafford, which was then a sleepy little market town, very English, Conservative and Protestant. I don't think he ever felt much at home there. He was a member of the Fabian Society, the avant-garde of Socialism in those days, an ardent Catholic, and still interested in Irish politics, sympathising with the Republican movement. Religion and politics were frequently talked about in our house, and although I didn't understand much of it, I formed a strong impression that my father was a fish out of water among his colleagues and acquaintances.

My half-sister Marion spoke about the relationship our mother had with her father:

She was very fond of him although he was very strict. I remember her saying that she was mad about learning to read and that she nagged her father. Every time he picked up a book she was asking him what the words meant and so in the end he sat her down and taught her to read, at around the age of three.

Pat backed this up, confirming that my grandfather had recognised my mother was a gifted child and that she was able to read and write on starting primary school. Pat also described the rented house in Stafford where they grew up as a spacious three-storey family home in a leafy cul-de-sac. It had three bedrooms, a couple of attics and a front and back garden. In the latter was an elder-berry and apple tree, and the local youngsters were free to come in and take fruit if they liked. Neighbours living in the adjacent semi-detached houses in this middle class area of Stafford included the owner of two coalmines and a prison parson.

My mother recalled:

Two things stand out in my mind about my mother. Firstly, her devotion to the Catholic faith, the obverse of which was a somewhat bigoted attitude to other denominations. Secondly, her poor health, which seemed to decline as the family increased. We lived in a safe area, and I can't pretend that the tragedies and triumphs of the Second World War made much impression on me. I vividly remember the civilian inconveniences; gas masks, rationing, having to share the school with evacuees, the blackout, and the sudden disappearance of organised amusement for my age group. My father did Home Guard duties in his spare time from work, and suffered a nervous breakdown, but recovered after a period of rest. I stayed on at school to take Higher School Certificate, the equivalent of the later 'A' levels, and then won a scholarship to Newnham College, Cambridge, to read Classics, in the last year of the war.

II

A Cambridge union

Dear Elizabeth

We were first contacted by your maternal grandparents when your mother was pregnant. We understood that your mother Mary Furlong was a student at Cambridge University who had completed two years studying Classics. She had become pregnant and as she was just beginning to show, her parents were keen to have Mary provided with accommodation, so as to conceal the pregnancy. Adoption was mentioned as the plan. At this time, we were advised that your father's name was unknown. It is probable that at this stage Mary's parents assumed he was white.

Letter from the Origins Social Worker at Father Hudson's Care, 14th September 2011

In 2011, at the grand age of 64, I at last decided to do something about what had been at the back of my mind for decades. Initially, I just wanted to find out if there were any photos of me during my nine years in the care of Roman Catholic nuns in

Birmingham. I only had one photo of me, aged about nine months, sitting on my mother's knee and clutching a rattle. There were also many questions about my early life which I now wanted answered.

Previous attempts at seeking information from my mother had gleaned some vital details, contained in two letters in 1972 and 1994 in response to my written questions. There had always been other family members present when I visited her, making it difficult to ask for sensitive material face-to-face. So letters had seemed the easiest way to communicate and this proved correct as she answered both of my letters asking for information, virtually by return of post.

The first was in March 1972 when I asked about my father. I didn't even know his name as I had been given my mother's maiden name as my surname. In 1994 I wrote again, to find out more about her own life. The details obtained were of intense interest, but although the letter provided a few significant facts about my parents, infuriatingly there were many that still remained outstanding. In addition, some of my mother's narrative did not fit in with my lived experiences, or what I had gleaned when living with my maternal grandparents and aunt.

It was only after my mother's death in 2003, and my retirement in 2007, that the time seemed ripe to start investigating my earlier life. The Sisters of Nazareth Archive at Nazareth House in Hammersmith advised that I contact the (then called) Father Hudson's Society in Coleshill, Birmingham where I had been looked after initially as a baby. I was contacted by phone and email by Siobhán, their Origins Social Worker. During the phone call she had informed me that unfortunately there were no photographs. Just as I was feeling disheartened, my spirits were raised when she informed me that there was, however, correspondence about me and invited me to meet her. It was an incredibly emotional encounter and one that was conducted very sensitively. The outcome went far beyond my expectations.

I was amazed to be handed a thick blue dossier bearing my name, which contained 57 documents, mainly correspondence between my grandfather, my mother and the Catholic authorities. Tucked neatly into the inside page of the folder was my original birth certificate – crisp and new. It was in such sharp contrast to the one I possessed, a tatty and torn copy that my mother had given me many years ago when I needed to present one to the hospital prior to commencing nurse training in 1965.

What was revealed in the folder surprised, shocked and pleased me, all at once. The documentation started in April 1947, a few months before my birth in July, and ended in September 1956 when I left Nazareth House convent to live with my mother and stepfather. It was an absolute eye-opener. As somebody interested in history and evidence-based materials it provided me with a goldmine of data. Yet the personal, revealing and poignant nature of it all was at times too overwhelming to take in.

The words that leapt from the pages of this original correspondence were incredibly vivid. They described the emotional impact on a devout Catholic family in the 1940s of the revelation that their gifted daughter was carrying an illegitimate child. The key players who wrote the letters were my maternal grandfather, my mother and Reverend (later Canon) Flint. The latter was Administrator of the Father Hudson's Homes in Coleshill and Secretary of the Birmingham Diocesan Rescue Society – the organisation that placed some of the many young children who were at the (then called) Father Hudson's Homes in Coleshill and older ones at Nazareth House Convent and Children's Home, Birmingham. The first few letters were written when I was still in my mother's womb. This struck me as amazing and it created a very weird sensation that took some time to wear off.

Before going through the dossier with me, the social worker had prepared a letter that summarised its contents. I learnt that my mother briefly went to live with a Birmingham family (where no-one would know her) before a place became available at the Mother and Baby Home; that she was now saying she would like to keep the baby; that she was wavering about going back to Cambridge; that she hoped to get a job to support them both; and that her parents and Reverend Flint were looking at ways to enable her to continue her education <u>and</u> keep her baby.

Letters went back and forth discussing the options, and right up until the summer it looked as if my mother might carry on with her studies after all. Her courage in deciding to keep her baby, whether or not she returned to Cambridge, deserves highlighting – as does the support she received from her parents, despite their misgivings. Illegitimacy was a huge stigma, and right up until the 1970s young women were persuaded (and sometimes forced) to give their babies up for adoption. Jane Robinson's book *In the Family Way* explores these issues in depth, and helps to put my mother's choices and decisions in the context of the time.

But in fact, the dramas were only just about to begin. According to my Aunt Pat the following plans were afoot:

Mum told me the idea was that Mary would have the baby in Birmingham and then Mum would adopt or bring him or her home and say it was hers. But Mary did not tell mum and dad that you were going to be a half-caste.

The letters written by my grandfather to Reverend Flint in the period up to my birth are short and to the point. But behind their formality is a sense of urgency that reveals the major fears, challenges, stigma and turmoil facing my mother and her family. Should she have me adopted? Should she return to Cambridge? Their correspondence also sheds light on the administrative details, hurdles and delays encountered in finding a nursery cot for me in this post-war era; and illustrates the substantial level of advice and financial support offered by the Catholic authorities to encourage my mother's return to her studies.

Siobhán, the Origins Social Worker, commented that this was not at all typical of the help that was provided at the time to single mothers in a similar position, including those from Ireland. I imagine this had something to do with my grandparents being solid, middle class, devout members of the Catholic Church and with a gifted daughter at Cambridge. If my mother had come from a different background, she might have found things even more difficult.

As it was, everyone involved was feeling the strain, and towards the end of April their anxiety is palpable:

Many thanks for your letter of the 18th inst. stating that you have arranged temporary accommodation for Mary. If it is at all possible I would be extremely obliged if the good people who are to afford Mary accommodation could be in a position to let her stay on the day that she visits them, subject of course to their being fully satisfied in every respect.

Mary is beginning to show and, the distance to the Railway Station being fairly lengthy, we do not want her to come under any possible scrutiny of neighbours that can be avoided. Subject to your ratification I suggest that when Mary travels to Birmingham she takes sufficient clothing with her to enable her to stay with the people offering the accommodation and thus prevent her having to make the second journey. Any further clothing or items that she may require could be sent on later and in the event of the people in Birmingham not wanting to put Mary up, which please God will not occur, I would bring the suitcase back with me.

Letter from my grandfather to Reverend Flint, 22nd April 1947

In fact, all went smoothly and my mother went to live with the Birmingham family for a few weeks until her place at the Mother and Baby Home became available.

Further tensions are revealed however. It became clear that my mother had definitely come to a decision that I would NOT be put up for adoption, and that she was beginning to think about getting a job rather than going back to Cambridge. While her parents were prepared to support her decision to keep her baby, they were less happy in the matter of her education and called upon Reverend Flint to help her see sense:

… Her mother has tried to reason her into accepting the situation as she, her mother sees it, namely that it would be better for her to go back to Cambridge, finish her course, and thus be in a position to obtain a better position and so enable her to provide better still for the baby … If you are in agreement with the idea that it would be better for Mary to return to Cambridge when the first term of next year commences I would esteem it a favour if you would use your influence to get her to see that such a course would in the long run be better for herself and her offspring.

Letter from my grandfather to Reverend Flint, 30th April 1947

Alongside this contentious subject, my mother's ration book took centre stage. It seems that the extra clothing coupons needed for the baby's layette were threatening to bring her pregnancy out into the open:

I have had a letter from Mary in which she told me of her visit and of your kindness and help in the matter of the ration book difficulty. Mrs Furlong has asked me to express

17

her gratitude to you for your help in this matter as it has been a source of great worry to her as it appeared to be an obstacle that we could not overcome and was likely to nullify all the efforts which had been made to keep the matter away from local knowledge.

I am also very much obliged for your talk to Mary on her future and your promised assistance in the matter of the child. We had a very sympathetic letter from the Tutor at Newnham College and one was also written by her to Mary. This letter, coupled with your assistance in the matter will, I feel sure, be sufficient to induce Mary to change her viewpoint and persuade her that her best course is to resume her studies at Cambridge at the commencement of the next year's course.

Letter from my grandfather to Reverend Flint, 14th May 1947

At the end of May, my mother moved in to the Catholic Mother and Baby Home, somewhat earlier than planned. Three weeks later the precious clothing coupons finally arrived, just two weeks before my birth.

Memo

50 Board of Trade clothing coupons sent to Mary Furlong on the 17th June 1947

I was born at Loveday Street Maternity Hospital on 2nd July 1947 and then discharged with my mother back to the Mother and Baby Home where, nine days later, I was baptised in the chapel. My Aunt Pat recalls how my grandparents discovered that I was mixed race:

It was only as they were walking along the corridor after you'd been born that the Irish nun turned and said to them, 'To be sure, the baby's a little dark'. And of course there you were and that put the kibosh on bringing you back home because you would have been the only coloured kid in Stafford basically. There might have been a few more because we did have American troops during the war. And, Mum couldn't possibly have said you were hers. Anyhow, the Parish priest said the gossip would be so bad, you know, and that it would have a very bad effect on the family.

It would take a further two months before my mother would reveal the name of my father to the nuns.

The next shock for my poor grandmother was that my mother wanted to call me Artemis, after the Greek goddess of the hunt, the Roman equivalent being Diana. This was firmly vetoed by her – what an almighty row must have taken place. They were both obstinate and determined women and I can imagine my grandmother saying something along the lines of 'Over my dead body!' Instead I was baptised Elizabeth Mary Furlong, having been born on the Catholic Feast Day celebrating the Visitation of the Blessed Virgin Mary to her cousin Elizabeth.

My mother had still not given any details to anyone about my father. They knew he wasn't white, that was for sure. She was also trying to decide whether to return to her studies, the option desired by her family and the Catholic clergy. Then there was the problem of who would look after me, now that my grandparents' plan to pass me off as their own was impossible. They briefly considered pretending that I was a foster child, but that too was considered unworkable. Putting me into care began to look like the best option.

It is therefore not surprising to read how stressful life became for my mother and my grandparents.

... I saw Mary on Sunday last on my visit to Francis Way and she appeared to be in a very low state and I think that she will need a holiday, of a bracing nature, before she will be fit to resume at Newnham. Mrs Furlong is not keeping too grand and will be going for a short holiday at the end of August. In these circumstances I am writing to ask if it is possible for you to say when Mary's child will be accepted into the Home and Mary be permitted to return to Stafford. I understand from Mary that you have a waiting list and I thus appreciate that the situation is difficult, but, if it is possible for an early admittance of Mary's child to be allowed it would facilitate matters greatly for me and would allow Mary to accompany her Mother on holiday and to get herself fit to resume her studies at Cambridge in October. If it will be of any assistance, or if you so desire it, either Mrs Furlong or myself will willingly come over to Coleshill to see you. Hoping that you do not consider this letter presumptuous, and thanking you for all you have done for us to date ...

Letter from my grandfather to Reverend Flint, 5th August 1947

At the end of August 1947, two months after my birth, my mother decided to give the nuns the name of my father: Lawrence Anionwu, aged 24 years, single, a student at Cambridge.

She did not reveal his identity to me until my request to her in 1972, when I was 24 years old myself.

III

Father Hudson's Homes

19th December 1947

> *Mother Dolores*
> *'Francis Way'*
> *Bentley Heath*
> *Knowle*

Dear Mother Dolores

re Baby Furlong

Miss Furlong may arrange to bring her baby to Coleshill on Monday next, 22nd inst. if it is convenient for you to discharge her.

Yours sincerely

Administrator

WF/mf

The news that everybody had been waiting to hear since my birth finally arrived. At the tender age of six months, I was to be separated from my mother and placed in St Teresa's Nursery, part of the Father Hudson's Homes Complex in Coleshill, while my mother went home to her parents in Stafford. I do wonder at the mixed emotions she must have experienced. While the long wait for a residential nursery place was now over, the date of our parting came just three days before what would have been our first Christmas together.

The letter she wrote in 1994 in response to my request for more information reveals something of the turmoil she was going through:

My parents had impressed on me that I could not keep the baby at home, and wanted me to have her adopted. This was against my wishes, and it was a relief to me when the nuns put an end to the argument, telling us categorically that there was no chance of finding adoptive parents for a coloured child. (It must be remembered that this was over 45 years ago, when a half-caste child in provincial England was a rare phenomenon). You were placed for the time being in Father Hudson's Homes, a well-known Catholic orphanage at the time.

I went home to Stafford, as there seemed no immediate alternative. I deferred to my parents' wishes by telling nobody of Elizabeth's existence, but I refused to go back to college. I didn't want to be parted from Elizabeth indefinitely, and the sort of academic career that I had hoped for simply would not have been open to a woman with an illegitimate child. The climate of opinion in such matters was very different in those days from what it is now.

I took a sketchy course at a business college, and got a job in a local office. It paid for my board at home, and the fees at Father Hudson's, but my aim was to find employment which would get me away from home and into a more freethinking atmosphere. Shorthand, which I was good at, seemed to offer a possible stepping stone to work as a journalist, and I went to advanced classes in the evenings.

My mother's decision not to continue with her studies must have come as a bombshell and a deep disappointment to both her family and the Catholic authorities – indeed, Reverend Flint had offered to waive the nursery fees to make it easier for her to return to Cambridge.

An independent, courteous and possibly obstinate character emerges from her letters. Equally clear is her appreciation of the temporary financial assistance from her father and gratitude to Reverend Flint for all his support. My mother wrote this letter one week after she handed me over:

Stafford
30 December 1947

Dear Rev Father

Would you please let me know when it will be convenient for me to come and visit Elizabeth, and what the usual arrangements are about visiting? If there is anything which Elizabeth needs in the way of clothes, perhaps you would send me her clothing coupons, and I will buy the necessary articles, and bring them with me to Coleshill when I come.

I appreciate very much your offer to look after Elizabeth without payment in order to allow me to continue my studies at Cambridge, but after thinking it over carefully I have decided not to return to college. I am hoping to obtain a post shortly, and I shall then be able to pay for the child's maintenance. In the meantime, my father is willing to accept responsibility for payment. Will you please let me know what arrangement in this matter will suit you?

I would like to thank you very much for all that you have done for Elizabeth and for myself. My parents and I are deeply grateful to you.

I remain,

Yours sincerely

Mary Furlong

A few days later she received a response. I was flabbergasted to read that:

… normal visiting days are the first and third Sundays of the month from two to four, but if Sunday travel is difficult for you I could arrange for any afternoon suitable to you if you will kindly let me know.

Letter from Home Administrator, 2nd January 1948

In trying to make sense of these seemingly draconian rules, it helps to remember the historical context. It was only just over two years after the end of the Second World War and a completely different era in respect to childcare practices, and before the advancement of knowledge regarding attachment theories and the impact of loss and separation in early childhood. Nevertheless, the combination of my health visiting experience and being a parent did make my heart skip a beat when I first read this letter.

$$- o - 0 - o -$$

My mother was issued with a pass that enabled her to visit me at the nursery for the first time on Saturday 10th January 1948. She next wishes to visit me on Wednesday 11th February. I am curious to know why a whole month had elapsed, but whatever the reason, my mother's self-reliant spirit shines through:

I am sorry that I have not been able to pay anything towards Elizabeth's maintenance. I have not yet obtained a post, as I am taking a three month's business course in order to qualify for a secretarial position. As you know, my father has offered to take entire responsibility for the child, but I am extremely reluctant to accept this offer. I feel that it is my own responsibility. I think you will understand my feelings on this point.

I would like to thank you very much for all that you have done for Elizabeth. I hope that it will not be long before I can arrange to have her with me and look after her myself, but in the meantime I know she is in the best possible hands.

Letter to Reverend Flint, 2nd February 1948

Her poignant conclusion suggests that the pangs of separation must have affected my mother greatly. After all, she had looked after me from birth to six months of age. It must have been incredibly sad – and more disappointment was to follow:

Dear Miss Furlong

Thank you for your letter received this morning. Unfortunately, I cannot enclose a visiting pass as, due to a recent outbreak of diphtheria, the Doctor has forbidden all visiting for the time being. Elizabeth is very well and I am hoping that we shall get no more than the three cases now in isolation.

Letter from Home Administrator, 5 February 1948

The letter went on to reassure my mother that maintenance fees would be withheld until she started work. She replied by return that she would like to come as soon as visiting recommenced – but astonishingly, nearly two months later, she was writing to Reverend Flint pointing out that she had not heard anything about her request for a pass, or the outcome of the diphtheria outbreak. She asks permission to visit me on Wednesday 31st March. This would make it nearly three months since she had been able to see me.

After this, letters are fewer and further between. There is a request from Reverend Flint to see my mother when she visits me, although the topic for discussion is not revealed. In August 1948 she writes to him announcing that she has commenced work and can now start to pay for my maintenance. Then on 3rd September it is my mother who makes a request to see Reverend Flint. Judging from a letter she writes on 23rd October, I believe the subject of this meeting to have been my father.

$$- o - 0 - o -$$

In the letter, my mother informs Reverend Flint that she will be seeing my father on Saturday 30th and requests a pass for him to accompany her on a visit to see me. That is (she adds), assuming that Reverend Flint will have no objection! I am nearly 16 months old and presume that this will be my father's first sight of me.

23 October 1948

Dear Rev Father

You may remember that, on the occasion of my visit to Coleshill about two months ago, we had some conversation on the subject of Elizabeth's father.

I received a letter from him today, saying that he will be in Birmingham next Saturday, 30th October. I am arranging to meet him on that date, and would like to bring him to see Elizabeth.

We have not yet reached any definite decision about our future plans, as I personally find it impossible to discuss such a question in letters, and I imagine that Laurie has the same difficulty.

I hope, however, that we shall reach some clear understanding when we meet next Saturday. I agree that it would be foolish to continue the acquaintance if it is not to lead to marriage.

However, I trust that you will have no objection to Laurie's coming with me to visit Elizabeth on this occasion.

Yours sincerely

Mary Furlong

In addition to this letter, there is an undated note from Reverend Flint to the nursery revealing my mother's hope of marriage; plans to return to Africa with my father; and that my grandparents are in agreement.

Somewhere in my memory is a recollection of being told that my father had visited me as a baby. But this is the first time I became aware that my parents had planned to marry and return to Nigeria together. This came as a huge (and pleasant) surprise because my mother had given me a very different version of the story in 1994:

> *Shortly after our brief romance he returned to Nigeria ... We exchanged occasional letters, and I learned from one of these, that he had married a lady of his own country.*

Without the correspondence with Reverend Flint, I would never have known that my parents' relationship had been longer and more affectionate than my mother had led me to believe. It must have been such a painful and traumatic period for her that she found it impossible to discuss the details with me.

$$- o - 0 - o -$$

Over two months elapse before my mother's next letter on 11th December enquiring about an illness in the nursery and asking when visiting is likely to be resumed. We spend another Christmas apart, and she asks whether it will be possible to visit me on Boxing Day – but the reply is in the negative for the reasons set out below.

13 December 1948

Dear Miss Furlong

Thank you for your letter received this morning. Elizabeth is quite well though we have had further cases of whooping cough among the young babies who were in more immediate contact with the original cases.

I am hoping that it will not spread to Elizabeth's side of the nursery and of course we are taking every precaution.

As we do not know yet the full extent of our troubles I am afraid I cannot give a definite date as to when visiting will be resumed but I am certain that we shall not be able to start visits again by Boxing Day.

With all best wishes.

Yours sincerely

Administrator

WF/mf

The outbreak of whooping cough was to linger on for several months. My mother is informed in February 1949 that I have caught it, and seemingly badly enough to warrant being able to visit me without restrictions:

I am sorry to have to inform you that Elizabeth has contracted the whooping cough and is having rather severe spasms. If you would like to visit her you may come at any time.

Letter from Home Administrator, 2nd February 1949

Further visits are recorded in April and May.
In July, my mother writes to (now) Canon Flint about the idea

of me coming to live with her and her parents. The pressure on cots must be immense, as he jumps at the suggestion, and hopes that my mother will collect me when she visits the following Sunday.

A month later there has been a complete change of plan. Hopes of taking me home were dashed when a planned move from Stafford to a completely new area failed to materialise. My mother spells out the continuing fears and stigma surrounding the risk of neighbours in Stafford discovering that she has had an illegitimate child. Even my aunts were still unaware of the existence of their two-year-old niece. The colour of my skin, together with my mother's eventual plans to join my father in Nigeria meant that I could not be passed off as a foster child. What a dreadful nightmare this all must have been for my mother.

4 August 1949

Dear Canon Flint

I think you will by this time have received a letter from our parish priest, Father Cregg. My mother has had a talk with him about the question of bringing Elizabeth to live with us, and he was very definitely against the idea, and promised to write to you to explain his point of view.

Unfortunately, I was unable to see either you or Father Murphy during my last visit to Coleshill, and so could not explain the position fully as I would have wished.

When I mentioned to you, some months ago, my intention of removing Elizabeth from the Home in the comparatively near future, I was under the impression that my father would be leaving Stafford, and that we could take her with us to a strange town where her appearance would cause less comment. This has not materialised, however, and it now seems that my family will be staying in Stafford indefinitely.

My mother thought that we might nevertheless bring Elizabeth here, and give people to understand that she was being looked after temporarily as a foster child, in response to the appeal for foster parents which has been read out in church recently. Father Cregg thinks, however, that this would be inadvisable, as people would not readily believe such a story.

I should explain that I am definitely engaged to marry Elizabeth's father, who has now returned to his home in Africa, as soon as he is in a better financial position. This may not be for a year or two, or longer and in the meantime I really don't know what to do about Elizabeth.

As you know, only one or two people in Stafford know anything about the child. Even my two sisters know nothing, and my mother is very conscious that they should be kept in ignorance. Father Cregg seems quite convinced that, if Elizabeth comes here, no matter what story we tell, the truth will come out, with very unpleasant consequences for both my parents and my younger sisters. He points out, also, that whatever we say now will have to be contradicted later, when I get married and take Elizabeth away with me.

I would be very glad of your advice in this matter, as I now feel very undecided. I realise that I was a little hasty in writing to you on the subject in the first place, and that I shall be causing inconvenience by changing my mind now. Believe me, I am very sorry about this.

If Elizabeth's place is urgently wanted for another child, I will try to make some other arrangement, but I hope it will be possible for you to keep her for at least a few months longer. I have been thinking lately of trying to get work in some other town, with a view to having her with me, but there are a good many difficulties in the way.

Apologising once again for being such a trouble to you, and thanking you for all you have done for Elizabeth.

I am,

Yours sincerely

Mary Furlong

PS I enclose £3 towards maintenance account. Will you please send me a pass to see Elizabeth on Sunday 14 August.

The powerful status and views of the Catholic clergy are clear. Goodness knows what my mother must have thought about Canon Flint's next piece of advice: to find a foster carer for me, who might be prepared to let her visit regularly. In the event, I stayed at the nursery until January 1951, during which time my mother gave her consent for me to have the diphtheria vaccine; I had bronchitis; and she was able to see me six times between April and December 1950.

$$- o - 0 - o -$$

3rd January, 1951

Dear Miss Furlong

Owing to the great shortage of nursery accommodation I have been obliged to transfer Elizabeth to Nazareth House, Rednal, Birmingham. You can rest assured that she will continue to receive the same care and attention which she received at Coleshill.

Visiting day at Rednal is the second Sunday for each month. I do not issue passes for this nursery.

I enclose directions from Birmingham.

Your maintenance contributions should be sent to me here as usual.

With best wishes.

Yours sincerely

Administrator

WF/mf

So, my stay at Father Hudson's was to end as abruptly as it had begun. I can hardly remember anything about the nursery, except that there was something like a patio at the back of the building where babies and toddlers were left out when the weather was fine. This memory was confirmed in 2011 when Siobhán showed me a photo in a brochure marking the 100th anniversary of Father Hudson's Homes.

I was now three and a half years old and, as far as I know, I had still not spent one Christmas with my mother.

IV

Memories of Nazareth House

*…Then on 3 January 1951 you were transferred to Nazareth
House, Rednal due to a shortage of nursery accommodation at
Coleshill. Mary was advised of this change and given direc-
tions, so she could visit you there.*

Letter from Siobhán, the Origins Social Worker

The years that I spent at Nazareth House in Birmingham (from
the age of three and a half to nine) provide the clearest recollections of my time in care. Even so, as I have always had difficulty
remembering names, it has been impossible for me to recollect
those of the nuns who cared for me during this period.

There are, though, many memories that stand out clearly from
my time at the convent. The first are the regular visits from my
mother when she would usually take me on outings that included
walks in the park, going to a café and having ice cream treats. One
image of her has stayed with me and I still cannot understand
why it fascinated me so much. It was a freezing day and she was
sneezing a lot and using a handkerchief. For one moment though,

a drip just hung from the tip of her nose and I just wondered how long it would stay there. Other recollections of her are of an incredibly well dressed woman and of how proud I was of my very pretty mother.

The visits would usually happen on a Sunday and I would wait for her arrival in the large recreation hall. This would be alongside a few other children who were not 'up for adoption'. I was conscious that this meant we were different from the other larger group of children who were playing at the other end of the hall. They would be the focus of attention of adults who trooped in. I later realised that the purpose of these visits was to look at them to see if they were suitable for adoption. During this era some of these children would be sent to various Commonwealth countries and there would be many heartrending accounts of the bitter experiences that they would encounter.

Many decades on, my then 11-year-old daughter became quite angry when I would not let her see the 1992 television programme *The Leaving of Liverpool*. Much later she understood why, after watching the emotional sections depicting the impact of the migration scheme on over 100,000 children sent to Australia, New Zealand, Canada and South Africa – some from Nazareth House convents, including the one at Rednal. Ironically, as an actress she was later to work with Christine Tremarco who had played one of the children, Lily.

The convent was situated on the Bristol Road in Birmingham, very close to the Lickey Hills. I have very fond memories of walking in a crocodile with other children in order to play in this green and leafy area. A particularly happy recollection is the fun of rolling down the steep grassy slopes. Opposite the convent was the very large Longbridge Austin car works factory. A 1928 photo capturing an aerial view of Nazareth House and the Longbridge motor works can be seen online, courtesy of English Heritage.[4] I remember looking out of the windows of the convent and hearing the workers, who were on something called a strike, singing lustily 'Keep right on to the end of the road' – which I only recently discovered is the anthem of Birmingham City Football Club. When I asked a nun for more details of what a strike was, none were forthcoming.

The Bournville Cadburys chocolate factory was not too far away and how pleased I was about that! The staff of the factory would regularly come to the convent to show us films such as *Laurel and Hardy*, which I really adored. The icing on the cake was that they would also bring along chocolate for us. My favourite was the very small bar wrapped in purple paper, and today the memory of opening and eating them reminds me of Roald Dahl's book *Charlie and the Chocolate Factory*.

Another film that I remember us all watching, this time on television and in black and white, was in June 1953 when we were all made to watch the whole of the Coronation of Queen Elizabeth II. I would have been nearly six years of age and all I can recall is seeing lots of ladies walking around wearing white gowns. Also, the Queen looking very tiny to have such a large crown on her head and that the programme went on, and on, and on. Around the same time, there was great rejoicing at the news that the New Zealander Edmund Hillary and the Nepalese Sherpa Tenzing Norgay had conquered Mount Everest on 29th May.

I clearly remember not being able to start school with the other children. I may have been one of the youngest in the convent at that time – the records from Father Hudson's Homes show that due to their shortage of cots, I was transferred to Nazareth House very suddenly, at a younger age than I should have been. The nuns must have become very irritated with my constant nagging to be allowed to start school. I was really envious of seeing the other children troop into their classrooms. While waiting for this special day to arrive, one of the nuns must have taken pity on me as she took it upon herself to teach me to tell the time. She took me into a corridor where there was a very large clock on the wall. I was absolutely delighted the day that I managed to understand the difference between the fingers pointing to the hours, minutes and seconds and correctly tell her the time.

I was thrilled at last to be told that I could indeed start school even though, it was impressed upon me, I was not yet old enough. The teacher was surprised to find that I could already read a bit – this was because one of my older friends realised that I loved to look at comics such as the *Beano*, and used to help me to work out what some of the words meant.

One teacher was impressed at how well ahead I was for my age in completing the regular spelling assessments. Then one year I repeatedly stumbled at the word 'knowledge', even though correctly spelling many of the subsequent words. It was a salutary lesson for me!

I recall that we used to be outside a lot and in all weathers. Favourite activities included races, skipping games, hopscotch (my favourite), leapfrog, tag, conkers and marbles. Making daisy chains was another regular pastime as was twirling buttercups under chins to see if friends wet the bed. I loved the countryside and while scared of bulls, remember observing that rhubarb seemed to grow out of cow manure.

It is a pity that the few photos I had of my time there have all been lost due to my various moves between the ages of 9 and 18. One was as a toddler riding a tricycle in the large recreation hall.

One of the nuns used to give piano lessons to me and a few other children, and when we had played particularly well she would take us into Birmingham city centre for the wonderful treat of a Knickerbocker Glory. These were sumptuous ice creams in what appeared to a small child to be very tall glasses, and eaten using a very long spoon. I always felt immense regret about never having further piano lessons after leaving the convent, but I have never forgotten some of the tunes the nun taught me, particularly Irish jigs, and today I still play them by ear.

The Irish influence of the Catholic nuns also came out in force when they taught Irish dancing to some of the children, including myself. I absolutely adored it and was over the moon when I was chosen to take part in competitions throughout the region, including Stoke on Trent. The excitement of wearing the green sparkly costumes and buckle shoes will always remain with me, together with the fast-paced and rhythmic music. To cap it all, I regularly won medals and was clearly the centre of attention as it must have been an unusual sight to see a young brown skinned girl in an Irish dance troupe. Maybe this is why I now love the Jamaican song *Brown Girl in the Ring*! Quite often adults, mainly men, would press money into my hand, including half-crowns. To my horror, they were always taken from me by the nuns and I would never see the coins again! At times I thought life was quite unfair and often wondered what happened to the money.

Pleasant memories include regular holidays, when we would swap our accommodation with children from a different convent. My ideal trip was the one to Nazareth House in Crosby, near Liverpool, as it was very close to the seaside. We would travel by coach and although I would often suffer from travel sickness, this was soon forgotten when I saw the sea! The sight of the blue water would never fail to thrill me, and still does to this day. Another trip that has always remained with me was when we went to Evesham in Worcestershire, and glimpsed fruit orchards for the very first time – I particularly remember the apple trees. It may have been on this visit that we were taken to see the shrine to Our Lady of Evesham, and I met a monk and was chastised by one of the nuns for daring to ask what he wore under his brown habit. It wasn't the first time I had made such a mistake – I also got into hot water for asking whether nuns had any hair under their veils, or were they bald?

A sadder memory is the first time I experienced the death of a child and the vague recollection that she had succumbed to leukaemia. We all lined the path as the car carrying the girl's coffin drove out of the convent grounds, and I remember feeling incredibly sad and scared.

- o – 0 – o -

It is not surprising that religion played a very important part in my life at Nazareth House and I have vivid memories relating to the rituals and events that were part and parcel of a Catholic upbringing. Preparation for my first confession caused me confusion and anxiety as I was about seven years old at the time and had to tell the priest what sins I had committed. It didn't help that I didn't really understand what a sin was and that I felt under immense pressure to come up with a good one. The best that I could admit to was stealing somebody's comic. This wasn't very successful as the priest gently pointed out that the comics belonged to all the children. Undeterred, I ploughed on, fabricating a story that I had fought with the child in order to read it. Satisfied with that, the priest gave me however many Hail Marys he thought necessary for my penance and I slipped away, chastened and probably feeling very smug.

Looking back, one sin that I never confessed to was joining in with friends to make the life of one older nun a great misery. Our antics always took place at night in the dormitory when, after the lights were switched off, a check would be made to see that we had all settled down to sleep. There was one particular nun whose steps we always recognised as she walked very slowly and with a stick. Shortly after entering the dormitory a kid from the other end would start meowing and the nun would try to hobble down to find the culprit. Of course, the noise stopped before she reached the relevant bed, and another one of us would start yapping like a dog down the other end. We were never caught, but fortunately for the nun she was eventually relieved of these duties and the burden of dealing with such horrid children.

My First Communion was an incredibly happy affair. There was huge excitement in the air and I remember my lovely white dress and shoes, together with the most wonderful white shiny prayer book and new rosary beads. The only blip was when I chewed the host, instead of swallowing it. One of the nuns pointed out to me that I had been eating God. I wasn't very upset, as even at that early age it did not make sense to me that God could be swallowed by all of the children. I loved the taste of the Communion host, so much so that a group of us got into serious trouble by raiding a large box that contained the unblessed hosts. We were caught in the act when found with a fistful of them stuffed in our mouths.

Sunday was the day of the week I most dreaded, as it entailed us having to go mass twice or even three times sometimes. First we would go to the Children's Mass, followed in the afternoon by the Benediction (the latter being the lesser of the two evils). The worst type of Sunday would be if we also had to attend the 11 o'clock mass, as this was usually extremely long and very boring. I took great pleasure in concocting various amusements that would make the time go faster, or at least make it more enjoyable while kneeling, sitting or standing in the pews. Making patterns with my rosary beads was always a favourite pastime as I loved the feel of the shiny, coloured glass beads, and my imagination knew no bounds with the shapes that I could make.

The funniest and scariest game I got my friends to play with me took place when the priest gave out the Holy Communion and the object was to see who could go up last to receive theirs. I usually won, as my trick was to make sure that I was seated at the end of the pew, and wait until the priest thought that the last person had received their host. Then just as he turned back towards the altar, I would start running down the aisle towards him, timing it to perfection. Eventually, the priest complained to one of the nuns and I got a severe telling off. It was worth it though!

One Sunday the thought of attending so many religious services was just too much for me. I decided to hide under my bed while all the other children went off to the Chapel. My name was being called out and I endeavoured not to move and to keep as quiet as possible. Unfortunately, unaware that I was allergic to house dust, I suddenly started to have a violent sneezing attack. I was dragged out and marched off to Mass and received no sympathy (or handkerchief for that matter, for my running eyes and nose). I had no problem about thinking up what sins should be recounted in Confession that week!

The smoke coming out of the incense boat used by the priest in the mass always fascinated me, and the scent for that matter. I was also captivated by the ritual of the priest drinking wine from the gold chalice. Some seemed to gulp it down, while others sipped it sedately. Then they washed and dried it quite fastidiously, and I would ponder why it seemed to take so long.

One event that I always enjoyed taking part in was the Twelve Stations of the Cross during Lent. Even if I was not totally clear about what was going on, there was something about the action involved in going to each one, stopping, lots of praying, and then proceeding to the next one that gave me great satisfaction.

What took place at Christmas each year should easily come to mind, but for whatever reason, that is not the case. There was only one year that stands out. We were all in the large recreation hall, and when our names were called we went up to the nun at the Christmas tree to receive a present. Mine was some sort of doll. It was a huge disappointment and made me cry – which makes me think that our Christmas presents were usually of a much higher standard!

There were also the times when we were allowed to light a brand new white candle, mutter some prayers, and stick it into a holder. The sight of candles in those little red ornate holders always whizzes me back to those convent days!

The nuns played the most important part in my life at the convent, whereas priests were usually seen at the altar or from behind a grille in the confessional box. It was clear though that the nuns treated them like gods, and were often at their beck and call.

While no longer a believer, I have been left with an abiding love of church choral music and I still enjoy watching television programmes such as *Songs of Praise*, much to the amusement of my daughter.

Not surprisingly, I will also watch any documentary about scandals concerning the Catholic Church. They horrify me and make me wonder if any children I would have known at Nazareth House were ever affected.

- o – 0 – o -

Very gradually, it became clear to me that my skin colour was not the same as all the other children's. I didn't want to be different and sometimes felt humiliated by being picked out in a variety of ways. One example was when we were watching a film about starving children in Africa, and being pointed and laughed at by some of the kids in the audience. Another time was when a nun whom I had never viewed as particularly friendly, suddenly became very pally with me. I clearly remember when she crouched down and informed me that a new 'coloured' child was coming to join the convent and that she would make a very nice friend for me. My suspicions were raised and I vividly remember being very sceptical about her being so pleasant to me in this very unusual way.

One day I ended up in the sick bay following my attempts to make my skin lighter than it was in order to look like all the other children. I had washed my face and arms at least ten times with red carbolic soap, and because of my sensitive skin and eczema it had caused a dreadful flare-up. I also used to wear a cardigan even if it was boiling hot outside, all in an effort to hide my skin colour, never appreciating that my brown hands and face were still showing.

Grooming my tight curly dark hair was clearly a problem for the nuns as I was the only black child in their care at this time. They soon gave up trying to use a normal comb, as I would be in floods of tears due to it being so painful. Instead they would take a bunch of my hair and tightly tie a red ribbon around it. While it might have looked pretty, it made my scalp throb so much that as soon as it was possible, I would loosen the wretched bow. But worse was to come when Nitty Nora, the nun who checked for head lice, tried to use a very fine-toothed comb on me with dire and painful effects. Fortunately, unlike many of my friends, I never had an outbreak of nits or lice in my hair so I was soon excused from this horrible, tear-inducing procedure.

One of the clearest and most hurtful memories of the effects of being a black child was when one nun overruled another who had chosen me to play Humpty Dumpty in a show that was being put on. She was of the opinion that Humpty Dumpty could not be black. My sobbing was so considerable that the decision was once more overturned, and I fell off that wall as the best and happiest Humpty Dumpty those nuns ever saw!

- o – 0 – o -

The environment at the convent was generally conducive to good health as we took regular exercise in the grounds as well as our trips to the Lickey Hills. I can't remember much about the food, but certainly don't recollect that it was dreadful. One day I sneaked into the kitchens, and before being chased out, was suitably impressed with what looked like a huge potato-peeling machine going at great speed.

Whether it was a bit odd or not, I always thoroughly looked forward to the daily queuing up for doses of cod liver oil and malt extract. We always had to brush our teeth using Gibbs Dentifrice, a pink paste contained in small tins. The more you rubbed the paste with your toothbrush, the more it frothed up, and I was often cautioned about using too much.

Although I was generally a healthy child, I had some chest problems – diagnosed as asthma when I was eleven – and quite severe bouts of eczema from a very early age. I regularly visited sick bay to see the 'white nun', so called because she wore a white, rather than a black habit. The areas most affected by eczema were my elbow creases, and in those days the treatment consisted of covering the red, itchy and painful skin with coal tar paste, followed by bandaging. Removing the bandages caused me great anxiety as they would be stuck to the dry skin and the procedure could hurt a great deal. I was so impressed with the way the 'white nun' always managed to distract me by using words which (at this tender age) seemed to be very rude, and not what you would expect to hear from such a holy person. One example that stands out was hearing her say the word 'bottom' – it always made me laugh, just at the moment she took the bandages off. It never failed to work! Then came the best part of the procedure, when the new dressing was applied. It was so cool and soothing, making me forget all the previous discomfort. I decided that this was the work I wanted to do when I grew up, and at some point discovered that it was called 'nursing'.

I remember having hot foments applied to my chest when suffering breathlessness and coughing fits. There are also vague memories, just before I had my tonsils out, of being on a trolley and smelling various vapours before being anaesthetised – the promise being kept that I would be able to eat loads of ice cream and jelly afterwards, which made the subsequent sore throat a bit more bearable.

My worst memories are of how the nuns dealt with children like me who wet the bed. The urine-soaked bed sheet would be draped over our heads and we would have to lift our arms out and stand very still. If they should start to drop one iota, we would be smartly rapped with a ruler. I knew even then that this was a very brutal punishment and not something that the Catholic nuns should be doing.

There have been some horrendous accounts from those who have lived in Nazareth House convents.[5] Barry Adams was six years old in December 1959 when he arrived at the same one I had left three years earlier, and in his traumatic 2004 memoirs, *Pater Noster*, he refers to it as 'Nazi House'. Judith Kelly spent the early 1950s in a Nazareth House convent in Essex, and in 2005 published her horrific account in *Rock Me Gently: A memoir of a convent childhood*. She came in for major criticism due to parts of her book being plagiarised, an accusation that she later acknowledged. However, in chapter 8 there is an interesting description of the punishment of a girl called Janet who had wet her bed. She had to remain in the dormitory and, as had happened to me, stand with a wet sheet over her head. I also remembered being told off for wetting a clean pair of knickers, but for some reason this ticking off didn't perturb me very much.

Later on in my life when working as a health visitor, I made sure to keep up-to-date with more humane treatments for bedwetting. I also tried to provide as much support to the child and their carers as possible.

A kinder experience that has always stayed with me concerned the cleaning duties that we were expected to undertake – including sweeping up dust, which made me feel very ill due to my allergy. One nun was insistent that I should carry on despite my discomfort. Fortunately another sister could see my distress and took me to see the Mother Superior, who agreed that I could be excused from this household chore. The alternative one was great fun as dusters were wrapped around my shoes to help me shine newly waxed corridor floors.

Canon Flint, who was so supportive to my mother and grandparents (as evidenced by their correspondence), was involved with the shocking Child Migrant scheme. It has been surprisingly difficult to unearth anything else about him, but some children of my generation were left traumatised and angry by his actions. Raymond Brand had been admitted to Coleshill in May 1948, just five months after my own arrival. He was one of the 'stolen children' shipped out to Australia in the 1950s. His poignant and devastating story is housed in the National Museum of Australia, and can also be accessed online.[6]

On a more positive note, I realise that overall, my experiences at Nazareth House in Rednal were a great deal happier than those set out in some of these harrowing narratives.

$$- o - 0 - o -$$

In August 1953, Mary wrote to advise us she had got married and that her husband would take responsibility for making payments towards your keep. They applied for a council house with a view to being able to have you come live with them. By August 1956 they had moved into one in Low Hill, Wolverhampton. Mary then finished her job on 31 August and on 2 September 1956, had you home from Nazareth House, after arranging for your discharge.

Letter from Siobhán, the Origins Social Worker

My departure from the convent was to be as sudden as my arrival six years earlier. On 14th August 1956 my mother wrote her final letter to Nazareth House:

Dear Canon Flint

As mentioned in my last letter, we have got a house, and my husband and I are both very anxious that Elizabeth should come home as soon as possible.

I shall be leaving my job on August 31st, and by that time Elizabeth's room should be furnished and everything ready for her.

I cannot adequately express my gratitude to you and the sisters for your care of Elizabeth during the past nine years, but as you know, it has always been my wish to have her with me as soon as circumstances permitted.

I hope, therefore, that it will be quite convenient for me to call for her on Sunday, September 2nd.

The clearest memory I have of this momentous day was the journey to Wolverhampton with my mother to start this new life with her and my stepfather. We took a bus from Birmingham and were seated on the lower deck at the back near the stairs to the upper deck. I was absolutely distraught at leaving my friends and the convent – the only home I had ever known – and started to sob uncontrollably. The conductor was clearly concerned and asked my mother why I was so upset. She tried to explain, but I think it must have been extremely embarrassing for her and also quite painful, in view of all the obstacles she had overcome in her efforts to provide a home for me at last. Little did either of us know that over the next twenty months I would be shedding many, many more tears.

Me aged 9 months sitting on Mum's knee in grounds of St Teresa's Nursery, 1948, Father Hudson's Homes, Birmingham

Nazareth House, Rednal, Birmingham. (Father Hudson's Care)

Great-grandparents John Furlong and Mary Kehoe. Granddad kneeling in front of them, aged 14 years (1910)

Great-grandfather John Sloan in Liverpool Docks Gateman uniform (Gran's father)

Aunts Pat, Sheila (nun), Granddad, Great-Aunts Lil and Kate, Gran.
Athlone, Ireland, 1955

Uncle Michael, Ship's captain

Mum as an infant 1927

Mum aged 18 years

Me aged 11 years
in Central Park,
Wallasey

FAMILY LIFE

V

Home to mother

In August 1953, Mary wrote to advise us she had got married and was now Mary Hart (living in Wolverhampton) and that her husband would take responsibility for making payments towards your keep. They applied for a council house with a view to being able to have you come to live with them. By August 1956, Mary had a house in Low Hill, Wolverhampton. She then finished her job on 31 August and on 2 September 1956, had you home from Nazareth House, after arranging for your discharge. So that completes the information we have about your background.

Letter from Siobhán, the Origins Social Worker

In September 1956, eight and a half years since my mother had last looked after me and a couple of months after my ninth birthday, I moved to Wolverhampton to live with her and her husband Ken. My stay here would last for a mere 20 months. By now they had a three year old son Michael, known as Mick. Also living with them was Kenny, nine months younger than me, and who was Ken's son by his first wife (according to my brother Frank, Ken wanted custody partly out of revenge after a bitter divorce).

There would be three more children after the birth of Mick in 1953. Frank was born in 1957, eight months after I moved in. Marion and Pam followed in 1961 and 1962. In spite of all the ups and downs I would always maintain a loving relationship with all four of my siblings.

Ken was originally from Bolton and came from a poor working class family. Born there in the winter of 1925, he had a sister Nellie and two brothers, Jack and Frank, who died quite young. Ken's father John Hart, a mill hand, was a gambler and his mother struggled to make ends meet. My sister Marion recalls Ken telling her:

... his dad had picked up his wages at the end of the week and gambled the lot on a horse, lost it and of course in those days there was no social security. His mum had to feed them and send them to school every day with something to eat and basically neighbours helped each other out. His mother baked bread and that's how she got by.

Ken joined the Royal Air Force and was posted to Gibraltar for two years before being transferred to a base in Stafford. I can recall seeing a photograph of him looking very smart in his air force uniform. Ken met my mother at a Fireman's Ball in the town and he would have cut a dashing figure.

My mother's account to me in 1994 was as follows:

In 1952, I met my present husband. He was in the Air Force and was stationed at a camp in the neighbourhood. We were married in the following year. My marriage caused a rift with my parents which never really healed, although, as will be seen, they were generous enough to help me out later. My husband had divorced his first wife after a brief and disastrous marriage ...

... This meant that the Catholic Church would not recognise his marriage to me, and in my parents' eyes I was proposing to live in sin, cut off from any hope of salvation. I could understand their attitude, knowing what the Catholic doctrine was, but I had had enough of living under a cloud of disapproval and in an atmosphere of secrecy. My husband had been offered a job in Wolverhampton on leaving the Air Force, and we went into lodgings there until we were allotted a council house.

As we had agreed at the time of our engagement, you came to live with us as soon as we had accommodation, as did the son of my husband's first marriage. By that time we had a baby son, and another child was on the way.

Ken had worked as a builder's labourer in Bolton. Marion said that the divorce from his first wife would have been a terrible trauma for him as he had been so besotted with her. My Aunt Pat recalled that when Ken was in the RAF he had visited Mum at their home in Stafford.

They were married at the Wolverhampton Register Office on 8th August 1953 and my grandfather was the only member of her family to attend. As a witness to the ceremony, his signature is included in the register book. Mick was born three months later. As a result of marrying a divorced man, who was also a Protestant, my mother was barred from receiving Holy Communion. However, my brother and sister recall that every Sunday without fail, the family still went to Mass. When Holy Communion was given, everyone got out of his or her pew, row after row after row went up, but Mum had to stay alone in her seat.

When Ken left the RAF he had a number of jobs before settling down to long-distance lorry driving, but his fiery temper meant he was constantly moving from one haulage firm to another.

It was unusual for women to work when they were married, but Mum did. She worked very hard doing office jobs, and always locally. First at ECC (Electric Construction Company) and then at Goodyear, both of which were big factories. It wasn't equal pay in those days, so Mum took home half the amount a man would have earned doing the same job, and had to give half of that to the childminder over the road. Lunch was bread and dripping every day.

It always seemed a terrible shame to me that Mum was unable to use her academic abilities in the way that she must have envisaged. In my younger days I was very angry about this. However, the two years of studying Latin and Greek at Cambridge University made a lasting impression, and she never lost her interest in languages. Pat told me about an amusing and enlightening incident that occurred around the time I had gone into the care of the nuns and Mum had moved back home to Stafford:

I remember when she stopped University and came back home that I used to get her to do my Latin homework because I was no good at it and I would clean her bike in exchange because she wouldn't do it for nothing. She was always reading and she switched off when she read, just like I do, but I remember once being in our sitting room downstairs and she was sitting in the big armchair with her legs curled up underneath her which was where she liked to sit and she was reading a book and I was sitting at the table doing homework. She put her hand round and said something to me which I didn't understand and I didn't understand it because she was asking me in Greek for the Greek dictionary on the sideboard. So, of course I was totally confused. Anyhow she said it in English and I got it for her.

Even as a nine-year-old I can remember Mum listening to radio programmes and occasionally hearing one in a foreign language. This was to become a lifetime habit and she was able to read novels and books in as many as seven or eight languages. When Frank joined the Army and was based in Germany he bought Mum a shortwave radio/cassette player. She'd never had a radio that could pick up so many foreign stations before. Mum loved it and would have it on in the front room when Ken was out at the pub.

Years later Mum told me how pleased she was to be asked to use her linguistic skills at work, but I was furious that it was never appropriately recompensed. She worked in the Traffic Office at Goodyear, although it was quite a menial clerk's job. The managers found out that she could speak German and Italian. So when the foreign drivers came in and they couldn't understand them, they used to call Mum down from the Traffic Office to do the interpreting. Later on Mum discovered that she could have been paid a lot more for this work, but it never happened.

That money would have come in really handy, as poverty was a constant and grinding reality. Things were so tough that the day-to-day shopping had to be put on a tab until Friday, when she received her wages and could settle all the bills.

The way Mum had to budget and penny pinch reflects the low wage she was on, but it also makes me wonder how the expenses of daily living were divided up between her and Ken. My brother Frank felt that Ken kept at least 50% of his wages to spend down at the pub. Mum never drank but as with many of their generation they both smoked heavily. Cigarettes seemed to offer one way of helping her to deal with stress. Once when she was upset over something, my brother Mick, who was a lovely natured little boy and very sensitive, said: 'Mum sit down, read book, have moke (a smoke).'

- o – 0 – o -

Stepping into my new home for the first time I was struck by the fact that there were no photos or flowers on the mantelpiece. Maybe this vision of a typical family abode had come from the children's books that I read avidly in the convent, such as the *Janet and John* series. Whatever the case, I was incredibly disappointed and felt bitterly let down. It was not the most auspicious start to this new phase of my life.

The house was on a council estate in Low Hill and was the first major housing development of its kind in Wolverhampton. By 1927 it consisted of more than 2,000 new council houses and was one of the largest housing estates in Britain at the time. But over the years it acquired an increasingly bad reputation and by the time my family had moved in there was a lot of poverty.

Ours was the second along a terrace of four houses and to get to our back door we had to walk round the side of the neighbour's house and across their back yard. It was small even by today's standards. Downstairs there was a tiny hallway. The living room had a lino floor and was the biggest room, heated by a coal fire. There was no heating anywhere else in the house. The black and white television set stood in the corner of the living room; there was a sofa and Ken's armchair.

A pantry off the living room featured a concrete slab to keep the milk and butter cool. Mum kept everything in there; food, ironing basket, coats and shoes. There was no fridge while I lived there; it wasn't to be acquired until the 1970s. A door next to the pantry led into the kitchen with a cooker and a clothes rack above it. There was a kitchen table and a sink unit under the window. Before she eventually obtained a washing machine, I remember Mum washing the clothes by hand and putting them through a wringer to remove as much water as possible before hanging them on the rack or outside on the washing line.

Off the kitchen was the coalhouse, about the same size as the pantry. The bathroom was also off the kitchen and as well as a bath there was a big green gas boiler with a tap above. We filled it up to heat the water and had to ladle the water into the bath. This was a slow and colossal task, so it is not surprising that having a bath was only a weekly event.

The back door led from the kitchen out to the yard which had a shed where Ken kept his tools and ladders. The back garden was surrounded by hedges and was turfed with a central path. It was always overgrown as neither Mum nor Ken did any gardening as both worked long hours.

The presence of large Alsatian dogs roaming around the neighbourhood seemed to be the order of the day. I was petrified of the constant barking as well as their black bushy eyebrows for some reason. So I was always fearful of going outside the kitchen door, whether to go round the neighbour's house to reach the street or just to get to the outside toilet – speed was essential. The toilet was freezing cold in the winter and there were only squares of newspaper hanging from a nail, instead of toilet paper.

There were three bedrooms, with Mum and Ken having the largest one at the front. The other two, at the back of the house, were very small and I slept in one of them. It could be freezing at times and I absolutely hated being cold, especially as it brought on wheezing attacks.

The street was my playground and people were generally friendly. In good weather I can recall sitting down on the pavement and just watching the world go by. My favourite pastime was going to St Christopher's Penny Bike Park in Fifth Avenue to learn road safety. Everything was kid-sized and roads were laid out with traffic lights and zebra crossings. It was within easy walking distance and a very cheap way to ride a bike. I seem to have spent hours there and it was huge fun.

- o – 0 – o -

In August 1956, a few weeks before my departure from Nazareth House, Canon Flint had communicated with Canon Woulfe, parish priest at Our Lady of Perpetual Succour Roman Catholic Church in Wolverhampton. It was to inform him of my new address and that having been in their care since birth, Elizabeth Furlong was 'being discharged on the 2nd September to her mother and stepfather, Mr and Mrs Hart, and I know you would wish to know of this addition to your parish'.

I was enrolled at St Mary's Roman Catholic Junior School and records show that my first day was Monday 3rd September 1956 – just one day after leaving Nazareth House. Rather surprisingly I have hardly any memories of my time at this school, apart from joining a library and the fact that there was no uniform. Instead, I always wore the same yellow dress, day in and day out. It was such a relief when it was washed at the weekend, so much so that I loved Mondays and Tuesdays as the dress would always feel fresh and clean.

Frank's arrival eight months after I came to Wolverhampton made me extremely happy, as he was such a gorgeous plump and cheerful blue-eyed little boy. One of my responsibilities was to go to the local Infant Welfare Clinic to exchange coupons for tins of National Dried Baby Milk and orange juice in glass bottles. The only other major errand I can vaguely remember involved walking some distance to collect coal.

The house must have been quite cramped with four children and two adults and the pram at the bottom of the stairs. It was enjoyable playing with Frank and looking after him and I developed a special bond with him. Mick was six years younger than me and was a gentle and quiet boy who loved playing football.

I also got on well with Kenny, Ken's son by his first wife, who was only eight months younger than me. At some point he left Wolverhampton but I don't know when or the details, except that he had returned to his own mother when her circumstances improved.

It seemed to me that Mum was mainly washing or cooking in the kitchen. I used to fear lentil soup day as although it was a tasty dish it was cooked in the dreaded pressure cooker. This could explode when the lid blew off and then the soup would splatter all over the kitchen ceiling. So I was always scared on hearing the hissing noise and seeing the black button rising from the top of the pressure cooker lid.

When Mum was in the front room her nose would be in a book, even while the TV was blaring. As I also loved reading there would be times when we were both curled up with a book which Ken would sometimes resent. He loved television and always determined what programme was chosen. Saturday afternoon seemed to be dominated by wrestling on ITV, a sport that I came to hate with a vengeance. It was utterly mindless watching huge men in skimpy outfits throwing each other around the ring and then leaping on top of their opponents with a deadening thud.

There were a few programmes that I enjoyed such as *Sunday Night at the London Palladium*, although the juggling acts left me cold. One of the first songs that I loved was 'He's got the whole world in his hands' and I have a crystal clear memory of watching a youngster performing it on television. Later on I discovered it had been a hit in April 1956 and sung by a teenager called Laurie London.

My asthma had not yet been diagnosed but I was always described as a 'chesty' child. A freezing outdoor toilet and a cold bedroom would not have helped, nor that Mum and Ken were heavy smokers. To add to my woes, pea-souper fogs were still a frequent occurrence in this industrial area of the West Midlands. Frank was also affected:

No wonder you and I had asthma, as it was a smoky place due to the coal fire and Mum and Dad always smoking. There were so many factories in the Low Hill area that had chimneys belching smoke out all the time. There was the Goodyear Tyre factory, which caused a stink around the place, and there was also a smelting furnace works.

The Clean Air Act was passed in 1956 but it would take many years before pollution-triggered fogs became a rare event.

I certainly experienced two severe 'bronchial' episodes. My Aunt Pat first met me on a visit from Stafford when I was quite ill and also hallucinating:

It was in 1956 and I was 19 when I met you for the first time. My Mum told me about you on the train going to see you and you were in bed and so I didn't really have a conversation with you because you were very chesty. I gathered from the conversation that we did have that you thought I was your teacher.

The second episode brought home to me that we were obviously very poor, and was extremely humiliating for my mother. The GP was examining me in the front room and asked my Mum if she had obtained something he had requested for me during his previous visit. While she was trying to explain that there was not enough money to pay for it, he exploded with anger, giving her some money and telling her to go to the chemist immediately. It was a shocking moment and I will never ever forget feeling so ashamed and embarrassed for my mother. This incident would have occurred sometime in 1956 or 1957.

Prescription charges had been introduced for everyone in 1952 at a shilling per prescription, and then in 1956 it was increased to two shillings per item. It would seem there were no exemptions for me as a child.

I am not sure when life started to become miserable for me, and Ken began to treat me differently from his own children. The first example etched in my mind was one hot day when he bought everybody ice creams except me. I sat on the pavement outside and just cried. It appeared that he enjoyed being awkward with me and asking the impossible; it felt that nothing I did would ever be right. Once I was in the kitchen doing the washing up and trying to dry some glasses, without much success as the tea towel was damp. He kept asking me to dry them again and again and when I pointed out the problem with the tea towel, he tore it from my hand and hit me with it.

I started to become scared of him as he began to lash out and slap me for no good reason, often when my Mum wasn't around. He had severe mood swings which were always due to drink. I dreaded his return to the house stinking of beer and smoke and quickly learnt to gauge his state of drunkenness. The least fearful one was when he was slightly tipsy, grinning and telling jokes. In the past, this would have heralded a time of laughter with all the family but later on I would be on guard as his mood could start to change. The darker stage began when he became argumentative and angry and my Mum and I would both be in the firing line.

Frank remembers that Ken:

… could be complimentary or cruel. Once he had had a bit to drink, he would be happy and hug us all. When he had had too much, his character would change and he could be a verbal bully and unpredictable. He was like a firework. The worst times were when he was so broke that he couldn't afford to smoke or go down to the pub to drink. I learnt to fight very quickly and was a bit of a lad, trespassing over the gasworks! Mick was a real gentleman, but his aggression was channelled into his football and athletics.

One day it must have all got too much for Mum as she left the house, pushing Frank in his pram with me and Mick alongside.

We walked and walked to a police station, if my memory serves me right, but I can't remember what happened next. We obviously returned home and it was the only time it happened.

Frank remembers when he was about eight, being very scared one Sunday afternoon and running to a neighbour's house for help. Ken was drunk and had lost his temper with Mum and started dragging her by her hair.

It would appear that Ken could not cope with the taunts at work about my presence in the home. According to Pat:

You were having trouble when Ken was having remarks made to him at work from what I could gather that you were black and what was he letting his wife do and he wasn't the sort of bloke who could take that sort of thing.

Frank told me that Ken used to keep a belt with his overalls on a hook on the coalhouse door and would use it on him, Mick and Kenny. In contrast, Marion remembers him only shouting at her or Pam, but never striking them. She never saw him ever use any violence against Mum, but when asked about this, Mum replied that when the children were a lot younger he did once raise his hand to her. My Mum picked up a broom and threatened him with it, warning him that if he ever laid a hand on her he would never see her again. Ken backed off, not saying a word, and never ever raised his hand to her again.

- o – 0 – o -

My mother's account of what led to my grandparents taking me in was at odds with what I remembered:

As the next few years went by, I became worried about your future. You were obviously highly intelligent, and in our difficult

66

financial circumstances, with other children competing for the available money and attention, it seemed unlikely that we could give you the sort of start in life that you deserved and needed. My parents had moved to Wallasey, a pleasant residential district of the Merseyside area where they had grown up. Their children were on their own feet, as one of my sisters had entered a convent and the other had qualified as an accountant. They kindly offered to have you to live with them until you were 16, as Wallasey could offer a more middle class background and better educational opportunities.

My recollection was of a more brutal denouement that led to me being rescued by my grandparents, and is forever etched in my memory. The incident that appeared to be the last straw took place one night after Ken had come home from the pub. I was by this time fast asleep upstairs. Mum told him that I'd kicked Mick earlier in the day, although for the life of me I cannot remember why I lashed out at my younger brother in this way. Perhaps poor Mick was on the receiving end of my pent up frustrations.

Whatever the reason, Ken was so angry that he came upstairs to wake me up, and then dragged me down the stairs to the front room. I was absolutely terrified. He struck me so hard that I fell across the room and hit my eyebrow on the edge of the hearth. It bled profusely and to this day it still hurts if I touch the spot above my left eye.

This must have been the breaking point for my poor mother who probably also felt enormous guilt at what had happened. So she decided to contact my grandparents and seek their help.

Until very recently I wasn't certain when my rescue took place. But with the help of Wolverhampton Archives and Local Studies records and my sister Marion recalling the name of my school, I was able to pin down the date. St Mary's RC Junior School's admission registers reveal that my last attendance was on 9th May 1958, and that I would transfer to St Alban's Junior School in Wallasey. Granddad came to collect me from Wolverhampton, and while sad to leave my Mum and brothers, I was overjoyed to leave a house that held so many awful memories. So two months before my 11th birthday, another move took place and a new chapter in my life was about to unfold.

VI

Rescued by my grandparents

It surprises me that I have absolutely no recollection of leaving Wolverhampton with my grandfather and travelling to Wallasey. Located on the other side of the river Mersey from Liverpool, Wallasey was often referred to as a dormitory town for commuters who would drive through the Mersey tunnel or go by the ferry (the latter to be made famous in 1965 through the hit song by Gerry and the Pacemakers). I embarked on this new phase of my life in May 1958, two months short of my 11th birthday, so it's difficult to understand why this momentous journey has been obliterated from my memory.

However, I was never to forget the impact of my new home and the contrast with the one in Low Hill. So what was my first impression? It seemed huge! It was a semi-detached house located on Mill Lane in the Liscard area of Wallasey. A gate opened up to a short path that led through a small garden up to a red front door with a large brass handle. Later on it would be my duty to make sure this handle always shone brightly, a task that I thoroughly enjoyed. I loved the smell of the liquid Brasso, pouring some onto a cloth, rubbing it on, seeing it go white and then giving it a good old polish. Watching the drab handle become a bright shiny gold colour gave me enormous satisfaction!

Living here were my grandfather, grandmother and my Aunt Pat – my mother's youngest sister, who was only ten years older than me. There was also a gorgeous little terrier dog called Whisky, who I adored – in spite of being diagnosed later with asthma and hay fever, caused by many allergies including dogs, cats and house dust. This was all discovered due to my constant coughing and wheezing when brushing the stair carpet, a household duty that I never had to do again!

There was a small hall containing an umbrella stand, a telephone on a tiny table and a place to hang coats. On the wall, and in a prominent position, was a large colour photograph of my grandfather, taken in Egypt during the First World War. He was astride a camel posing in front of the pyramids.

Carpeted stairs led up to a landing where there was a bathroom and four bedrooms; one of which would be mine.

Downstairs there was a front room, a dining room and a large kitchen. The latter was divided up into three sections. There was a pantry adjacent to a very cosy area that was heated by a coal fire. Here was a large Formica topped table and chairs where we generally ate. The radio was usually on and I could look across to the cooking and washing up area and chat to my grandmother as she prepared the food. A door led outside from here to an additional toilet, a bicycle shed and a large back garden. The dining room was at the back of the house and was only used for special occasions. Christmas was one such event and later on I will describe the very first one that was to be etched in my memory and the wonderful dinner and family celebration that took place here.

My grandmother was exactly how I envisaged she should look. Short and plump, with the most wonderful smile and great sense of humour, she dressed in bright colours. When preparing to go out I would watch how she positioned her hat with a large and dangerous pin and worry whether she would pierce her head with it. Looking back, her appearance reminded me of the late Queen Mother.

Pat recalls her initial memories of my arrival:

You were very quiet. I think you were rather sort of flabbergasted. The thing I remember the most was that Mum nearly cried when she unpacked your suitcase because there was so little in it and what there was wasn't fantastic. She took you out to Marks and Spencer's one Saturday and kitted you out with new underwear etc.

I was to find out many years later that Gran had never liked Ken and thought that he had treated me very unfairly.

Pat came with us on that shopping expedition and it was one that I would never, ever forget. It was the first time that I remembered ever having been taken shopping for clothes. The store appeared immense and very bright and there were so many beautiful clothes hung on see-through plastic hangers. Pants and vests were purchased alongside crisp white shirts, white socks, grey skirts, cardigans and black shoes for my new school uniform. My poor brain just could not take it all in.

I was immediately admitted to St Alban's Roman Catholic Junior School and attended there for the few remaining months of the summer term – so perhaps it's not surprising that I have virtually no recollection of my time at this school. I can just about picture the iron railings surrounding the small playground and also attending mass at the adjacent church.

The first photos of me taken in Wallasey were shot outside the house in Mill Lane and in the nearby Central Park. They show me in the clothes I wore to St Alban's School with Kenny and Mick, who were visiting from Wolverhampton.

The school was also in Mill Lane and just ten minutes' walk away, so I was able to come home for lunch. This was always very enjoyable, not only for my gran's lovely cooking but because we could listen to the radio while we ate – enabling me to explore my fledgling interest in classical music. It started when watching a black and white film about the life of waltz king Johann Strauss the Younger (shown at school I think) and I remember being entranced by my first hearing of the *Blue Danube* waltz. I wanted to hear more music by this composer, so would pore over the *Radio Times* to see when any of his work was being played. My grandmother was quite happy for me to twiddle with the radio buttons and tune into a concert. There was always a thrill when discovering more of his compositions, such as the *Tritsch-Tratsch* and *Thunder and Lightning* polkas – and I quickly discovered other music that I liked by Schubert, Mozart, Beethoven and Dvorak. Later on at secondary school, when striding into a morning assembly, I was delighted to recognise that it was to the resounding rhythm of Franz Schubert's *Marche Militaire*.

The radio was a great source of entertainment. Saturday morning, for example, meant it was time for *Children's Favourites* with Uncle Mac. Many years later I would introduce my daughter to some of the songs heard regularly on this show such as *Nelly the Elephant* and *There's a hole in my bucket, dear Liza, dear Liza.* Radio was to open up other wonderful delights. The humour of Ken Horne and his team on the brilliant comedy series *Beyond Our Ken* suited me down to the ground, although most of the double entendres went over my head. In contrast I couldn't stand it when Bill Cotton bellowed out 'Wakey, Wakey!' as it also heralded the start of his *Bandshow* programme that, to my mind, was never very entertaining. I preferred listening to comedy and a wide range of most types of music, a habit that has lasted to this day – I was never to be a Radio 4 listener. There was no television in the house until just after I left in 1963.

My grandfather and I developed a close and warm friendship. To begin with he seemed rather a stern figure, quite tall and very engrossed in his newspaper and doing the crossword. I was quite taken with how smartly he dressed and that he always wore a hat at quite a rakish angle. It didn't take me long to realise that he had a wonderful sense of humour as he would recount funny and interesting stories. We used to go for walks together and he discovered that I was interested in history and soon started to talk to me about Ireland. He seemed quite pleased that I loved to listen to Irish music and he would explain to me the meaning of some of the songs. One was *The Wearing of the Green* concerning the banning of the shamrock. The opening verse is:

Oh, Paddy dear, did you hear the news that's going 'round?
The shamrock is forbid by law to grow on Irish ground
Saint Patrick's Day no more to keep, his colour can't be seen
For there's a bloody law again' the Wearing of the Green.

The arrival of a small parcel of shamrock from Ireland was an annual event, and my gran would pray fervently that it would come in time for St Patrick's Day on 17th March. We would all have a bunch pinned to our coats.

Every morning before Granddad travelled to work at the Customs and Excise Office in Liverpool, Gran would prepare his special breakfast, which consisted of a whipped-up raw egg with milk. I would sit in the kitchen and watch this daily ritual with utter fascination and then see how fast he would drink the concoction. It seemed a revolting mixture but he always swallowed it very quickly.

I can only recall one time when he was ill. Gran was upstairs and shouted down to me in the front room that Granddad wasn't well and to turn the music down. Pat told me later that he had suffered with frequent bouts of bronchitis so this was probably the trouble – but what killed him, just 15 months after I arrived, was a heart attack. This shattering event happened when he was only 62 years old. He collapsed at work and was admitted to the nearby David Lewis hospital, and at first seemed to be on the road to recovery. But nearly two weeks into his stay he died in his sleep, on 6th August 1959. I didn't go the funeral but heard many years later that my devastated mother did attend, looking exhausted (according to Pat), having travelled on the very early 'milk' train. Pat didn't see her again for another 11 years until Gran's funeral in 1970.

- o – 0 – o -

The person I had most contact with during that first year in Wallasey was my grandmother, and she always appeared to be smiling and laughing. Religion was very important to her and she was incredibly respectful towards the local priests and attended mass regularly. I loved her cooking, in particular her soda bread, lemon meringues and currant buns. Baking the latter was always a treat. A small amount of the mixture was always left for me to spoon out into a special bun case and once baked I was able to eat it straightaway. It was the first time I had ever been asked to help in a kitchen and we would have great chats together.

It won't come as a surprise therefore that Sunday was a very busy day, firstly going to mass, followed by a classic Irish fry-up for breakfast. This was my introduction to black pudding, which I loved so much in those days! The wonderful smell of sizzling bacon, fried eggs, tomatoes and toast meant we would be soon called to sit at the kitchen table. Sunday lunch was always a succulent roast joint accompanied by vegetables, roast potatoes and gravy. If I was in luck, the most delicious lemon meringue pie would then follow it. It is clear from the few photos of me from this period that I quickly put on a bit of a weight. As usual the radio would be on and we would listen to *Two-Way Family Favourites*. I was fascinated by the letters that were read out from families who wanted a special request for a relative in the Armed Forces (usually based in Cyprus or Germany). This was when I first came across the beautiful voice of Paul Robeson, as his rendition of *Ol' Man River* was frequently played.

The front room was where I found other sources of entertainment that would keep me occupied for hours. The most exciting discovery was the pianola that included a mechanism for inserting pianola rolls punched with perforations. A huge number of these rolls were stored inside the piano stool and it was a journey of discovery picking one out at random and slotting it into place. Then pumping the pedals of the piano resulted in the roll turning, and producing music ranging from Scott Joplin to Chopin. I was absolutely beguiled by the process and would listen to the resultant music for hours at a time. When tired of this I would play the piano by ear, trying to remember some of the tunes I had been taught during my piano lessons at Nazareth House. My favourite was the Irish traditional melody *The Rakes of Mallow*, particularly as it was one of the tunes I danced to during my Irish dancing days at the convent.

Another magical item in the room was a brand new combined stereophonic record player and radio, a 21st birthday present for Pat. There were plenty of shiny black long-playing records that varied from Irish traditional music to jazz, the latter a favourite genre of my Aunt Pat and including Ella Fitzgerald and Dinah Washington. In those days I wasn't that keen on jazz, but I fell absolutely in love with all the Irish music, particularly listening to the wonderful voice of John McCormack. One of his albums had a stunning photograph of him on the front cover where his eyes appeared incredibly beautiful. There were so many of the songs that I loved, and still do, including of course *The Wearing of the Green*. There were also records by a singer called Guy Mitchell and I was to play *Singing the Blues* repeatedly, along with *She Wore a Red Feather*. The other one I nearly wore out was *The Story of My Life* by Michael Holliday. Radio also introduced me to pop music and I adored Eddie Cochran's *Summertime Blues* and *Three Steps to Heaven*, Joe Brown and the Bruvvers singing *A Picture of You* and anything sung by Buddy Holly and Adam Faith. In 1960, as a teenager all of 13 years of age, I never took to *Cathy's Clown* by the Everly Brothers, preferring Adam Faith's *Someone Else's Baby*. A couple of years later my records of choice were to be the Beatles' *Love Me Do* (October 1962) and *Please, Please Me* (January 1963) the latter becoming their first number one. I was also starting to become interested in folk music and songs such as *Dirty Old Town* by The Spinners.

My other pastime was reading, and it was a joy to be in a household where everybody seemed to be a bookworm! When I was older it was my responsibility to cycle to the library to return our books. Armed with their list of titles/authors I would select a fresh batch for Gran, Pat and myself. It was always a pleasure as it meant I could spend a long time there. The librarians knew me and would take great interest in discussing the books I enjoyed and also suggesting new authors and titles. Some of these were to get me into trouble, but more of that later.

Newspapers were part of my reading routine and those delivered to the house included the *Express*. One day I couldn't find the newspaper and hunted everywhere until I discovered it stuffed down the back of the sofa. On the front page was splashed the 1963 Profumo scandal that involved the Tory Secretary of State for War, John Profumo, model Christine Keeler and a member of the Russian Embassy. Fortunately being a fast reader I managed to finish the whole article quickly and hide the paper back where it had been originally concealed.

- o – 0 – o -

One of the first challenges facing my grandparents was that my 11+ exam results had somehow gone missing between Wolverhampton and Wallasey. There was great consternation as I was due to start secondary school in three months and the results would determine whether I went to a secondary modern or grammar school. As Pat recalled:

So, my dad, sort of like stirred things up and as far as I know they sort of said, look this child's got to know where she's going when she moves from junior school and we hadn't got much time so get your finger out and do something about it. Because they weren't sure whether you'd passed the 11+ or not, they put you into Wallasey Technical High School.

The all-girl school turned out to be ideal and it was an extremely happy period for me, although it was all a bit scary to start with. On the first morning I was accompanied by my grandmother and I have a vivid picture of entering the playground with her and being overwhelmed at the sight of so many girls who seemed amazingly tall and adult. Fortunately my memories of the next five years are incredibly positive.

Every four years or so all the pupils and staff would gather to pose for a school photograph. My original one was lost decades ago, but courtesy of Facebook I recently managed to obtain a copy. Taken in 1960 during my second year, it's clear to see that I am the only black pupil in the entire school. Sitting next to my neatly dressed friend Mary Parry, my appearance is more akin to that lovable scruffy hero of Richmal Crompton's famous *Just William* books. My hair looks unkempt (I didn't possess an Afro-comb in those days), my tie is askew and I am squinting at the camera. It wasn't long after that the French teacher realised I couldn't see anything on the blackboard and I was diagnosed as being very short-sighted.

Each morning I would enjoy walking the short distance to my friend Mary Parry's house where I waited for her to finish her breakfast before we set off for school together. As an only child she was doted on by her parents and fussed over by her mother making sure she ate everything. Her mum was very kind and always offered me a cup of tea and would chat away with the pair of us.

My best friend was Jennifer Salisbury, aka 'Salty', who was an excellent athlete and great fun to be with. Sadly we were only able to maintain contact for a few years after I left school.

The school provided me with a sound academic education alongside fantastic sporting activities. Apart from white shirts and socks, the colour of our uniform was green – skirts, summer dresses and the most unbelievable baggy green knickers. We were allocated to a School House, all named after famous women such as Edith Cavell and Mary Slessor and each had their own coloured tie. Mine was to be Helen Keller and our tie was green!

Although I have managed to mislay all of my school reports, there is an inkling of the progress I was making during that very first term. Courtesy of my cousin Anne, I have a copy of a letter written on 12th December 1958 by our grandfather to her father, my Uncle Michael who was serving in the merchant navy. He always looked so handsome in his uniform and would ultimately rise to be a captain of his own ship. I would have been at Wallasey Technical High School for three months when Granddad wrote:

Elizabeth seems to be getting along OK at school & has got an 'A' for Maths (in which I can claim a share) and is expecting an 'A' for French (no thanks to me but Pat helps a bit).

He also notes that 'Mama & Elizabeth are going over to see Mary at Wolverhampton on Sunday so Pat will have to be the chef.' (Interestingly I have no recollection of travelling with Gran to see my mum, or of any visits she made to Wallasey to see me. Then again there are so many things I have forgotten, but it is strange that I can remember her visiting me as a young child at Nazareth House convent.)

The letter demonstrates Granddad's affectionate nature in this sign off to his son:

Cheerio for now Michael, love from all at home. Looking forward to seeing your smiling face in the very near future.

A few weeks later I would celebrate a wonderful Christmas with the family, including Uncle Michael and his wife Doreen who was now pregnant with their first child Sean. Born the following year he was the sweetest little boy and I would take a great deal of pleasure entertaining him when he came to stay. As a toddler his favourite pastime was when I perched him on the front gate so that he could shout out whenever he saw a car or a bus.

That first Christmas in Wallasey was to remain etched in my memory. The dining room was decorated and we all sat around the large table to eat a wonderful Christmas dinner. I became so excited that Uncle Michael quietly told me to calm down. He had bought me some mechanical windup toys from Hong Kong – how I adored them! Other presents received were books (including a much loved copy of *Old Possum's Book of Practical Cats* by T. S. Eliot), jigsaws and clothes.

By now I had settled down well with my grandparents and felt very safe. It took me some time to realise that I was hardly ever flinching at unexpected movements or sounds in fear of being hit.

At school my favourite subjects were English Literature, French, Geography, Biology and History and I was to pass them all at 'O' level as well as English Language and Maths. I was a very fast reader and one day this caused me some embarrassment. Our English teacher had issued the class with brand new copies of *Pride and Prejudice* and brown wrapping paper, instructing us to cover the book and bring it back the next day. Before the lesson had started I happened to mention to a friend that it was a fantastic novel. 'Miss, Miss!' she shouted out, 'Elizabeth says she read the whole book last night!' As we were filing out of the class the teacher asked me to stay behind and asked a few questions about the novel. While initially mortified, I managed to answer her questions correctly. On escorting me out of the room she said well done and patted me on the back. Although pleased, I secretly vowed to never allow such an incident to happen again. It was, though, to remain one of my favourite books of all time.

Geography was always interesting and particularly so when the Queen's 1959 Royal Tour of Canada formed the basis for many of our lessons that year. I used to love being provided with the itinerary and being asked to search an atlas in order to trace the progress made.

Maths had started off well, as can be seen from my granddad's letter. Unfortunately we then seemed to have a teacher who failed to keep my attention and I started to lag behind. Many of us began to hate maths until a wonderful new teacher arrived. She started off by stating that most of us would fail the GCE exam if we did not pull our socks up. After a discussion with us about our problems, she gave us the most incredible pep talk ever and committed to working as hard as she could to help us. More importantly her teaching methods were marvellous as she steered us through seemingly impenetrable problems. Our confidence restored, we were then able to start thinking for ourselves. I thought she was a great educator and this was proved when many of us *did* pass the exam!

In addition she introduced me to a couple of new hobbies. One was chess, which I played during the school lunch break and the other, via her husband, was collecting matchbox labels. He gave a talk about his hobby, Phillumeny, and I was entranced and soon to become an enthusiastic collector, otherwise known as a Phillumenist (Lover of Light). It would not take me too long before I accumulated several albums of matchbox labels from all over the world. The box needed to be soaked in water in order to peel off the label, and once dried, pasted into the album. I joined the Phillumenist Association and was then able to correspond with people in far flung corners of the world and exchange labels. The letters would arrive with beautifully coloured stamps on them from around the globe, including Russia. This might have raised a few eyebrows, as it was the Cold War era when the West was petrified of a possible nuclear war. But it was a suitable escapist pastime for a teenager who was to be increasingly confined to home in the evenings and weekends, as my gran was to become progressively preoccupied with keeping an eye on me. Much later on, I discovered that she was petrified I would follow in my mother's footsteps by meeting a boy and 'getting into trouble'. Even so, I discovered that a fellow Phillumenist lived quite near Central Park and would visit him and his wife and play with their baby.

Back at school it became clear that I was ridiculously cack-handed and as a result often struggled with art, domestic science and needlework, managing to get thrown out of the latter two classes. Part of domestic science involved various activities in a purpose-built flat, where we were taught to make beds, cook and clean. One day we had been left on our own for a short while and I started to muck around and do handstands on the bed. So I was upside down, balancing against the wall, skirt having fallen over my head revealing a pair of brown legs and baggy green knickers. Unbeknown to me, in walked both the teacher and head teacher who were accompanied by some dignitaries.

Needlework was just incredibly difficult and I was always far behind my classmates in whatever garment we were supposed to be making. One day we had to model our latest item of clothing (which happened to be pyjamas) to some sort of audience. I had not managed to complete the sewing and so had just tacked them together but not very well. Sniggers greeted my appearance as the gaping holes showed sections of my skin. I also had to hold up the pyjama bottoms, as there had been insufficient time to insert a cord into the waist area. While thankfully being removed from these classes to double up on other more enjoyable ones, these mishaps never seemed to get me into serious trouble with any of the teachers. I can't remember any diabolical encounter with a teacher; in contrast it was more a case of being on the receiving end of a lot of encouragement and good humour.

According to my Aunt Pat:

When you went to the Technical High School, with being the only black kid in the school I think you got a bit spoilt. I mean that was only my impression but you got away with murder basically. I remember you saying once that somebody got told off for doing something and you'd done exactly the same and they didn't tell you off, you know. But no, I think, as far as I remember you quite enjoyed the Tech. You weren't somebody who was looking for people to help you with your homework particularly. You seemed to cope with all that yourself.

I thoroughly enjoyed sports activities and seemed to be an all-rounder in P.E., netball, rounders and various types of athletics.

This extended to representing the school in the 100 metres, relay and throwing the discus.

Back at home my relationship with Pat was excellent. As I got older and Gran became more unpredictable, Pat would always support me in her quiet way. One leisure activity that we shared was cycling. It was a huge thrill when I obtained my very first bike, a second-hand red one from the shop that was virtually next door. The owner always took time out to help me with any odd problems that I might experience. Pat and I would often go out for bike rides and she recalled one interesting episode:

I remember we were out on our bikes on the promenade near New Brighton. We had a break and sat on the bench and this elderly lady trotted along and sort of nodded and smiled and we smiled back. Then she got into a bit of a conversation and she said to you, 'you must find it very cold compared to where you're from?' And you said, with your Midlands accent, 'Oh no, it's not as cold as Wolverhampton!' Then you and I nearly had hysterics only we were too polite, so she trotted on, and she was taken by surprise. She took it for granted you were from abroad because there just weren't any black people around here at all. We got on ok.

My grandmother signed me up to a couple of clubs run by the local Catholic Church, the first being the Girl Guides. It was quite fun doing all the activities required to obtain the various badges. There was even a camping trip, which (apart from singing round the campfire) wasn't particularly enjoyable. I woke up exhausted and wheezing due to the cold lumpy ground and being petrified of the cows mooing in the adjacent field. One evening there was an international extravaganza at the town hall and we were issued with a flag and then processed up to the platform. I was somewhat bemused by being issued with one from an African country because the Patrol Leader said 'I looked the part'.

The other group I was obliged to attend was the Children of Mary. We had to listen to boring talks by nuns, and were told that as Catholics we were better than those who practised other religions. Once I challenged this and pointed out that as children did not choose their religion, they shouldn't be penalised just because they happened to be a Protestant, Buddhist or Muslim. This was not taken kindly and I was told to be quiet. So I started playing truant and visited my Phillumenist friend and his family instead, until my grandmother was eventually informed about my absences.

A pleasurable pastime was going to the local cinema in Liscard for the Saturday children's matinee. There was always a serial that ended in a cliff-hanger, so that you couldn't wait to return the following week to find out what happened (well, what do you know, there would be yet another ending full of suspense)!

As I grew older I was able to watch films in the afternoon. One that transfixed me was *The Quiet Man* starring John Wayne and Maureen O'Hara and set in Ireland, with the added bonus of all the brilliant Irish music that was played throughout the film. It even included *The Rakes of Mallow* as the backdrop score to the famous fight scene. I stayed on to watch it a second time, and on exiting the cinema bumped into Pat and her boyfriend (later husband) Alex. She warned me that Gran wouldn't be too happy with me. It was worth the risk though, and I can't remember getting into any serious trouble on my return home.

- o – 0 – o -

My Aunt Sheila, still a nun at a convent in Stafford, came to visit. At about the age of 11 or 12 I had wanted to follow in her footsteps but when she heard about this, she informed somebody in the family that

I would not be suitable. Although a bit miffed at the time I did later realise she was absolutely right, as my faith began to fade away rapidly.

My grandmother had always been very loving, but around the age of 14 or 15 I gradually became aware that she was becoming forgetful and also very difficult with me at times. It probably didn't help that during this period I ceased to believe in the existence of God. My reading was wide and varied and at some point the local parish priest discovered me with a book by Somerset Maugham. I was informed that it was on the Index, a list of books that Catholics were banned from reading. When replying that I wasn't aware of this, I was informed it wasn't possible to know what was on the list. It all seemed quite farcical; fortunately the Index was discontinued in 1966.

As it became clear I was losing my faith, it was decided to dispatch me off to a Catholic retreat in Liverpool. I was the youngest person there and a monk extracted from me the reason for my presence. I poured out my heart to him concerning my difficulties in believing there was a God and the various methods I had used to try and prove there was indeed one. This included goodness knows how many recitations of the rosary and looking for a sign from the statue of the Virgin Mary. Having been well and truly indoctrinated in my early life, I would hope to see blood flowing from her heart or some such miracle. The monk started to smile and said that I should stop worrying, and that my faith may or may not be restored in the future. Then he asked if I wanted to go back home and burst out laughing when my quick-fire response was 'No!' It was like a holiday for me, as I was away from my gran's near constant nagging. He really went up in my estimation when he not only allowed me to stay, but also promised to have a word with our parish priest.

Liverpool was also where I spent several very pleasant holidays with my great-aunts (sisters of my grandfather). Kate had been a teacher and Lil a seamstress, and they lived in the West Derby area of the city. Although they seemed incredibly old and extremely religious, I was pleasantly surprised at how much good fun they were. They taught me to play the card game Canasta and I was initially taken aback when one accused the other of cheating until seeing the smiles on their faces.

One incident has remained etched in my memory. We were out walking and met one of their neighbours. I was amazed when one of my great-aunts introduced me as having been adopted by my grandparents. This was a lie being told by a deeply religious person and made me realise there must be stigma felt due to my illegitimacy and skin colour.

The other holiday I remember was a cycling one to Llandrindod Wells in Wales, organised through our local church. We were a bunch of male and female teenagers and it was my first real contact with boys. I was very shy and kept away from them as much as possible, having a great time with the girls instead.

These were welcome breaks from what was becoming an increasingly gloomy time at home.

- o – 0 – o -

Life had gradually become more difficult for my grandmother following Granddad's death, three weeks before his 63rd birthday. She had a history of poor health due to conditions such as pernicious anaemia and a weak heart – and it's lodged in my mind that in the early days (so the story goes) her treatment for the anaemia included eating raw liver sandwiches. Gran's sense of loss and isolation must have been exacerbated due to Granddad having always taken responsibility for so many aspects of the household management.

There were severe restrictions on my external activities, and I was not allowed to go to the youth club. This was the period when the Beatles performed locally in New Brighton and the Twist was all the rage. Years later my friends could not believe that I couldn't do this iconic dance. They instructed me to pretend that I was drying across the top of my back with a towel whilst stubbing a cigarette out with my foot. Sadly, I never quite mastered it!

I also had to go to bed at 7.30pm every night. Gran insisted that the light had to be switched off promptly, and she told me off if she caught me using a torch to read a book under the blankets. Pat recalls:

I'm quite sure that she was so difficult with you was because she was running scared of something happening to you or you doing something that you shouldn't do and the whole thing being repeated all over again. It would, she felt, be her responsibility because she was the one who was bringing you up and looking after you. I'm sure that that had a lot to do with how awkward she was with you sometimes, because she was quite unreasonable on occasions.

A couple of years after I arrived in Wallasey Pat started going out with Alex, a South African who worked in the Vauxhall car factory in Ellesmere Port. They had met at a New Year's Eve dance in New Brighton, becoming engaged in 1962, and were married in October 1963 – the first wedding I had ever attended. While I remember being delighted with a home-made orange dress, the group wedding photo shows me in the back row, looking anxious and peering between Pat and Gran. Perhaps it was a portent of what was about to transpire.

VII

Sudden departure at 16

Following their marriage in Wallasey in October 1963, Pat and Alex travelled to Ireland for a week's honeymoon. It was during this time that my gran dropped the bombshell that I would be returning to Wolverhampton immediately.

I had now been in the Lower Sixth for a few weeks and was enjoying it immensely. The teachers knew that my heart was still set on becoming a nurse, but often told me that I had the ability to obtain a place at university. When the head teacher heard from my gran that I would be leaving, she and the French teacher came to visit her to plead my case. I was so touched by this, and that they tried their best to comfort me during my utter sense of shock and desolation at this awful news. Until recently I assumed her decision had been due to my 'bad behaviour' relating to once staying without permission with a friend in Central Park until 5.30pm, truancy from the Children of Mary and my lack of faith.

To my surprise, Pat recounted a completely different reason:

When I got married and went to Ireland on honeymoon I didn't know you would be leaving and you'd gone when I got back. Nobody had told me and I got the impression that because Alex was South African (English South African), my Mum thought that he wouldn't want to live with a black child in the house. I don't know. She never said anything to me. It was presented to me as a fait accompli. She said you'd gone to do a nursing course. I mean, as far as I knew, that was that. I rather gathered when you got older that she had thought that it might cause friction, which I don't think it would have. But, I wasn't her and I don't know how she viewed Alex, you see. She might have viewed him in a different way.

I would never see my gran again and unbeknown to me, she died in February 1970 while I was living in Paris. A few years later I would once more visit Wallasey and be delighted to reconnect with Pat and her family.

Another forgotten experience is my return to Wolverhampton, and whether I travelled there on my own. It is difficult to understand how I can recall my journey to Wolverhampton from the convent in Birmingham at the age of nine, and yet have no memory of this one that I made at the age of 16. Possibly, I was in a dreadful state of shock. I could have been in a rage as well – I must have felt antagonism towards my grandmother for taking me away from the school that I loved, as well as suddenly having to leave my friends. There would also have been fears about the situation I was returning to in view of the circumstances that led to my departure just five years before.

My mother had not been in a position to visit me during the time that I lived in Wallasey and my feelings towards her were now very mixed. On the one hand she had sent me to a place of safety to get away from my stepfather's treatment. On the other, she had not been able to prevent my grandmother sending me back to a place I now hated with a vengeance. After all, in spite of the later difficulties with my grandmother, I had really enjoyed my stay in Wallasey and dreaded the contrast with what life would be like in Wolverhampton.

The family composition had changed somewhat during my absence. Kenny was now back living with his mother in Bolton, and my mother and Ken had had two more children – both girls. Mick was now ten, Frank six, and the young girls were Marion (age two) and Pam (age just one). I can't recall the sleeping arrangements exactly – presumably the boys were in one of the bedrooms and Pam was with her parents, and there is a vague memory of bunk beds in the smaller third bedroom for Marion and myself.

There was no question of my returning to secondary education, so the first priority was to get a job. This was where Ken came in to his own as he was familiar with the process of looking for jobs, following his habitual altercations with various bosses. It was an era of virtually full employment in many parts of Britain, and he was keen to escort me to the job centre. He looked on proudly when I answered questions about my educational qualifications and we both noted the look on the interviewer's face when my seven GCE O-level subjects were set out. With my desire to be a nurse I was immediately found a post as a school nurse assistant at Park Lane Infant Welfare Clinic.

Fortunately for me the clinic was within close walking distance of the house in Low Hill. It was the very same one from which, five years or so earlier, I had obtained the dried infant milk and orange juice for my brother Frank. My duties were to assist the qualified school nurses and to help out with any other work that was needed. It was an enjoyable time and I seemed to get on with all the staff, although it was not without hiccups – for example, when operating the small telephone switchboard I managed to cut off a call to one of the doctors. Fortunately no one got cross, but I was never asked to do this task again.

My very first pay packet contained notes and cash in a small brown envelope and I felt like a proper adult. I used it to buy a set of cutlery and crockery for my mother, as I was appalled at the grotty knives and forks in the house.

During this period I applied to several London teaching hospitals to train as a nurse, including St Bartholomew's (aka Bart's), St Thomas' and Great Ormond Street Hospital for Children). There was not one acknowledgement, in spite of my decent exam results. All the application forms required a photograph of yourself plus details of father's occupation – which I had left blank.

The Medical Officer at the clinic, who thought highly of me, was shocked and amazed that I had not received a reply from any of these hospitals. He advised me to write off to his alma mater teaching hospital, St Mary's in Paddington, and stated that he would give me a reference. By mistake I applied to the nearby non-teaching hospital, Paddington General in Harrow Road and was invited for an interview. Travelling there with my mother, it was my first taste of London (maybe for her too), and the number and diversity of the people I saw on the bustling Harrow Road really struck me. My mother sat in on my interview with the matron and a couple of other women, and we soon learnt that I had been accepted! The three-year State Registration Nursing course would start in September 1965 when I would be 18 years of age. I couldn't wait ...

- o – 0 – o -

Meanwhile the stress of living with my mum and Ken in a cramped, damp house where both adults were heavy smokers had started to affect my health. My asthma became worse, not helped by the dreadful pea souper fogs. Wolverhampton remained a very industrial city and it was still common to see smoke billowing from the tall chimneys of many factories in the area. One day there was a particularly nasty fog, but although I was feeling unwell and wheezing quite badly, nothing would stop me from going to work. The fog was so dense that it was only possible to see a yard or so ahead, so you had to put your arms out in front of you to feel your way, which was quite frightening.

Coughing and spluttering, I carried on, as the clinic was quite near. All of a sudden a man put his hand on my shoulder and asked me what was wrong. I was unable to answer him due to being so breathless. When he proceeded to lead me into Park Lane Clinic I tried to explain that this was my workplace. He told me that he was a doctor and that I was to stop trying to talk any further, although he soon discovered that I worked at the clinic. It turned out he was a Medical Officer of Health, and this meeting with him would prove to be a turning point in my life.

While my asthma attack was being treated I could hear hushed voices discussing my home situation. They were obviously very concerned about me and it was decided that I would be transferred immediately to work as a school nurse assistant at Kingswood, a residential open air school for delicate children in Albrighton, on the border with Shropshire. While close to Wolverhampton it was in a rural area and near to the Cosford Royal Air Force base. Three years earlier in 1960, the school had moved half a mile to purpose-built premises, so at the time of my arrival it was virtually brand-new. It was run by Wolverhampton Education Authority in collaboration with the local health authority. The children had a variety of chronic conditions such as asthma, heart ailments and cerebral palsy. There is no record of when I moved to this new job, but it was probably just a few months after starting work at Park Lane Clinic.

I have never forgotten this act of compassion towards me by those managing the child health services. Their intervention helped me enormously during this traumatic phase of my life, and I stayed for nearly two years before going to London to study as a nurse at the age of 18. It was a wonderfully cathartic interlude, something I've always appreciated and feel incredibly lucky to have experienced.

For the first time I felt truly independent and I savoured every minute of it. My role was once again to assist school nurses, the older of whom was also resident. The younger one seemed more like a model and her husband was a racing driver. There was also a cleaner who always wore a gingham overall. She loved to have a good old gossip and was pleased to see that I listened to every word of her tittle-tattle. While I was initially a bit in awe of the younger nurse, she and all the other staff were very helpful and friendly.

My main responsibilities were to assist the nurses in caring for whichever children had been admitted to the sick bay. This included making beds, bathing, toileting and giving the children their meals. One pupil I remember was a young South Asian girl with moderately severe physical and learning disabilities due to cerebral palsy. Always smiling and laughing, she was an absolute delight to look after. With more experience I was taught how to do inhalations and take temperatures. We would also go across to the main school to inspect the children's hair for nits and lice. It was no surprise to be called 'Nitty Nora the Great Explorer'. The authorities organised for me to attend a one-year day release pre-nursing course at a college in Wolverhampton. This was another agreeable experience where I was to make friends, and learn first aid and human biology – as well as thoroughly enjoying the chips that were on offer in the local canteen.

At Kingswood I was allocated a comfortable bed-sitting room in the medical building that housed the sick bay, which was adjacent to the school block. To have such wonderful accommodation was an absolute luxury. From my weekly wage I saved up to buy books and my very first record player, a Dansette, which was all the rage at the time due to the reasonable cost. It was possible to stack and play several records, one after the other. The first singles I bought included my favourite singers Bob Dylan, the Rolling Stones, the Supremes and the Liverpool folk group, the Spinners. I also bought classical records such as Beethoven's 5th Piano Concerto (*Emperor*) and the music for the ballet *Giselle* composed by Adolphe Adam.

The headmaster Mr Frank Macmillan and his wife and twin adult children lived in the head teacher's cottage that was down a little lane around the corner from school. A long drive led up to the entrance of the school and we could see it from the medical block. So it was easy to see when Frank (as everybody called him) arrived, motoring up the driveway in his beloved green Austin Mini Countryman with those distinctive wood inserts in the rear body of the car. Tall and walking with a stoop, he was a gentle giant and a wonderful teacher.

Everybody seemed friendly and I remember being invited to the home of a younger member of staff who lived on a local farm. Lunch consisted of a buttered roll containing cheese and apple, a combination I had never encountered before but turned out to be extremely tasty. I was also surprised to see how many pairs of stockings there were hanging out to dry and asked whether they all belonged to her. When she said yes I decided that it might be a good idea to buy a few more for myself!

- o – 0 – o -

I can't remember ever visiting my mother and family in Wolverhampton during this period – I didn't want to be in contact with them and harboured feelings of anger and resentment towards both her and my stepfather. Meanwhile, at Kingswood I became very independent as well as quite adventurous – characteristics that were to remain with me over the years. Salty was one of the few school friends from Wallasey I kept in touch with. In the summer of 1965 (just before I moved to London) we went on the first of four consecutive annual holidays together, one in Cornwall, one in London and two overseas. In Cornwall we travelled all the way down to Land's End. I still have some lovely photos of us both at that time. Lack of money was no hindrance, as hitchhiking was our mode of getting to wherever we wanted to be. It didn't seem as hazardous for 16 year olds as it might today and it was a fairly common sight back then.

We always stayed in Youth Hostels and there was a very puritanical view about how we were supposed to travel (i.e. healthily hiking from one establishment to another), so we would ask to be dropped off within reasonable walking distance and then pretend to huff and puff our way to the reception. We became skilful liars when comparing details of our itinerary with the more serious walkers who would also be spending the night at the hostel. In exchange for an incredibly cheap overnight stay we were rightly expected to take part in the rota of cleaning duties. We would generally sleep in large dormitories on bunk beds, tucked into our sleeping bags. This was when I became aware of my snoring habit, due to often being shaken during the night by an exhausted individual desperate for some sleep. In the end I would just warn people, apologise in advance and suggest that they stuff something into their ears. It was only during my first year as a student nurse that it was discovered that I had a major blockage in one nostril that required surgery.

Another holiday I undertook, this time by myself, was to cycle from Kingswood all the way through Shropshire to a convent in Llandrindod Wells in Wales. This was in order to stay for a week with my Great-Aunt Kate who was now living there since the death of her sister Lil. Looking back, the whole venture seems a bit crazy – but thank goodness for youth, as it never entered my head that I would encounter any problems. It was a distance of between 70 and 80 miles, and at some point I remember cycling along the banks of the beautiful River Dee. All seemed to be going well until I noticed that it was starting to become so dark that, even with the front light of the bike on, it was impossible to see what was in front of me. Suddenly I jumped out of my skin when I bumped into something soft, followed by the sound of bleating from goodness knows how many sheep! After shooing them away, I looked around and was relieved to see lights on in a nearby building. Slowly edging myself towards it, I knocked at the front door and was greeted by a gentleman who told me he was a farmer. When I told him what had happened he called his wife over and they both started to laugh, while reassuring me not to be worried.

They said I was very close to Llandrindod Wells, but that it was far too late for me to try and cycle there, and that they would put me up for the night free of charge. His wife gave me some delicious hot soup and then showed me to my bed, which I needed to climb up to. It turned out to be one of the best night's sleep that I ever had, due to the most incredibly soft mattress. Next morning, the farmer's wife woke me and brought me up a cup of tea. She later showed me to the bathroom where there was the most enormously deep bath that I have ever seen, into which she poured hot water from a large jug. After my bath I was invited me to join them for breakfast and they wanted to know more of my adventures. They said I was one of the funniest people that they had met in a long time, and wished me well on the last leg of my journey.

The farmer drew a map of the route to Llandrindod Wells, and as a result I arrived at the convent in less than an hour. This was long before the era of mobile phones and my poor great-aunt had been frantic with worry. I don't think that I had even made a note of the convent's telephone number. My return journey passed off without incident except for the onset of short bouts of excruciating acute pain, shooting halfway down my left leg. It lasted on and off for over three decades but fortunately this wretched problem disappeared as suddenly as it came on.

The two or so years I spent at Kingswood Open Air School passed by very quickly without any negative experiences whatsoever. While very sorry to leave, I was really excited to be moving to London to start training as a nurse. My new trunk was packed with all my worldly possessions, a new suit had been bought and I was ready for the big city!

Section of Wallasey Technical High School photo March 1960 – spot me!

Aunt Pat's wedding October 1963 and me peering between Pat and Gran

With sisters Marion and Pam

Preliminary Training School, Paddington General Hospital.
Me standing, back row, 2nd right. 1966

1st year student
nurse, Paddington
and so proud of
my white boots!

Staff nurse at
Paddington
General Hospital,
1968

In Paris with Martine and Jean-Christophe, 1970

Police camions, Paris, 1970. Photo that got me into trouble with a gendarme

NURSING, FRANCE
& POLITICS

VIII

Becoming a nurse but not a midwife

My life as a student nurse began in September 1965 when I arrived at the nurses' home of Paddington General Hospital in north-west London, with a new trunk containing all my worldly possessions. It was situated on the bustling Harrow Road, next to the local police station, and in a photo taken outside – with seven of the twelve students who had also arrived that day – I can be seen proudly wearing my brand-new suit. Looking at that image we appear quite fuddy-duddy for 18-year-olds!

Twenty years on I would discover that the grave of Mary Seacole, the Jamaican-Scottish Crimean War nurse was less than a mile down the road. In the future I would become very involved with the fundraising appeal for her memorial statue at St Thomas' hospital, overlooking the Houses of Parliament, but I heard nothing about her during my entire training.

We all had to live in the nurses' home for our first year. To start off with I was quite happy living in the allocated small room on an upper floor of the building. There was just enough space for a bed, cupboard, desk and chair, and I found room for my beloved Dansette record player by placing it on top of my trunk.

The toilets and baths were further down the corridor. There was a call box on the ground floor, and if you were lucky someone would be passing by when the phone rang. They would rush up and bang on your door and shout out that you had a call. Then it was a matter of running downstairs as fast as you could, hoping that the person was still on the line.

A dragon of a woman (a former nurse) was in charge of the home and she took great pride in keeping a steely eye on our whereabouts. Fortunately there was a fire escape and some of us came to know it quite well (a 3rd year student had advised us how to keep it slightly ajar). This came in handy when the front door was locked and we needed to creep back into our rooms in the early hours of the morning.

In those days most nurse education programmes were undertaken in a School of Nursing that was part of a hospital (and not a University, as is the case today). We studied for three years to obtain our State Registered Nurse (SRN) certificate. In the late 1970s I would undertake a one-year Diploma in Advanced Nursing at Manchester University to bring my qualification up to degree level. This idea had not even entered my mind at this point; I was just thrilled to be starting a nursing course at last.

Paddington General Hospital had been established in the 19th century with links to the local workhouse. This might explain the oft-held sentiment that we were seen as the poor sister to St Mary's Teaching Hospital in Praed Street, although the two institutions merged in 1968. By then I had qualified as a nurse and would only stay for a further six months or so. Renamed St Mary's Hospital, Harrow Road, it ceased operation in 1986 and the buildings were pulled down and replaced with flats.

We spent the first three months of our course attending the Preliminary Training School (PTS). Our small cohort included several overseas students: two from the Caribbean and one each from West Africa, Finland and Hong Kong. The remainder of us had come from various towns and cities in England. This was my first opportunity of living and working with such a cosmopolitan group of people and I enjoyed it immensely. Fifty years later, I continue to be friends with two of our group, namely Sue and Janet. They have both reflected on their first impressions of me, as well as some of our shared experiences over the years.

Sue:

I remember your keen intellect which enabled us to have pithy conversations (neither of us liked small talk, although we loved to laugh). The zeitgeist – idealism, left-wing politics, doing the Guardian crossword under our desks in PTS lessons, joining the local Labour Party – full of coughing, smoking & drinking older men. Later on, you with your straightened hair, in a black and white plastic mac with white plastic boots. (I have a photo of me in May 1966 proudly wearing the latter!)

It's hard to believe now, but I think you found socialising quite difficult in your late teens – the combination of your not suffering fools gladly, plus being mixed race (your 'difference' in other words) alienated you; you seemed English in so many ways but were black & I think this confused people & made you stand out. I don't remember you talking about your dad in those first few years, but I do remember you talking about going to the convent where the odd nun was cruel to you; your mum & stepfather & how horrible he was to you and how you were left out by him for being black. I think this engendered in you a sense of not belonging, which you carried forward with you in life until you finally found your dad.

Janet:

I think the first impression was that you had a good sense of humour, I remember that, and you laughed a lot but you were not that confident. But you were very English, and I think that's why I never saw you somehow as black. You know, you were just English and I think that's partly because of your accent. You had a very strong mix of Liverpool and Wolverhampton accents, which actually almost identified you really, and perhaps it was that. We spent a lot of time together in London and what I liked about you, why we got on so well, is that you were always game for anything. You would always come with me and if I suggested we should have a curry somewhere, oh yes, you'd say, I'll come. So whereas you were shy, you had that good sort of spirit, I think that was very noticeable to me, and also the ability to talk about things and understand. There was never anything we couldn't talk about really but I think I would say that to me you were very English, who happened to be black.

This was exactly how I felt, having to this point grown up in a totally white Irish/English culture, with no contact or knowledge of my Nigerian family. In contrast, I was acutely aware that society viewed and labelled me as coloured, half-caste or black.

- o – 0 – o -

Nursing turned out to be better than I had ever hoped. It was the combination of studies, idiosyncratic tutors and, most importantly, caring for patients with an incredible variety of illnesses. My favourite subject throughout training was medical nursing, but most of the other disciplines were of interest too. Our standard textbook was the 1965 edition of Toohey *Medicine for Nurses*. I can't remember that we were ever encouraged to read articles from journals. Many years later when working as a health visitor in Wembley, I had two Caribbean families on my caseload with young children affected by sickle cell anaemia. It is a painful inherited red blood cell disorder that primarily affects people from the Caribbean, Africa, the Middle East and South East Asia. I knew nothing about this condition and was quite ashamed of my ignorance. Out of curiosity I went back to my old textbook only to discover that the illness was not included. Looking back it is surprising that we never had a lecture about it, considering the significant Caribbean population then living in the Paddington area.

There was a small group of nurse tutors who included Miss Papadopoulos, Miss Dunstan and Mr Adigun. Most of the lectures were quite interesting, although Sue and I were told off for doing a crossword puzzle during a particularly tedious session! Doctors also contributed to the course and I always enjoyed the input of Dr Simon Cohen, a senior registrar who later became a consultant physician in East London. He had a flair for explaining the symptoms of a condition clearly, together with the relevant physiology and anatomy. It was obvious that he enjoyed keeping us awake by a mixture of telling jokes and firing questions at us.

Miss Papadopoulos, or Miss Papa as she asked us to call her, was our sharp and extremely knowledgeable principal tutor. She did not tolerate ignorance kindly and could be quite caustic when questions weren't answered quickly enough. Having said that, she could occasionally stun us with her wicked sense of humour. Complications of poliomyelitis resulted in her needing to walk with a stick, so we could always hear her approaching the classroom. This was useful for some students who were petrified of her, as she could throw a most withering look when displeased. Fortunately she took a shine to me and was delighted to inform me that I had been awarded the second year prize. Asked to select books up to a certain value, I still have them to this day. They were Philips' *Record Atlas* and Cassell's *French-English dictionary*, presented to me on 18th October 1967.

The mock-up ward in the School of Nursing was also used for medical students' practical examinations. Real patients were brought in for the day and on several occasions Dr Cohen obtained permission from Miss Papa for me to help out at the sessions. During one of these times he asked me to consider studying medicine adding that he'd be happy to explore this if I was interested. While very touched, I explained that nursing was exactly the career for me and did not wish to switch to medicine – it's a decision that I have never ever regretted.

After PTS we were kitted out in our mustard and white student nurses' uniforms in readiness for our first ever ward experience. We stayed here for about three months and I was delighted that my friend Lynne was on the same placement. In those days student nurses were part of the actual ward workforce and not supernumerary, as is the case today. Apart from study days our rota mimicked that for the qualified staff, including night-duty. As students we could easily have times of actually being in charge of a ward – frightening to look back at now!

We constantly moved to new wards or departments and these were the scariest periods during those three years of training. The first few days in a new environment were the worst by far. Being shy was a terrible hindrance as there were so many staff to get to know, never mind the patients. My stomach would be in knots during those first days, so whenever possible I would escape to the sluice and pretend to be busy washing bedpans. Nursing activities on the ward included bed making, bathing patients, cleaning lockers, giving out meals, doing dressings and the drugs round. There was also the regular recording of patients' temperature, pulse and respiratory rate, together with their blood pressure reading.

If possible, I would keep clear of the doctors' rounds with all the fuss and pomposity that surrounded most of them. We nurses were expected to be busy little bees completing all our tasks – not talking to patients and/or sitting on their beds. This was severely frowned upon. It posed a major problem, as I loved reading the patient's notes and then getting to know the person. It was clear to me that understanding something about their background and condition impressed and reassured them. So whenever the opportunity arose, I would just ask a few questions and listen to their answers. The best opportunities arose when giving a bed bath, doing a dressing or accompanying them to the bathroom. Most patients poured their hearts out and I soon became acquainted with a rich and diverse Paddington population. There were a significant number of Irish patients and they were usually very surprised to hear of my own origins; some would have me in fits of laughter with their jokes and stories.

In contrast there was a minority of patients I used to dread having to look after. One was an older woman on an orthopaedic ward recovering from a hip operation that hadn't gone very well. As a result she had been on the ward for a very long time and seemed to take pleasure in picking out one new student and making their life hell. Unfortunately I was one such target and once she made me go back to the kitchen three times to boil an egg to her exact standards. I finally refused at the fourth demand. After that bruising experience I would often speed past her bed acting as though deaf, blind and dumb – not the best nursing care of course. It was therefore not a shock when she reported me to the sister who, to my eternal gratitude, listened to my account and had a quiet word with the patient! However she did give me a few tips on dealing more compassionately with a so-called 'difficult patient', including discussing issues with experienced staff on the ward.

My weak area was poor manual dexterity, otherwise known as cack-handedness. I would envy those nurses who could, for example, speedily and efficiently remove stitches. One surgeon had me thrown out of the operating theatre when I dropped an instrument on the floor. He was quite tall and I had already irritated him due to not being able to secure the back of his gown quickly enough. It didn't help that he kept wandering about, as I had to leap up behind him trying in vain to tie the tapes. He was absolutely right to get rid of me and I was quite pleased, as theatre nursing frightened the life out of me.

Whilst some ward sisters were absolute dragons, most were helpful and some even good fun. The one I was to remember most was in charge of my very first ward. Lynne and I had been told to go and lay out a deceased man. It was our first contact with a dead person and we were both petrified. Peering around the screens surrounding the bed, we both gasped. There was what appeared to be a huge body beneath the sheet, as his abdomen was enormous due to fluid that had collected from complications of his illness. Our initial job was to wash the body and this entailed turning him over to wipe his back. Lynne and I were on either side of the bed and, as we were both very short, had difficulties working out how we were going to complete this task. We looked at each other, with anxiety, across the bed and then I proceeded to roll him towards Lynne. We suddenly heard what sounded like a sighing noise emanating from the body, which frightened the living daylights out of us. Our immediate reaction was to laugh hysterically, which we knew was totally inappropriate. All of a sudden the screens swished to one side and the face of the ward sister glared at us.

Silence ensued and we were marched off to the office, where we both burst into tears. Very quietly she asked who had asked us to perform this duty. The 3rd year student nurse responsible was called in and, in front of us, was brusquely told off by the sister for not staying with us and supervising everything. Before all three of us went back to complete the unfinished business I was amazed when she made tea for everybody, and chatted about coping with the experience of the death of a patient.

Caring for a dying patient would never be easy, but her words of wisdom helped enormously. One other incident has always stayed with me and this concerned the searing grief of a bereaved mother. During my final year I was working in the very busy casualty department when a young adult male was admitted following a drugs-related incident. Whilst being examined, he suddenly collapsed and had a cardiac arrest. The team immediately started trying to resuscitate him but without success and he was declared dead, much to the shock of all the staff. He had appeared so physically fit and strong. One of the nurses phoned his mother and I will never forget the sound of her piercing shrieks on hearing of her son's death.

Night-duty could be both wonderful and fearful. We would gradually be given more responsibilities during these shifts. Generally it was less busy, and opportunities arose to spend more time with patients who were anxious and couldn't sleep. Other times we would be absolutely frantic and just prayed that there was a senior manager available, who would actually roll up their sleeves and help us on the ward. Also that the doctor on call would respect your judgement that, yes, they really *did* need to come now to see the patient. The phone call informing us of yet another admission was what we all dreaded. Tea and meal breaks went out of the window, and in the morning we were just about able to stagger to the hospital canteen for breakfast.

One night an incident happened that caused me to get more sleep than I could have ever dreamed about. I was a first-year student and suffering from a particularly severe bout of hay fever.

To relieve the symptoms a doctor gave me a small blue Phenergan tablet, a medicine that I had never taken before. It clearly must have knocked me out as the next thing I can remember was waking up in my room some 12 hours later!

The group of student nurses I started the course with in 1965 was a small one. As such we generally stuck together and were fortunately able to share the worst and best experiences of hospital life. After the first year we were allowed to move out of the nurses' home and quite a few of us couldn't wait for this moment! Four of us rented a flat in Harvest Road that was within walking distance of the hospital. Lynne, Helen, Jane and I were to remain living here until after we qualified and were finally ready to leave Paddington General Hospital.

- o – 0 – o -

Shyness caused no end of problems during my first year and made me quite hesitant about going out to socialise. Instead, I would tend to stay in my room and read, play records or listen to the radio. My taste in music was becoming quite catholic, ranging as it did from The Rolling Stones to *Rigoletto*. There was a residents' lounge in the nurses' home where I would occasionally watch television. Above all, one of my favourite pastimes was sleeping! It took me some time to adjust to the physically demanding life of nursing. At times I found the combination of long hours on the wards and revising for exams utterly exhausting. Many years later when I told my friend Sue that I was pregnant, she wondered how on earth I would cope with sleepless nights. She recalled the times when I was off-duty, sleeping for up to 24 hours following a particularly tiring set of shifts.

My nascent organising skills came into play at this time as I got involved in setting up a local student nurses association, probably linked to the Royal College of Nursing. A lasting memory is being invited to visit Germany in March 1968, with a group of student nurses from all over the UK. One photo shows a group of us in blue and white uniforms looking quite cold outside the entrance of a hospital. Others were taken at Heidelberg Castle, outside Goethe's house in Frankfurt, and at a grisly first-aid demonstration in Wiesbaden.

We were invited to several official events and I was very impressed that classical music was played during these functions. However, I will never forget my intense embarrassment at a dance we all had to attend, as we were matched up with a male cadet for the evening! In contrast I thoroughly enjoyed our trips to see other hospitals, although I was shocked at the severe restrictions imposed on parents wishing to visit their small children. They were only able to peer at them through a window of the children's ward.

There were to be other trips abroad during my student days. I was still in touch with Salty, my school friend from Wallasey. In 1966 we hitchhiked to Switzerland, and spent a wonderfully hot day in Lindau on the shores of Lake Bodensee. There was a scary moment while hitchhiking when Salty dragged me back from a car that was pulling up to give us a lift. Not always known for being very observant, I had failed to spot that the driver had exposed himself.

The following year our hitchhiking adventures took us to Germany, where a less worrying but quite embarrassing incident occurred. A very stern policeman approached and informed us that, unbeknown to the pair of us, we were hitchhiking illegally on the autobahn (motorway). Ordering us to stay where we were, he proceeded to peer at the licence plates of oncoming traffic until a British car approached. To our utter amazement he ordered the driver to stop and give us a lift. We crept into the back, apologising profusely, but fortunately the driver had a great sense of humour and was not at all annoyed. One of the few photos taken during this holiday is a lovely one of Salty at Koblenz Castle, overlooking the junction of the rivers Rhone and Moselle. This was to be our last trip together as Salty got married and I sadly lost touch with her.

My final hitchhiking holiday was with Josephine, a Spanish nursing friend who hailed from Aduna in the Basque province of Guipuzcoa. Her family would have been horrified to know of our travel plans, so we just hitchhiked across France until we got to the Spanish border. We then took a train to her hometown where her brothers met us; they remained none the wiser and we managed to have a great holiday in spite of our limited budget. On the way back my French came in handy when we thumbed a lift in the south of the country from a lorry driver and his mate. I overheard the driver whispering which of us he would go off with when they stopped at a café. Poor Josephine had no idea what was going on when I suddenly pretended to retch and double up in pain. The men were clearly astonished that my French was good enough to demand that they stop the lorry so that we could get out. It was only after they had driven off that I could explain everything to her.

In 1968, my final year as a student nurse, I took my first flight on a holiday with Sue to a Spanish seaside resort. While not at all fazed by take-off or landing, the bouts of turbulence petrified me, and always have ever since. Consequently I gave up flying in 2005, with the exception of one short flight in 2015!

- o – 0 – o -

Looking back, my social life as a student nurse was a bit tortuous at times. I was somewhat frightened of meeting men and was happier going out and having a laugh with our set of student nurses, who all happened to be female. The odd date that I did have never led to a lasting relationship, as one or other of us would finish it after the first or second encounter. I was in awe of friends like Janet and Sue who seemed to be so much more at ease in any social setting.

Nurses used to organise dances at the hospital and invite policemen from the local station to come. I went to a few but didn't enjoy them, as I was unable to participate in the small talk that often led to dates for many of my friends. In addition I didn't know how to do popular dances such as the Twist, and just felt too embarrassed to get onto the floor and have a go.

Rose, a fellow student nurse, took pity on me and suggested that I accompany her to small parties, organised in the homes of her fellow Jamaican friends. I even went with her a few times to the famous Cue (later Q) Club in Paddington that was run by the late Count Suckle. It was here that I first heard and fell in love with ska and then reggae music, adding (to name a few) Prince Buster, Peter Tosh, Toots & the Maytals and Desmond Dekker & the Aces to my growing record collection.

Friends who noticed how tense I was at social events suggested alcohol could help and this led me to try gin and tonic. It worked for a short period before I started to feel depressed and someone told me that this was a classic side effect of gin. So I switched to rum and coke and this suited me better, and certainly helped me become more relaxed. It took me many years though to stop being so self-conscious and thinking that people at parties were always watching me due to being so uncool. This was the swinging sixties after all! Fortunately I never became drunk, as I didn't enjoy the taste that much, and was able to unwind with just a small amount of alcohol. In addition, the smell of alcohol always reminded me of Ken's drunken antics and rages.

My friend Janet was a few years older than me, and struck me as extremely worldly-wise. She had a lovely car, a small green mini, and would take me with her on wonderful outings that included shopping sprees. As she relates:

I had a lot of Chelsea friends and was always sort of wanting to try new fashions, because of course it was the time in the 60s with the mini skirts and things like that, and so I did have some white boots and a white hat. I knew you liked them but I didn't realise how much until the next time I saw you, and you were wearing a pair of white boots and a white hat! It caused me great amusement because you looked quite incongruous with your black hair and black skin and white boots and white hat, which of course were unseen in Chelsea, and not generally common anywhere in those days.

I agreed to go with Janet to a dance in London's Leicester Square ballroom; goodness knows why, as apart from Irish jigs and reels, dancing was then a no-go area for me. The place was packed and quite overwhelming. At one point an African man came up to me and said how pleased he was that my hair was natural and then asked for a dance. That was it! I suddenly became quite anxious, said I needed to go to the toilet, and just fled the venue without even telling Janet. My lack of social contact with black men must have been a factor in this reactionary response, alongside my inability to dance.

Janet's reflections shed light on my behaviour:

I never thought about you getting married because you didn't seem to like men too much. It wasn't that you disliked men particularly but you were slightly, I don't know whether afraid is the right word, but timid, unsure. The image that I had of you when I first met you was that you wouldn't have been brave enough to go out with a man, you know, white or black. I remember you saying, 'Oh, I never want to be with a black man', because you never had that connection and they would be alien to you.

Not very long after this incident my friend Rose persuaded me to get my hair 'relaxed': in other words, straightened. It is clear from my first passport photo in July 1966 that I still hadn't mastered moisturising and combing my natural hair. She took me to the local black hair salon for my first experience of the process, which involved using fiery chemicals that burnt some of my scalp. While expensive and painful I liked how my hair looked immediately after a hairdressing appointment, as seen in a photo of me taken in October 1966.

My hair would soon become stiff and straight requiring it to be put it in rollers to keep it wavy, and after a few years I became really fed up with it all. In addition, spending some time in Paris opened my eyes to the ideas of self-esteem and black identity. On returning from France in 1970 it was a pleasure to revert permanently back to my natural hairstyle – particularly as the wonderful Afro comb had now made its appearance! During the 1970s I took great pride in having a huge Afro.

The late 1960s was a period of unrest in many parts of the world, and there were some that I followed with particular interest. These included the Biafra War in Nigeria (July 1967–January 1970), the May 1968 upheavals in France, the US Civil Rights movement and the growing international protests against apartheid in South Africa. In the late 1960s, and much closer to home, there was continued police harassment of the West Indian owned Mangrove Restaurant in Notting Hill. It culminated in a demonstration against the police, whose heavy-handed tactics resulted in violence.

There followed a well-publicised trial in 1970 of the Mangrove Nine that included Frank Crichlow and Darcus Howe, all of whom were acquitted of the charge of incitement to riot. Robin Bunce and Paul Field (2014) clearly set out the historical context of these events in *Darcus Howe. A Political Biography.*

On a more personal note, I was very relieved to pass the final exams in October 1968 and become a State Registered Nurse. Unfortunately a couple of our cohort had to re-sit their papers. The satisfaction I gained from those hospital nursing days was from making a sick, frightened person as comfortable and reassured as possible, while also trying to understand their condition, treatment and prognosis.

- o – 0 – o -

Once qualified I successfully applied for a position as a staff nurse on a medical ward and worked there for about six months. It was a thoroughly enjoyable experience, and the extra responsibilities were a welcome challenge, in a ward that was generally adequately staffed. I was totally unaware that Janet was worried about the impact that racism would have on my future promotion prospects:

You were doing well in nursing, but I do remember saying to my sister that it's a shame that Elizabeth will never be able to go very far in nursing because of her colour. To my knowledge, I don't know whether this is true, but there didn't seem to be any black ward sisters and hence the chance of you being one. I mean we were all aspiring to be ward sisters ultimately. I remember when my ward sister was off sick and I was in charge of the ward. I don't know what stage that was but I mean I was a complete novice, and we would be in charge of a whole ward. So we were led to believe that ultimately we would be in charge of a ward, be a ward sister. But there was always a thought; well Elizabeth sadly won't get there.

You came over as being so bright and I know you got very into politics and were always enquiring and asking questions. I didn't really consciously think about it, but I think society has an impact on us all really, and maybe my feeling was that blacks were less intelligent than whites. I mean, where would I have got that from? I don't remember thinking that, but society bombards us with this propaganda and therefore to see Elizabeth, you know black, but a clever girl, was perhaps different. So therefore I thought what a shame almost, what a shame Elizabeth is black because she won't be able to move forward in her career.

None of this was at all obvious to me at the time so Janet's comments came as quite a revelation.

The relationship with my mother was probably at its weakest during this period, as I never had any great desire to visit Wolverhampton. Friends were plentiful, nursing kept me busy and interested and I was very happy with London life.

While having enjoyed the experience of being a staff nurse I had itchy feet and wanted to move on. In those days it was the done thing 'to do midwifery' after qualifying as a nurse, even if you had no intention to practise as one. So began the process of looking around for a suitable maternity unit. I chose to go to Scotland, as it was a country that had fascinated me since a teenager in Wallasey. In those days I had spent many enjoyable hours cutting out a series of Highland figures in kilts from the back of Quaker Porridge Oats boxes! There was no doubt that I had a very romanticised view of the country, perhaps from also listening to a lot of Scottish traditional songs and dance music on the radio.

My location of choice was to be the beautiful capital city of Edinburgh. I got a place at the Simpson Memorial Maternity Pavilion Hospital, and started in May 1969, on the first 1 year integrated midwifery course. Up until then it was usual to do a six-month Part 1 course and if you wanted to become a fully-fledged midwife then proceed to Part 2. This again lasted six months and could be taken at the same hospital, or you could move to another one.

There were 12 of us on our course and the cohort photo shows that we were a fairly diverse group. I was to discover quite quickly that the Simpson Memorial Maternity Pavilion was a much more traditional and hierarchical place than Paddington General Hospital. On our first day we were issued with a sheet of questions to help us familiarise ourselves with the history and layout of the hospital. It included finding some sort of reference to the first antenatal clinic having been established there in 1915. More interested in chatting and getting to know each other, most of us did not take the task too seriously. We were to suffer as a consequence! The tutor was so angry; I really thought that she was going to burst a blood vessel. She reminded me of the lead character, played by Dame Maggie Smith, in the 1969 film *The Prime of Miss Jean Brodie*. Our punishment was to be sent back to the wards immediately, with a firm warning that we were not to return until all the questions had been answered. Oh dear, what an introduction to midwifery training.

On a lighter note I shared a lovely huge flat with some other students; it was situated in Marchmont Crescent, close to the greenery of Bruntsfield Links and The Meadows. Some of my friends in the cohort included Gerry, Sue and Moggy and we enjoyed exploring Edinburgh together. This included a dawn climb of Arthur's Seat, which students rudely dubbed as Arthur's Arse. The hill is 822 feet high and overlooks the city. I was still very keen on improving my French so registered for lessons at the Institut Française. It was also a must for me to go to the Edinburgh Festival, and I will never forget seeing a magnificent performance by Ian McKellen, in Marlowe's *Edward II*. The play had a shocking end when the homosexual king was killed through having a scorching hot poker put up his backside. It was performed at the Prospect Theatre and unsurprisingly caused a storm of controversy.

Back at the 'Simpson' I was enjoying midwifery, particularly time spent with the women and their babies on the post-natal wards. To start off with I experienced difficulty understanding those who spoke with a strong accent. One day there was a great deal of laughter when I asked for a 'translation' of the following rapid sentence addressed to me: 'Would you get me a wee goonie (nightgown) for my wee bairn (little baby).'

Student midwives needed to deliver a minimum number of babies by the end of their first six months. Achieving this was not at all straightforward for several reasons. Firstly, as a teaching hospital there were many medical students competing for deliveries. Secondly, it was a major referral centre for women with complex obstetric histories often leading to a Caesarean section or forceps delivery. There was also a great deal of research undertaken at the hospital. One of our tasks seemed to be forever collecting huge bottles of 24-hour urine samples from the women, without any explanation. The doctors were treated like gods and it was clear that student midwives were at the bottom of the pecking order – no questions were ever encouraged. I can recall that epidurals were still a relatively recent procedure for pain relief during labour. Unfortunately it went disastrously wrong for one poor woman and as a consequence she had been unconscious for some time. All I knew was that she was being nursed in a side cubicle but was never to find out what happened to her.

By five months or so into the course I was way behind in completing the required minimum number of normal deliveries; and a weird system had been developed to address the problem.

Those of us in dire need of a delivery were issued with a number. Every so often a midwife would come running into the ward and shout out a number – it seemed similar to ordering a Chinese takeaway. If your number came up, you then needed to rush out and rapidly follow her down to the labour ward.

On arrival there was barely time to say hello to the mum-to-be before washing my hands and gowning up. Then I would get on with the delivery under the supervision of one of the labour ward staff. The most appalling incident was when a midwife was actually holding back the head of the baby so that I could deliver it. It was only when it was all over that you could chat to the mother and write up the records and your own notes. The most memorable experience was when I had just delivered a baby and it soon became clear that another, and unexpected one, was on its way. Although everyone was caught on the hop, twin two came safely into the world, much to the relief of the mother, me and everyone else!

The hierarchical and illogical behaviour of some of the staff was starting to get me down. The final straw was getting into trouble with the sister of a post-natal ward for becoming 'too involved' without her permission. It concerned an older middle class woman who was both depressed and struggling to breast-feed her baby. I spent some time at her bedside successfully helping the baby to suckle at last. The mother was very exhausted, and her depression developed into the more severe mental illness of puerperal psychosis.

She was transferred to a psychiatric unit in a different part of Edinburgh. After some time her husband, a journalist, contacted me saying that his wife wanted to see me. I went and was delighted to see the improvement in her state of mind, and how well she was bonding with her child. On my return to the hospital I was summoned to see the ward sister and shocked when she gave me a dreadful dressing down. A friend of hers at the psychiatric unit had informed her of my visit. All I can remember her saying repeatedly was 'Just who do you think you were? Who gave you permission to visit her?' It seemed to be such a daft and unjust admonition that after her dismissal of my initial response concerning the husband's request, it seemed better to just keep quiet. Once out of her office, I struggled to stop the tears from running down my face and felt a sense of blackness surrounding me.

There was no way that I wanted to continue my studies and I decided to look into how to become a health visitor. The idea of working in the community and visiting families in their own homes to promote health appealed much more to me than working in a hospital. In the meantime, continuing with French classes at the Institut Française helped to lessen my feelings of depression. One day I saw a small announcement on the notice board, stating that a family living near Paris were seeking a person to speak English to their two children. My mind was made up; this would be my next move!

Around the same time, while walking along the hospital corridor, the matron, Miss Margaret Auld, stopped me in my tracks. She asked me why I was looking so despondent and, lo and behold, the tears started flowing again. So she invited me to come to her office, and over a cup of tea asked me why I had changed so much from the cheerful student of six months ago. I was amazed that she even knew me, never mind the degree of sympathy and support offered, so I just told her all my problems.

Firstly she said that she would speak to the sister in question, as I had been quite right to visit the psychiatric unit. Then she proceeded to enquire about my future plans, and promised to give me a reference when I applied to become a health visitor. She reassured me that the obstetric experience I had gained at the hospital was sufficient to meet the requirements of the course. Finally, she told me to apply for the job in Paris and to let her know the outcome. When I heard that the job was mine she was one of the first to offer her congratulations and wish me well in

France. So in December 1969 at the age of 22 years, I was about to embark on my first ever experience of living abroad.

IX

Nine months in Paris

I arrived at the Gare du Nord railway station in December 1969 clutching a photograph of Madame Lacroix. She was co-owner of a maternity and surgical clinic in the Paris suburb of Vitry-sur-Seine, quite close to Orly airport. We had exchanged photos, and the plan was that she would collect and drive me to what would be my home for the next nine months. This didn't quite work out, as on my arrival there was a huge crowd and unfortunately I was not able to spot her in the throngs of people milling about.

After hanging around for a bit I decided to find a taxi, confident that my French was good enough to communicate the address to the driver. This proved to be the case, but what I hadn't reckoned with was that the trip involved crossing half of Paris. I was staggered at the cost of the fare and thoroughly disheartened at such an expensive start to my stay. Fortunately Madame Lacroix, who arrived back from the station at around the same time, took pity on me and paid the fare. She was as friendly and as chic as she appeared in her black and white photograph.

We entered the clinic reception and after a few quick introductions to members of staff, took the lift up to the family flat. Once inside, all the family came to greet me and I was shown around their large apartment that took up a whole floor above the clinic. Both Monsieur and Madame Lacroix were doctors, he an obstetrician and she a neonatologist (a specialist in newborn babies). Monsieur Lacroix was well built, had quite a Germanic appearance and welcomed me with a smile and a few words of English. It was clear that he adored his wife and that this was a mutually loving relationship. Their son Jean-Christophe was ten and their daughter Martine eight.

Although my role was principally to help the children with their English, the family were delighted that I spoke some French and could understand them quite well (although the children spoke far too fast for me at times). Jean-Christophe was asked to take me to my room and as we went, chatting in French, he asked me why the British had killed Joan of Arc. Welcome to France! I can't remember my reply but he appeared satisfied, and we were to get on extremely well during the next nine months. He was a serious, gentle and quiet youngster, and I was really pleased to discover that he had a great sense of humour. Martine was bright, like her brother, very chatty and could be quite feisty at times. She had a great sense of fun and we also got on fine, once I had set a few boundaries.

One of the first jokes I played on them was when they asked me to explain a word I had used, namely 'berk' for somebody who was stupid. I said it was too rude to explain and wouldn't let on, despite their pleas, throughout my whole time there or on subsequent visits to see the family. However, eventually I caved in on a trip to Paris about ten years later. They were studying at university and invited me out for a meal in the Latin Quarter, as they knew it was one of my favourite locations. I was amazed to find that they had not forgotten the word and agreed that as they were now both adults it was time for me to reveal the meaning.

They were genuinely surprised at my answer, but saw the funny side of it all. To my horror, I later discovered that there is indeed a ruder definition of the word but am not sure whether they ever discovered it.

The apartment comprised four bedrooms, two bathrooms, a kitchen and an L-shaped dining room/library. Hanging from ceiling to floor of the library wall was a most beautiful tapestry. There was also a very large balcony that took up two sides of the building and included a small sports area. Everybody made me feel extremely welcome and all occasionally tried to speak some English, with Madame Lacroix being the most proficient. I was asked to consider myself a member of the family and to take all my meals with them. The food was an eye-opener and I was introduced to a wide range of delicious French cuisine! Over and above the fish, steaks, cheese and patisserie, the children insisted I try their snack of a buttered baguette sandwich containing chocolate squares. They were delighted with my very positive reaction. It didn't take me long to become accustomed to strong black coffee, as well as tea with lemon rather than milk.

There was one unfortunate outcome for me that was thought to have arisen as a complication of eating steak tartare. This is made from raw ground beef, a raw egg and various seasonings. Madame Lacroix began to get worried when I developed a flu-like illness and swollen glands and promptly referred me to a medical specialist in the north of Paris. He seemed to be a very efficient doctor but a man of few words. I'd hardly sat down when he asked me: 'Se pourrait-il que vous soyez enceinte?' – 'Could you be pregnant?' My immediate thought was 'What the …?' but in spite of my shock I was able to splutter back 'Pardon?' It turned out that he was a specialist in toxoplasmosis, an illness that can cause complications for the unborn baby in early pregnancy. The infection, which I did indeed have, can be acquired from cats or eating uncooked meat. There was no treatment given and my symptoms gradually subsided, but the experience put an abrupt halt to eating any more steak tartare.

The need to improve my French was brought home to me pretty quickly when I decided to venture alone into Paris for the first time. The trip entailed taking a bus to reach the nearest metro station. I confidently tried to purchase a ticket from the driver only for him to start talking to me very quickly. My mind froze, as nothing he said seemed to make any sense. By now a queue of people had formed behind me, and I was feeling very foolish for holding everyone up. Some of them joined in this one-way conversation, making the situation even more incomprehensible. Then a man speaking some English explained that for frequent journeys it would be cheaper to buy a book, or carnet, of tickets. So that's what the poor driver had been helpfully trying to tell me!

Prompted by this experience I registered for French lessons at the Alliance Française in Paris, where I met an American called Sarah, who was in France to study the language. We are still friends, over 40 years later. There were a few initial misunderstandings between us due to our different interpretations of certain words. Two examples come to mind. During a break in the lesson Sarah asked for directions to the bathroom. 'What,' I responded, 'don't you have a bath where you live?!' not realising that she only wanted to find the toilet. Another time she asked me to pass her purse and looked askance when I started to ferret around in her handbag. Fortunately we both had a good sense of humour.

Sarah recalls some memories from our time in Paris:

We were the only English-speaking students and quickly found each other. We were both young, single and on small budgets! We bonded over croque monsieur or cheap hot dogs for lunch and our almost daily indulgence – French pastries with afternoon tea. You were Elizabeth Furlong then. We talked about everything and anything – the way 22 year olds do. You told me about your family, mother and school experiences, particularly an unhappy episode with nuns. Race did not define our relationship – you were Elizabeth, I was Sarah and we were friends.

We enjoyed walking all over the city, visiting museums, going to cheap afternoon movies and talking, talking, talking. The franc was only 20 cents, and, therefore, five francs to the US dollar. Paris was not horribly expensive then. [It was for me though!] A decent steak/frites dinner might be 10 francs. Not that we splurged on that very often. We talked about so many things: French history, English history, literature (we both loved to read), English attitudes, American attitudes, French music, the funny differences between American English and English English, crossword puzzles, and, of course, boys. Or men, since we were both in our early 20s. We were still so young and carefree and innocent in many ways.

$$- o - 0 - o -$$

I was a keen photographer and would often go into the city on my own, camera at the ready. To understand what happened next it is important to remember the context. I arrived in France about 18 months after the period of rebellion by students and workers that is still referred to as simply 'Mai Soixante-Huit' (May '68). The unrest had been particularly intense in the Latin Quarter of Paris where the Sorbonne University is located. Everything was being questioned and challenged, from the education curriculum to the power of the police. Massive demonstrations and strikes had thrown the country into utter turmoil and near-collapse. While the

131

iconic President de Gaulle survived the immediate crisis, he was to resign in April 1969 following the rejection of his referendum proposing reform of political institutions.

Sometime in 1970 I decided to take a stroll around the Latin Quarter. There was a small side street lined with police vans (camions) that reminded me of the old British Black Marias used to transport prisoners. These camions were painted in pale and dark grey, and had crisscross grilled bars on the two back windows. A police siren light was on the roof. Out came my camera and I took a photo. Suddenly an armed policeman appeared from nowhere, screamed something at me while lunging at my camera and then tore it away from me. Deaf to my attempts to explain, he was incredibly rude and sneering, telling me that he was taking me to the police station for questioning. Although initially petrified, a sort of calm came over me as I decided to keep quiet until we arrived. As soon as we went through the doors into the reception I started to insist very loudly in French that he ring Madame Lacroix at her clinic, stating that she was my 'patron' or boss. His face registered shock at this information and the sudden change in my behaviour. Without any argument he immediately phoned the number and I explained to her what had happened. After she spoke with him, he became very conciliatory and allowed me to leave – with my camera. The photo taken that day is still in my collection. Madame Lacroix was extremely angry about the way I had been treated, discussing the hostility towards the police in 1968. For my part, I became more vigilant when taking photos, ensuring to keep well away from gendarmes!

Madame Lacroix and I got on extremely well and we loved telling each other funny stories. Very early on during my stay she decided to take me into the city centre for a shopping spree. I squeezed into her little sports car and off we sped on what was to be a quite zany ride. Parking seemed to be impossible near the huge department store of Galeries Lafayette. Then I experienced how it was done! Madame Lacroix bashed her way into an impossibly tiny space. Seeing the fear in my eyes, she told me to relax as cars had bumpers for a reason! We had such a great time that it was repeated several times during my stay.

The family invited me to spend Christmas 1969 with them. It was a wonderful day and I was delighted and touched by their great presents – chosen I think to encourage my developing enthusiasm for French culture. There was a newly-published biography of Edith Piaf written by her half-sister Simone Berteaut. While I knew and loved her songs, it was fantastic to find out more about her – and get to know her repertoire better listening to the French radio. I also received an LP by the singer Guy Béart, whose sublime voice and lyrics I had already encountered on the radio. I just wanted to hear more, and went on to buy most of his recordings. His death was announced while I was writing this book, so I took the opportunity to listen to his songs again, now on my iPod.

There were times that I had difficulty in understanding some of the 'argot' or slang words used in Berteaut's book, as they were not always to be found in my French-English dictionary. One day I made a note of a particular word and at the dinner table asked what it meant. Monsieur Lacroix choked on his food at the other end of the table and his wife tried not to smile, saying it was quite a rude word and she would explain it to me later. It was another salutary lesson – this time to choose a more appropriate time and place to ask questions!

Another book Mme Lacroix bought me was *Papillon* by Henri Charrière, for my birthday in 1970. Published in 1969, it was the autobiography of a prisoner who had escaped from a notorious jail in French Guyana, sparking my curiosity by the immense coverage it received in the media.

The Christmas gift I chose for the children was a record of the musical *Oliver!* that had been such a worldwide hit when it was released in 1968. Explaining the songs to them provided me with an opportunity to talk about the novels of Charles Dickens. They adored the record and soon learnt many of the lyrics.

- o – 0 – o -

It did not take me long to discover that most French people take immense pride in their language and can be quite abrupt with anyone who doesn't appear to be trying to learn it. This was certainly the case for Ann, an English nurse I knew who was working at the American Hospital in Paris. She was finding it very difficult to speak French and her stay in the city had turned out to be so utterly miserable that she was planning to return home. My efforts to encourage her to stay fell on deaf ears. For my own part, speaking French as much as possible and not being embarrassed about making mistakes seemed to help, as did not being fazed when corrected sharply by all and sundry!

Nevertheless, speaking mainly French and hearing very little English in those first few months brought on a mild bout of depression. It was a struggle to find the right French words and to speak the language in a grammatically correct manner. I really missed the opportunity of speaking, reading and listening to the English language – later, these experiences gave me some insight into how non-English speaking people must feel when first coming to live in Britain.

It helped to go to the WH Smith bookstore in the Rue de Rivoli and browse through the newspapers and books, while listening out for people speaking English. I was also a regular visitor to the British Council Library, located in the Rue des Écoles, just off the Boulevard St Michel in the Latin Quarter of Paris. Nesta Roberts was the Paris correspondent for the *Guardian* newspaper, and I learnt a great deal from her writings – so much so that I wrote to her, and to my amazement she replied, inviting me to tea at her apartment in Rue de Grenelle in the 6th arrondissement. Her sharp and incisive observations were incredibly refreshing and informative. When she discovered my interest in the events of May 1968 her enthusiastic analysis was probably equivalent to a university tutorial!

My vocabulary gradually expanded through reading French books, and I particularly enjoyed those by Maupassant. The hypocrisy of the French bourgeoisie appears to be a constant theme in his writings, an aspect that I found incredibly entertaining. Françoise Sagan's novel *Bonjour Tristesse* had been a massive hit when published in 1955. It wasn't too difficult to read and it became one of my favourite French novels.

Television programmes were initially very difficult to follow, but I was determined to persevere. An interesting example was the weekly *Les Dossiers de l' Écran*. It featured a film about a topical subject, which I would often find educational and entertaining. There then followed a discussion with a panel of experts, that seemed to just go on and on with everyone shouting over each other. At times it was so frustrating and confusing that I would reluctantly give up and retire to bed with a book. This domineering way of debating appears to continue, judging by current French programmes. Is it a British upbringing that still causes me to find this style of discussion so irritating?

Having said that, I noticed after a while that even this type of debate seemed a little easier to follow. Then came the realisation that I was thinking and counting in French – et voilà! The transition had been made, and life started to become so much more bearable and interesting.

But although my French was becoming more fluent, I still wasn't happy with my English accent. Then I read somewhere about the differences in emphasis between syllables spoken in

English and French. In the latter it mimics a machine gun, with a very even emphasis given to every section of the syllable, unlike in English. I decided to practise this in my room for the rest of that evening. The next morning I conversed in this way with the family at breakfast and, to my utter pleasure, was congratulated on not sounding so English!

During the school holidays I would take the children into Paris to wander around the parks and museums or to see a film. One day I took a trip on the metro with Jean-Christophe, Martine and the 3-year-old daughter of a French African midwife who worked at the clinic. The little girl began to get very fidgety, so much so that the woman sitting opposite her pulled a face. Unfortunately the child turned to me and said that the woman was ugly: 'Qu'est-ce qu'elle est moche!' I immediately reprimanded her and apologised to the woman. She was delighted with my response and said that it was fine and that our children can sometimes embarrass us in public. When I said that the child wasn't my daughter and that London was my home, she complimented me on my French and apologised for her assumption.

My carte de séjour or residence permit had been issued in January 1970 and I was thoroughly enjoying my time with the children. The parents provided me with free meals and accommodation together with a small allowance that was a reasonable amount for the limited amount of work that I was doing. The downside was that the cost of living in France was incredibly expensive. While there was plenty of spare time to explore Paris on my own or with Sarah, I just couldn't afford to. So it was with a heavy heart that after three months I decided to tell Madame Lacroix of my decision to quit and return to London. She was horrified, and sat me down with her husband to discuss an alternative proposition. This was to work nights at the clinic while still continuing to speak English with the children.

- o – 0 – o -

As I was not a qualified midwife my areas of work would exclude the labour ward, thank goodness! Rather, I would help the staff to settle the babies and their mothers for the night, and then assist with feeds and breakfasts in the morning. This was ideal, as I adored comforting fretful babies and chatting to the mums, who took great pride in teaching me new French words and correcting my grammar. In the evening I would feed some of the babies with a sort of pulped carrot juice, that sent them soundly off to sleep for the night. Fantastic!

The work offered me the opportunity to not only earn some extra money but to practise my French with staff and mothers alike! It was often quiet after midnight, and the staff would let me have a nap for several hours, so it was the best of both worlds. In the morning I would have breakfast with the family upstairs, and then usually still have enough energy to set off to Paris to spend time with my friend Sarah. What was even more incredible was that no tax was deducted from my earnings.

Those last six months of my stay were wonderful as I was very busy and had so much more spending money. Sarah was adept at budgeting and noted all her daily income and expenditure, a concept alien to me. A few weeks before returning to London I decided to buy a short-wave radio to enable me to continue listening to French radio programmes. To Sarah's horror, I rapidly chose and bought one without checking out other stores for a better bargain. It would take many years before my finances would be managed in a more sensible manner. The radio was fantastic though, providing many hours of listening to those French songs that I had come to love during my stay in Paris!

While working at the clinic I became friends with Paula, a French-African (Benin) midwife. She was to play such a crucial role in widening my wider political education and enabling me to embrace my black and African identity. It started off during a coffee break when she asked for my opinion about who was the 'better' colonial power, France or Britain? I honestly hadn't a clue what she was talking about, admitting that my knowledge in this area was non-existent. Paula suggested various books to read and the one that had the biggest impact was Frantz Fanon's 1952 *Black Skin, White Masks*. The title says it all. Fanon had practised as a psychiatrist in Algeria and became a political activist in the revolutionary movement for liberation from France. He was to die in 1961 of leukaemia at the age of 36 years, just three months before Algeria achieved independence.

It was fascinating to explore his ideas on the psychologically damaging effects of colonialism on black identity. It abruptly woke me up to the realisation of my own sense of inferiority due to skin colour. The memories of repeatedly washing my face as a child to become white suddenly came flooding back. It was a relief to discuss it all with Paula, but it also made me wonder why I had never properly pondered over these issues before. This longstanding negative attitude changed overnight and it was also at this point that I decided to stop straightening my hair. I was imbued with a quiet self-confidence, together with a keen desire to challenge racism whenever possible. There was also a burning need to widen my reading, as I was genuinely horrified at my own ignorance concerning black culture and politics.

While still enamoured with French culture, I was becoming conscious that their media content was extremely white and Eurocentric. For example, it took many years after leaving Paris before I became aware of the French Caribbean départements of Guadeloupe and Martinique and that the latter was the birthplace of Frantz Fanon. A novel that I should have discovered much earlier is Joseph Zobel's acclaimed autobiographical novel *La Rue Case Nègres* (1950, *Black Shack Alley* or *Sugar Cane Alley*). It is set in the 1930s

French colony of Martinique and follows the educational success that Zobel achieved, in spite of intense poverty and racism.

My ambition to become a health visitor never wavered and I made several trips back to London to ensure my place on a course as well as sponsorship from an employing authority. The Hovercraft was my favourite form of transport across the English Channel. During one such trip in January 1970 I noticed a black man was constantly staring at me. He eventually approached and apologised for bothering me, but wanted to know where I was from. Here we go again, I thought, and trotted out the standard refrain: 'Half-Irish, half-Nigerian and born in Birmingham, England.' He immediately responded with 'But there's no such place as Nigeria, don't you know there's a war on?' The Biafran War had been raging from July 1967 and was due to end in the next week or so. The images of pot-bellied starving children had sent shock waves around the world.

While aware of my Nigerian heritage I had no knowledge of my father, not even his name, and thus felt no personal link to this conflict. The man continued: 'You look like an Igbo, it's really important that you find out about your father.' It was so interesting to hear him talk about the war and about the plight of the Igbo people. Many years later I was to read of a similar encounter experienced by Jackie Kay, the Scottish/Nigerian poet and novelist who had been adopted from birth. In *Red Dust Road*, her 2010 memoirs of tracing both biological parents, she describes how a man she met on a train in Manchester told her that she looked Igbo. It was to prove correct for both of us.

The Hovercraft encounter, together with my greater interest in black history, convinced me that I needed to discover more about my Nigerian father. First things first though, as by now I had been offered a place to study health visiting at Chiswick Polytechnic. The London Borough of Brent had also agreed to sponsor my place and provide me with employment once qualified.

The young woman who returned to London in the summer of 1970 was very different from the one who left nine months before. Now fluent in French, I was more mature and self-confident, and much happier. I was looking forward to starting my health visiting studies, and I felt more at ease with both my white Irish and black Nigerian heritage. I was also keen to widen my horizons and become involved in black community activities, and I was determined to learn more about my father. And you never know, I might even search for him one day!

X

A radical health visitor

On returning from France I needed to find accommodation urgently in readiness for the health visiting course at Chiswick Polytechnic College. Fortunately it wasn't that difficult and I was soon sharing a flat just off the High Street in Acton with Pippa, a student teacher. It was to prove a great success as we hit it off straightaway.

The one-year programme was a combination of college-based lectures and observation visits followed by a two-month supervised placement at a child health clinic in Wembley, Brent. Life outside studies proved to be much more attractive and while enjoying some of the lectures, others were somewhat tedious. The Principal Tutor was a far cry from Miss Papa of my student nursing days. Let's just say that I wasn't one of her favourite students, although I was never quite sure why. So it was extremely enlightening to receive this recollection by Sue H, a fellow student at the time: 'My lasting memory of you is of a feisty and questioning fellow student – displaying extreme tolerance of that awful Principal Tutor and her racially discriminating attitude towards you!!'

On returning there years later to give a talk on sickle cell disease, a former tutor informed the class that a public health doctor had complained to her once that I was doing a crossword puzzle during his lecture. That particular session must have been incredibly boring as it was one of my favourite subjects.

Being on placement at the child health clinic was so much more interesting as it included visiting families in their homes, predominantly focusing on mothers and their young children. The community was very diverse, comprising mainly white British, Caribbean and South Asian families. Many of the latter had recently been expelled from East African countries such as Kenya and Uganda. It took a few years for a Gujarati speaking health visitor to be appointed to help support and signpost them to local health services. I was to learn a great deal from her about their cultural beliefs in respect to nutrition, childbirth, and parenting.

I still have a small red diary for 1971 in which for some unknown reason I decided to record brief notes concerning daily activities and occasional observations. This was the only year I documented my life in such detail, as I normally only use diaries to remind me of forthcoming events. It has turned out to be a very useful record and something of an eye-opener! Some of the comments now seem naïve and occasionally downright crass, but most are helpful recollections of my life and views as a 23/24 year old. Without it, there is no way I could have recalled the minutiae of what had clearly been an incredibly hectic period. Over and above my studies it comprised a growing political and community activism together with a very lively social life. There is also evidence of the vast number of books I was reading, the frequency of severe asthma attacks and a great deal of travel. It was somewhat exhausting to read back through all the details – and I can imagine that such a frantic pace of life would perhaps have had an impact on my health. It was a great time though!

The diary revealed an unhealthy start to 1971 due to becoming ill with bronchitis and asthma. The end of the year was no better apparently, as my mother comments in a letter to me in early 1972: 'I hope you are keeping well, and not overdoing it. You didn't seem at all well at Christmas. Look after yourself.' There is a brief entry about spending a few days in Wolverhampton at Christmas. I can't remember any details, but by now I was in more regular contact with my mother, and this holiday visit was a rare overnight stay. A month later, 10 year old Pam wrote a sweet letter thanking me for the very popular present of a record player. She added that as a result it cut down the amount of time they were now watching telly and 'It stops mum putting so much money in to the TV slot meter.'

Apart from college lectures, the months that followed were occupied with going to hear a host of speakers at meetings arranged by the Fabian Society, Labour Party, Socialist Medical Association (SMA) and the more radical Needle health group. The latter was my favourite organisation and I was involved with it for a couple of years. The name came from the title of a magazine they produced, the purpose of which was to well and truly 'needle' those trying to dismantle the NHS. Members were drawn from all sectors of the health service and included nurses, students, technicians, porters and doctors. Although unable to recall meeting her then, it turned out that one of the medical students had been Dr Moira Dick. She was also a member of the Socialist Medical Association. I came to know Moira well in the 1980s through our mutual work in sickle cell when she was a consultant community child health specialist in south London. It was only after we had both retired that these common links became apparent. As well as that, she had studied at Newnham College, Cambridge. What a small world! Needle challenged, amongst other issues, the growth of private practice within the NHS, nursing culture, inadequate mental health services and reorganisation of the NHS.

Through attending these various meetings I was able to listen to Martin Ennals, human rights activist and Secretary General of Amnesty. Other speakers included Labour politicians such as Ennals' brother David, Harold Wilson, Barbara Castle, Richard Crossman and Dr John Dunwoody. There were also talks by newspaper editors such as the *Guardian*'s Alastair Hetherington and William Rees-Mogg of *The Times*.

By now my pride and joy was a wonderful orange Mobylette scooter, purchased through monthly payments. It was in France that I first appreciated their incredible popularity as they were such an inexpensive form of transport. The Mobylette offered me a brilliant and cheap way of zipping around London (and going to France for a summer holiday) as the petrol consumption was very efficient, although it was prone to breakdowns. One day I took my friend Helen (sitting on the passenger seat) on a trip to Hyde Park Corner. When we prepared to leave the scooter wouldn't start and I had to push it 5 miles back to Acton. The only comment in my diary is 'Exhausted'. It took nearly a week to repair the damage, which it transpired had been caused by somebody putting ½lb of sugar in the petrol tank. A year on, when a motorist ignored my right of way and crashed into me, I reluctantly decided to think about saving to buy a second-hand car.

The House of Commons became a regular place to scoot off to, as it was possible to obtain tickets from the local MP to attend Prime Minister's Question Time and debates. These experiences widened my understanding of the process of legislation as well as the opportunity to spot politicians seen in the newspaper or on television. It was a huge shock to watch the rowdy behaviour of some of the MPs.

In between all this external activity there was also time spent at home tidying up, watching television with Pippa, knitting, listening to music and reading. Unsurprisingly during this phase of my life, many of the books were political in nature. One that had a great impact was the fantastic and searing *The Ragged-Trousered Philanthropists*, the working-class novel by Robert Tressel.

My diary entry for Sunday 21st February records: 'Woke at 10am, bright cold day. Went to Trafalgar Square to watch TUC demonstration, had a good view – sunny day. Watched TV & finished book.' Searching the Internet helped me discover that over 200,000 people had marched that day from Hyde Park to Trafalgar Square, protesting against the proposed Industrial Relations Act.

During the Easter holidays of 1971 I flew to stay with a friend in Dublin. On a hot Easter Sunday we visited Phoenix Park followed the next day by a trip to Glendale. We also visited Avoca in County Wicklow, the incredibly beautiful town which many years later would be the location for the television programme *Ballykissangel*. The following Tuesday, we hitchhiked up to Belfast to start our travels around Northern Ireland staying at Youth Hostels and once with a friend's relative.

Our itinerary included Belfast, Downings in County Donegal, then Portrush and along the stunning North Antrim coast, taking in the magnificent Giant's Causeway. This was three years after the start of the Troubles. We were to learn the opposing points of view as we obtained lifts from both Protestants and Catholics. One of the latter told us proudly that he had nine children and that there would be more in order to ensure that the Protestants didn't wipe them out. A Protestant driver addressed our ignorance concerning William of Orange with a history lesson about the Battle of the Boyne. As we had reached our destination before it was finished, he just pulled over and continued for about 15 minutes!

Young and perhaps naïve, we had little sense of fear throughout the journey, although quite conscious of the on-going conflict. While aware of my family links with Wexford in the Republic of Ireland, I later discovered that my grandmother's family originated from Moygannon, as well as Rostrevor and Warrenpoint in County Down. They became part of Northern Ireland following the partition of the country in 1921.

- o – 0 – o -

Back in London I was becoming more involved with the local Labour Party and became Assistant Secretary and then Treasurer. My diary records canvassing with my flatmate for the May 1971 local elections and that Labour gained a majority of seats on the council. While interested in listening to visiting speakers and attending demonstrations, there was a more tedious side to some of the meetings. An observation made about the Annual General Meeting was: 'usual stifling petty arrangements'. There were also very few, if any, discussions concerning minority and immigrant communities and I was conscious of being the only black member at meetings.

As a result I volunteered in June 1971 to do Saturday work for Ealing CRE (Council for Racial Equality) and helped out at various local school projects. The first one was held at the Dominion Cinema in Southall where helpers taught 40 children. On Saturday 9th October I became involved with one in Acton: '1st day of Saturday school. 64 children arrived. Bit chaotic but worthwhile'. The following week 65 turned up and it was more organised and settled. That same evening I went to Ealing Town Hall for the COA (Caribbean Overseas Association) anniversary dance where a steel band played. A few months earlier, the COA hall had been set on fire and I noted that this was now the 3rd arson attack: 'wrecking hope of having project there. Wrote letter to *Acton Gazette*'. I cannot recall if it was ever published.

Through being involved in local activities I became acquainted with Jessica Huntley and her fellow Guyanese husband Eric. They had established in Ealing one of the first UK black publishing companies, Bogle L'Ouverture Publications that was named after the freedom fighters Paul Bogle (Jamaica) and Toussaint L'Ouverture (Haiti).[7] I began to help sell their books at community events all over London and when I had a mini, further afield, such as at St Pauls Festival (now Carnival) in Bristol. This was really when my black history education began! Sitting behind the book-stall before the event kicked off or during a boring session gave me a chance to pick up a book and read. Over the years these included *The Lonely Londoners* (1956) by Trinidadian author Samuel Selvon, Eldridge Cleaver's 1968 memoirs *Soul On Ice*, the 1971 edition of Paul Robeson's 1958 *Here I Stand*, and Walter Rodney's 1972 *How Europe Underdeveloped Africa*. Bogle L'Ouverture published the latter and Jessica asked me to help Walter, a fellow Guyanese, by driving him to various meetings during his visits to London from Tanzania and then Guyana. We were to become firm friends.

Other literature that made a big impression on me included Nelson Mandela's 'I am prepared to die' speech at the start of the Rivonia Trial in 1964 and *Angela Davis: an autobiography* (1974). It was thrilling to hear her speak at the London Keskidee Centre on 10th December 1974 and I still have the black and white photos that I took of her at this event.

- o – 0 – o -

Back in June 1971, having finished the written health visitor exams, I went by scooter to Paris for a holiday with the Lacroix family. What a crazy journey it turned out to be! My suitcase constantly sagged to the right, even though I had fastened it as securely as possible at the back of the scooter. Motorists were constantly hooting to alert me, so to avoid stopping all the time I would just do a thumbs-up and sail on.

Sunday 6th June saw me setting off at 8.15pm for Newhaven planning to catch the 11.45pm boat to Dieppe. Unfortunately I missed it by just 5 minutes due to scooter problems encountered on the South Circular, apparently because of poorly mixed petrol. So I slept in the waiting room before boarding the boat at 7.30am. My diary records leaving Dieppe at 11.15am, eventually arriving in Paris at 4.30pm. The only scary time was negotiating access on to the Boulevard Périphérique, the dual carriageway that encircles Paris and one of the busiest routes in Europe. Goodness knows what a sight I must have been! Not surprisingly I was very tired on reaching Vitry-sur-Seine. After a refreshing bath I joined the Lacroix family and their relatives for a meal to celebrate La Fête des Mères (Mother's Day).

Back in England I commenced a two-month period of supervised health visiting practice in Wembley. It proved to be a happy and interesting experience as it involved having a very small caseload of families with young children. This was under the supervision of experienced health visitors until they felt confident enough to let me visit on my own.

All appeared to be going well until I spotted an anomaly in the way that one portion of the weekly statistics were being completed. Health visitors were asked to record the number of families they had seen who were from the 'New Commonwealth'. When I asked the first health visitor for the definition of this term she was quite upfront and said she wasn't sure but thought it was non-white families. The next one replied: 'Well, people like you dear'. This patronising comment galvanised me into questioning as many other health visitors as possible. Their answers included 'black people', 'Indians', 'non-English speakers' and 'recent immigrants'. Me: 'From any country?' Reply: 'Err no, just countries like Africa'. Me: 'That's a continent'. Silence. Finally, this intriguing one: 'You know, people with funny names'.

The New Commonwealth was a term referring primarily to recently decolonized and predominantly non-white countries in the Caribbean, African and South Asia.

I explored the reason for collecting these statistics and discovered that it was in order to claim 'Section 11' funds. These were available from the Local Authority for the provision of services specifically relevant for immigrant communities.

So my new query concerned the use of any funding obtained as I had observed that there were no interpreters to assist health visitors. This was a step too far for Mrs Lines, my overall health visitor supervisor. Notwithstanding her previous glowing reports, she determined that my attitude was not conducive to health visiting and proceeded to fail my practice assessment! This meant that I would not be able to become a health visitor. Fortunately I was advised by a member of the Socialist Medical Association to speak with Dr Ernest Grundy, the local Medical Officer of Health. What a breath of fresh air it was to meet up with him, never mind being congratulated for my actions. He subsequently ordered a review of how the 'New Commonwealth' statistics were being collected and the use being made of any funds obtained.

Representations were also made to the College about the threat to fail me. I was called to appear before a panel to confirm my final results. My diary records on Friday 22nd August that I sat outside room 222 for one hour before being informed 'that there would be no necessity for me to see the examiners'. The next day a letter arrived confirming my status as a qualified health visitor – phew!

In this same month I record my first taste of public speaking – travelling by scooter to the venue, all the way over in Leytonstone, East London. I don't mention the subject of the talk in my diary, only that it was 'Not too bad' which is interesting as this was something that I was to enjoy doing a great deal in the future.

- o – 0 – o -

From September 1971 I was to work as a health visitor for three years, and it was a wonderful experience. My base was a small child health clinic located in the grounds of One Tree Hill Park in the Alperton district of Wembley. At this time community child health services were managed by the Local Authority (their transfer to the NHS took place in 1974). Miss Sansom was the only other health visitor there, a much older and very experienced practitioner who I liked and greatly respected. She was happy to advise me in those early days and then allow me the freedom to innovate where I saw fit. This included collaborating with a male social worker to set up a Mother and Toddler group that for the first eight months met on a weekly basis in the clinic. When the numbers regularly reached 20 to 30 it moved to larger premises in a local youth and community centre, courtesy of the Education Department.

The group was established after I observed that many mothers came to the clinic every single week to weigh their healthy, thriving babies. One day there was an incredibly long queue and I apologised for the delay but also asked why they came so often. The response of one mother: 'To get out of the house and have a chat with an adult!' was greeted with nods and a round of applause! The successful outcome of the group in reducing their feelings of isolation was written up in my first ever-published article. On re-reading it so many years later I note my observation that while Asian and Caribbean mothers attended, they were few in number. It appeared in 1975 in the now defunct *Nursing Mirror & Midwives Journal* and was entitled 'A mothers' group in Alperton'.

It was liberating to have the freedom to make links with a wide variety of people who could help solve problems encountered by families. For example a local councillor was quick to resolve one for a family with three small children. Visiting them during a particularly cold spell I discovered the mother and toddlers huddled around an open oven in the kitchen. They had no heating in their council house and were just being passed from pillar to post by various officials. The councillor and I were to become close colleagues and he often expressed a wish that more professionals would contact him about issues in his local ward.

I made it a priority to visit the general practice that many families were registered with and was fortunate to meet Dr Walker, the senior partner, and Megan, the practice nurse. She recalls:

You came as our new health visitor in 1971 and were very different from any previous ones we had ever had. You weren't just interested in health; it was also the much broader aspects of people. This was because the area that you were working in had quite a lot of social and financial problems. You certainly would come back and discuss with Dr Walker and put people in touch with the right people to make sure they were getting the correct benefits. This may well have been your role but I can't ever remember any other health visitor talking about that sort of thing before. So I was very conscious of the fact that you connected with people on a different level. You were concerned about them and you wanted to help them. It wasn't just going to see the baby, which people often thought that's what a health visitor did – no, it was far broader. I remember you being happy and confident.

This last sentence is striking, as Megan was the first person to describe me as being confident. It is a sharp contrast with that shy student nurse in Paddington, and can be attributed not only to maturity but to a growing inner sense of self-worth, gained from my wider experience of life and growing radicalisation.

Megan continued:

You've never been a pushover at all, but you've always had a strong sense of justice and you feel strongly about things that you consider right.

There were three families on my caseload that had children with genetic blood conditions. The first had a boy and a girl who were non-identical twins whom I visited frequently from birth. Their mother was very anxious as they were her first and only children, and the initial problems were typical queries relating to feeding and sleeping patterns. She was also very isolated and at times felt tired and depressed. As the twins got older I would see them peering out of the window and becoming more excited as I walked down the path to their front door. They were a delightful pair! One seemed to be underweight and pale so I asked Dr Walker for his advice. He asked to see the two of them, and to everybody's shock, blood tests revealed that both had Thalassaemia Major. This is an inherited anaemia due to inadequate haemoglobin production and requires lifelong blood transfusions. At this time in the UK the condition was mainly seen in Greek and Turkish Cypriots and South Asian communities. One reason for our surprise was that one of the parents was white English, although I later learnt that the latter have a 1 in 1,000 chance of being a healthy thalassaemia carrier.

Two other children on my patch had sickle cell anaemia – another inherited anaemia that causes severe, painful crises. One of the mothers had gone to the public library to find out more, only to be devastated on reading that it was a disease 'that affected Negro children who rarely survive beyond the age of 2 years of age'. This information was grossly out of date in both prognosis and in the use of the word Negro. At that time I didn't know anything about either thalassaemia or sickle cell disorders and couldn't have predicted that I would specialise in both and reconnect with these children into their adulthood.

- o – 0 – o -

On 11 September 1971, a few weeks after qualifying as a health visitor, I embarked on my first trip to the USA. It was organised at a very affordable price by the Fabian Society in partnership with Americans for Democratic Action (ADA). Our three-week programme of activities commenced in New York before moving on to Philadelphia and ending in Washington, D.C. Ann Clwyd MP (then Ann Roberts, working as a journalist) was one of the members of the group and we were to become friends. At the time she was on the Welsh Hospital Board as a lay member. It ran the whole of the health service in Wales until the Tories abolished it in 1974, transferring its responsibilities to the Welsh Office. She recalled:

We were with a group of people who had a particular interest in the health service, do you remember? We started talking and sort of palled up together. You came over as a very caring person, very determined, you asked questions that some people might not ask, you weren't afraid to ask them. I just saw you as a sort of fellow spirit actually.

Then she described an incident that I had completely forgotten:

I remember on our first stop in New York, we were sitting on high stools in the breakfast room and this porter just fell. You thought he might have had a heart attack and as a nurse you immediately went over to him. I remember the scene very well and you tried to loosen his tie and they said 'Stop, don't touch him'. I remember how surprised we all were! 'You've got to first check his medical insurance status'. They decided which ambulance to call. That gave me a shock and I'm sure it certainly gave you one as well.

That was our introduction to the USA health service!

Ann remembered that a lot of people wanted to meet us to learn more about the NHS. 'This was particularly the case for those who were then prominent in the Democratic Party, so we met people like Hubert Humphrey and the Kennedys.' Our meeting with Senator Ted Kennedy in Washington, D.C. remains a vivid memory, together with his searching questions about health visiting and community health services.

During a sightseeing trip to New York's Times Square on 13th September, I happened to look up at the zipper (moving illuminated bulletin board). It was showing news of the deaths of ten hostages and 29 inmates following the storming of Attica prison by state troopers. Governor Nelson Rockefeller had given the order after a four-day occupation following a riot about prison conditions and the murder of a prison guard.

Before leaving London I was given the address of a New York Chapter of the Black Panther Party, somewhere off Harlem's 125th Street. It was a time of great tension between the police and this radical organisation. When asking for directions the person realised I was from England and said he would take me there, as it wasn't advisable to wander around on my own. On our arrival, someone peered through a grill asking for the name that my London contact had given me, then unlocked the door. I was immediately escorted downstairs to a small basement room where a group of about 14 youths were huddled together taking turns to read aloud from a book. This turned out to be *Soledad Brother – The Prison Letters of George Jackson*, published in 1970.

154

Silently they shuffled up to make a space to sit, and then I waited somewhat nervously for the book to reach me. When I began to read there were shocked faces and shouts of incredulity. 'You from England sister?!' The book was taken from me and friendly questions were fired left, right and centre. When the session ended and it transpired that I was on my own, a couple of them were charged with accompanying me back to the subway. It was an exhilarating meeting and was one of the most incredible and heart-warming experiences of my stay.

Another unforgettable event in New York was when our British delegation met Bayard Rustin, the noted African-American civil rights and gay activist. He was the organiser of the 1963 March on Washington for Jobs and Freedom, attended by over 200,000 people and led by Rev. Martin Luther King Jr. and others. I was enthralled by his succinct and vivid accounts of key moments in the history of the civil rights movement. He also provided background information about the Attica prison situation. So it was with utter horror and embarrassment to hear one of our group smugly state that Britain did not have any similar incidents! Quick as a flash and in his impeccable way of speaking, Rustin retorted sarcastically: 'Didn't you all have something called the Notting Hill riots in 1958?'

When the meeting ended one of the organisers handed me a note from Bayard Rustin asking me to come and have a chat with him. At this period I had a huge Afro and during the trip was often mistaken for an American. As soon as I said a few words of greeting Rustin burst out laughing and said he had been wondering why I was with the group. We discussed the nature and objectives of the trip in more detail. He asked me whether I would like to learn more about civil rights during my stay in Washington, D.C. and of course the answer was a resounding Yes! To my astonishment he asked me to accompany him to a room where there was a phone, took out his bulging address book and proceeded to call several people. They were informed about my impending visit and asked to brief me on their history as well as show me around various projects and organisations. One such person was Marion Barry who would be elected eight years later for the first of four terms of office as mayor of Washington, D.C. Back in that autumn of 1971 Marion took me on a conducted tour of an organisation he had co-founded called Pride Inc. It offered an opportunity for jobless black youths to work their way up the employment ladder. This started with rat catching and cleaning streets, with the possibility of progressing on to leadership roles in petrol stations owned by Pride.

There is no doubt that I returned to London a changed and more informed person particularly in respect to the US black civil rights movement.

Ann was the only member from the British group that I would continue to keep in touch with. She was to invite me regularly for wonderful visits to Cardiff where I met her journalist husband Owen, who later became Head of Programmes at BBC Wales. One memorable trip included several days on the beautiful Gower Peninsula. Owen was an erudite and gentle person who was later diagnosed with multiple sclerosis. It was devastating to hear Ann speak in Parliament about the poor care he received at the time of his death in 2012.

In the autumn of 1972 my local branch chose me as a delegate to attend the Annual Labour Party conference being held in Blackpool. Ann was also going and invited me to share a flat she was renting for the week. As a result of her contacts and introductions I was able to observe at close quarters key players within the Labour Party. While it made for an incredibly interesting week it was here that it dawned on me that I wasn't cut out to be a party activist.

Back in Ealing, a few members were privately raising concerns about discriminatory behaviour towards Asians attempting to join a particular Labour-run social club. I was very disillusioned by the apathetic responses that led to no action at the time. It reminded me of the notorious colour bar in 1964 at a Labour club in the west Midlands town of Smethwick. Ironically, in this general election year when Labour won, Smethwick bucked the trend and voted in Peter Griffiths, a right wing Tory. The following slogan was daubed locally: 'If you want a nigger for a neighbour, vote Labour.' Two years later the actor Andrew Faulds regained the seat for Labour.

While appreciative of many of the Labour Party priorities it became clear to me that I was living in two worlds. There were so many problems affecting minority communities that were barely being addressed. This was the reason I eventually decided not to renew my membership. An example that comes to mind was the bussing of black and minority ethnic pupils in Southall to schools outside the area. This policy was in place where such pupils exceeded 30%, and had begun in Ealing in 1963 due to the concerns of white parents. It would result in the murder of Shakil Malik in 1974 after being bottled to death when boarding his school bus. Following the prosecution of Ealing Local Education Authority in 1975, bussing on the grounds of ethnicity alone was ruled discriminatory under the 1968 Race Relations Act.

In 1972 I met Peter Moses, another activist friend of the publisher Jessica Huntley. Born in Dominica in 1945, Peter sadly died of leukaemia on 20th December 1972 at just 27 years of age. His death occurred only months after he had fulfilled his dream of setting up the Marcus Garvey Supplementary Saturday School in Hammersmith, where I became a volunteer. Peter had also been very active in raising funds for other projects, such as the first ever Black Arts Festival in 1972. It was held at St Thomas Hall in

Shepherds Bush and my diary records that I attended the event on Sunday 28th May. This was the same venue where hundreds of us would gather the following year at a cultural memorial concert to celebrate Peter's life and honour this charismatic and committed activist.

Peter had invited me and a group of like-minded black volunteers to help out at a Saturday School that he had co-founded with Dada Imarogbe, a fellow Dominican. It was inspired by Bernard Coard's 1971 book *How the West Indian Child is made Educationally Sub-normal in the British School System*. The school was held in the afternoons in a small basement off the Uxbridge Road. I was to work there for more than two years with a group of enthusiastic activists, some of whom are still my friends to this day. The project was self-organised and located in a cold basement, kept warm by paraffin heaters. Over 40 years later six of them met up with me to record our memories of those heady times. As well as Dada, they included Marvlyn, Sandra, Florence, Rose and Mariamma. We recalled trips made with the children to places they had never been – Brighton comes to mind – and to the Tutankhamun exhibition at the British Museum. One of our charges was the future film maker Steve McQueen, who for a brief period came to the school with his sister when he was very young.

My friends remember me variously as 'always questioning, wanting to know everything', 'an eager beaver', 'into text books' and 'prepared to put the effort in'. As far as my being mixed race was concerned, none of them seem to have thought about it. Most just assumed that like them I would have a Caribbean or West African heritage, remembering me as friendly and with a big smile – noting my big hair, that I came 'from somewhere up North', and even that I was 'very posh'! It was wonderful to chat in this way and the surprise was how so many memories came flooding back. The group were probably unaware of the influential role they played in assisting me to absorb so much about black British history and culture. This was a period of transition from a virtually all-white environment to that of a more ethnically diverse one.

It did bring home to me though that there was a missing piece in the jigsaw puzzle in respect to my own dual heritage. So in March 1972 I at last wrote to my mother asking her for the name and any other details concerning my Nigerian father.

Dad, Nigerian Ambassador to Italy greeting Pope Paul VI. 1963

Dad in centre – on left is best friend Mr Albert Osakwe. Onitsha

Dad, in Rome as Nigerian Ambassador to Italy, 1963

Aunty 'C' – Nnabuenyi
Mrs. Cecilia Nneka Ikeme

Anionwu family, Onitsha, 1950s. Back row, far right: Uncle Sunday. Centre row from 2nd left: Aunty 'C', Uncle Chike and wife Angie, Dad and wife Regi

Back row: The Ndichie of Onitsha. Centre is Dad – lead Counsel. Source:
Onitsha Market Case The Rt. Hon Dr Nnamdi Azikiwe P.C. 1976

With Dad at Onitsha, 1978

Photo I took of Angela Davis at Keskidee Centre,
London. December 1974

In Los Angeles, August 1977

With Jessica Huntley
(Bogle L'Ouverture Publisher) at
Notting Hill Carnival, 1977

BECOMING ELIZABETH NNEKA ANIONWU

XI

Finding my father

I can understand you wanting to know about him, if only because your friends are bound to ask questions about your nationality etc. And if you are mixing with Nigerian people, you just might, by some wild coincidence, meet him, or people who know him. But although I have given you all the information I can, such as it is, I would advise you against making any effort to trace him. At this stage it could have the effect of causing embarrassment to him and his family, and I can't see that any good would come of it.

Letter from my mother, 14th March 1972.

This advice from my mother was well intentioned but it would be ignored, as the letter contained the crucial information that I had needed to know for so long – the name of my father.

I have meant for some time to tell you about your father, but as you say it isn't easy here. He is a Nigerian from Lagos. (His hometown was in fact Onitsha in south-eastern Nigeria). His full name is Lawrence Odiatu Victor Anionwu. He used to be known as Lawrence, or Lawrie, among his English friends, but preferred to use his Nigerian name, Odiatu Anionwu.

It was such a strange sensation seeing the surname of my father for the very first time and uppermost in my mind was how I should pronounce it. My mother continued:

I met him when I was at college. I was 19 at the time. He was quite a bit older. He had been studying law in England for some years, and was on the point of being called to the Bar. Shortly after obtaining his final qualifications to practise as a barrister, he returned to Nigeria, permanently. He had a great love of his own country, and had no wish to stay in England.

I didn't tell him about you until it was too late for him to alter his arrangements about going home. By that time I had realised that his feelings about me were less serious than I had imagined, and I was just an episode in his life. We did exchange a few letters after his return to Nigeria. Some years later he married a Nigerian girl. I was married to your stepfather by that time. The last I heard from him must be about twenty years ago. He was living in Lagos then, and from what I know of his plans, it seems reasonable to suppose that he is still there.

This letter must have been quite difficult to write, as it would have brought back such a painful period of my mother's life. Much later, when I obtained her correspondence with the Father Hudson's Homes, I realised that this account differed with how she had written about it at the time – in this letter there is no mention of my parents' engagement or of her plans to join my father in Nigeria.

But back to 1972. Apart from noting my father's full name at the back of my diary, I did nothing else with the information for three months. This was probably down to its psychological impact, but also because I was unsure how to proceed. It was unsettling and tumultuous at the same time, and it didn't occur for me to even discuss it with close friends. But I was determined to make enquiries about him, with the huge hope that we might even meet one day.

I pondered over who might be the best person to help me unearth the Nigerian origin of the Anionwu name. Due to the Biafran War I became aware of three main ethnic groups in Nigeria, but later discovered that there were well over 250 others. Could his surname be Igbo, Hausa/Fulani or Yoruba, or was it from one of the many other groups? There was no Internet in the 1970s! More importantly I had no contact with Nigerians at this time and my black friends were mainly of Caribbean origin.

Much of my local social life was spent at a club called the Caribbean Overseas Association, or COA, that used to be based in Acton High Street. It became a meeting place for people like me who were involved with the Saturday supplementary schools for young black children. It was also the HQ for a steel drum band and their rehearsals. One person who regularly attended was the now deceased John Roberts, a barrister from Sierra Leone who in 1975 became the first black person to be made Head of Chambers and the first to be appointed a Queen's Counsel in 1988. Married to a nurse, he also taught Nigerian law students. So I decided to show him my father's name in the hope that he might recognise which part of Nigeria it originated from. It had taken me until the evening of Monday 10th June 1972, three weeks before my 25th birthday, to work up to asking John the question.

John answered that he wasn't sure, but that he promised to investigate further and get back to me. I assumed that this would entail a discussion with some of his law students. On Wednesday, just two days later, he phoned me at the clinic in Wembley where I was catching up with some health visiting paperwork. To my utter amazement he told me that he had found my father and had already spoken to him! I was absolutely flabbergasted and in a total state of shock. All I could say was 'What, you've spoken to my father in Nigeria?'

His reply was even more extraordinary: 'No, in London, in Palmers Green.' I felt dizzy and faint; it was all so sudden and unbelievable. John gave me my father's phone number and said that he was expecting me to call him. That is about all I can remember of the conversation and I'm not even sure whether I thanked him.

Much later on it occurred to me that I hadn't even asked John how on earth he had managed to locate my father so quickly. My assumption that it was through one of his Nigerian law students proved incorrect. At the time John would occasionally collect his 10-year-old son from school. The Nigerian mother of one his friends would also be waiting, so John decided to show her my father's name. To his utter amazement she said that her husband was an Enwonwu and related to my father's wife! They were currently living in London and she immediately gave John the details.

While absolutely stunned at this development I didn't waste any more time. Once the conversation with John was completed I instantly phoned the number he had given me. Asking to speak to Mr Anionwu, the man at the other end said 'Speaking'. So it was that I heard the voice of my father for the first time. I can't remember the gist of the conversation, except that it resulted in an invitation to visit him and his wife the next day.

So as my diary notes, I 'met F' for the very first time on the evening of Thursday 15th June 1972. He and his wife Regina lived in a three bedroomed semi-detached house in Palmers Green in the north London Borough of Enfield. It was just off the North Circular Road and it was an effort to keep focussed while travelling by scooter in the rush hour along this extremely busy dual carriageway. Pulling up outside the house, the nerves kicked in and I could feel the butterflies in my stomach. I was both anxious and excited as, after taking a very deep breath, I knocked on the front door. A short, rotund, bespectacled and very dark skinned man opened it and I knew immediately it was my father. He beamed at me, looked me up and down, hugged me, stood back, gazed at me again, smiled and said 'Welcome!' I can still remember the sensation of his warm embrace and the tears that came to my eyes. It was as though they completely washed away my mother's concerns (and mine to a lesser extent) that tracing him would result in rejection and embarrassment.[8]

My father's wife Regina also came to the door and said hello, then stared at me for what seemed like a very long time. We all entered the house and Regi, as my father called her, went to prepare a meal while he took me into the sitting room. There he took out some photographs and showed me pictures of when he was a student at Cambridge and an Ambassador in Rome. Looking at one of him wearing white cricket gear he told me how much he loved all types of sport. He asked me about my mother and I told him she was fine. Then he wanted to know all about my career to date, and seemed to be very proud of my achievements.

Regi called us into the dining room and we sat down for my first introduction to Nigerian food. It was okra (ladies' fingers) stew with pounded yam, the latter looking like mashed potato. I was invited to eat it using a knife and fork although I noticed that my father dipped his hand in water before scooping a portion of yam and stew into his mouth. The first spoonful of the okra stew made me gag because it was so slimy, and there was laughter around the table. Something else was offered, but I refused as I wanted to try this new dish – and I am very pleased that I perse-vered, as it is now one of my favourites. But the one that comes top is egusi soup, made from ground melon seeds, crayfish and much more. Other dishes I've come to thoroughly enjoy include jollof rice, fried plantains (dodo) and Moin Moin (a spicy steamed bean pudding).

How to address my father was a problem for me, so I called him Lawrence, as I was not ready or brave enough to start calling him Dad – it just felt too strange, as I had simply never had a father figure. The first few letters he wrote to me were also signed Lawrence. But after a few visits my stepmother Regi took me aside, saying that I should not be calling him Lawrence as he was my father, so from then on I started to call him Dad. I later discovered that my father and his wife had lost their only child in infancy, a daughter called Genevieve. It was clearly a major cause of distress and stigma for a woman to be childless, which must have been exacerbated for Regi on discovering that her husband had other children. I was his eldest child and there were another five children by three different Nigerian women, some of whom I would meet.

- o – 0 – o -

My father was born in Onitsha, an extremely large market town on the eastern banks of the River Niger in the south-eastern state of Anambra. Across the river is the town of Asaba, and the magnificent Niger Bridge connects the two. Historically Onitsha comprised the traditional community of Inland Town and Onitsha Waterside. Inland Town (Enu-Onicha) is composed of many villages or quarters and the Anionwu family hails from one called Ogbeli-Eke. They come under the heading of Nwanna Ugwulu and the sub-heading of Okagbue Oduah. Anionwu then sits within a group of names that includes Amechi Agha, Agbapuonwu Ojiba, Uyanwa Ijagwo,

Ifenu Omodi, Onwualu Agba, Ofokansi Nwalie, Chugbo Akwue, Egbuniwe and Nnosa.[9]

My father's entry in the 1943 admissions register to Trinity Hall, Cambridge says:

born on the 5th May 1918, the son of Julius Olisa Anionwu of New Market Road, Onitsha, Nigeria.

However, the date of birth on both his death certificate and Burial Programme is recorded as the 5th May 1921, making him three years younger. This tallies with the record of his admission to Lincoln's Inn in November 1946, which gives his age as 25.

I am extremely grateful to all my Anionwu relatives for providing me with so much information about the family, in particular my cousins Joy and Osita.

My grandfather Akunne Julius Olisa Osakwe Anionwu worked at the United African Company (UAC) Ltd in Onitsha. I was informed that he was 'on the quiet side, with impeccable character but quick tempered'. He had a total of 17 children, his first two (Walter and George) by a woman from the Nzegwu family of Ogbeoza village. Walter, who was a teacher, became deputy headmaster of St Philip's Central School, Akpakaogwe Ogidi – attended by the acclaimed writer Chinua Achebe from 1936. In Ezenwa-Ohaeto's 1997 biography of Achebe, he notes that Walter Anionwu was strict and flogged pupils excessively.

My grandfather had four wives who had 15 further children. His first wife, my grandmother, was Madam Hanna Echiana Anionwu, née Ejor, from Umuaroli village. The eldest of her four children was my Aunty C, Cecilia Nneka Nnabuenyi Ikeme (1915–1997), followed by my father and then uncles Akunne Frederick Chike (1924–1994) and Onoenyi Sylvester Sunday Onyekwelu (1925–2005).

The other wives (and children in brackets) were:

Nwawuluaru Afulenu née Obiozo Onya from Ogbeoza village (Odera Ifenyinwa Mrs. Ozobia and Beatrice Nwanyife Ugonwanne Okadigbo)

Grace, née Chukwukelu from Ogbeozoma village (Okwuonitcha, Ikem, Adiba and Onochie)

Ziem, née Chukwurah from Umuiseli Quarters of Umudei village (Edna Mrs Egbunike, Azuka Mrs Obieze, Akunnia Orakwue, Nkemdilim and Nwabufoh)

According to cousin Joy, the daughter of Aunty C:

Your father did not believe in anybody but my mum because their mother died when they were very young. My mother, being a girl, married very early and was like a guardian to all of them because by then their parents were dead and everybody lived with her. This included your Dad until he went to read Law at Cambridge and Uncle Sunday before he also left for England.

My grandfather's brother was Simon Anionwu who had four wives and a total of 12 children. I came to know two of his sons very well from when they were in London; uncles Akudo from his second wife and Obiozor from his third one. I was fortunate enough to meet many of these generations of Anionwu relatives, most of whom are now deceased (including uncles Akudo and Obiozor).

It will not be surprising then, that during my first visit to Nigeria I would be introduced to countless aunts, uncles, cousins, nieces and nephews. There were many others who might or might not be more distantly related, and it was quickly pointed out to me that as a mark of respect for elders, I should address them as uncle or aunty. It wasn't a problem though, as all of a sudden I was part of this vast extended family. It was wonderful to learn how to pronounce the array of Igbo names of my relatives that also included Nkiru, Nnamdi, Emeka, Chinwe, Ngozi, Chioma and Obiageli. That's just to name a few!

Several family members had been authorised to purchase a traditional Onitsha Ozo title. The Ozo title society for men is called Agbale Nze. Uncle Chike was known as 'Akunne' and Uncle Sunday as 'Ononenyi'. Otu Odu was the equivalent titled society for women and also required a considerable outlay of money. Aunty Cecilia was addressed as 'Nnabueyi' and her daughter, cousin Joy, is 'Ugobueze' whilst several female relatives chose the title 'Amalunweze'. My father had never been interested in buying one, even though he was often encouraged (and also teased) by Ozo titled men that he was wealthy enough to do so. The Ozo title was the level below the Ndichie Chiefs (red cap chiefs) who are a council of ministers appointed by and to advise the Obi, or king, of Onitsha.

From all accounts my father was a very bright child and commenced his education at the Holy Trinity Primary School, Onitsha before travelling to Lagos for his secondary education at King's College. Sports that he loved playing included football and hockey. He returned to Onitsha for a short spell as a tutor at Christ the King College. Then in 1942, in the midst of the Second World War, he sailed to the UK via the Caribbean, travelling with other students including his very good friend Mr Albert Osakwe.

Dad commenced his Law studies at Trinity Hall, Cambridge in 1943. Records show that he achieved a third in both parts of his exams. In 1946 he proceeded to Lincoln's Inn to complete a Master of Arts degree followed by an LLB degree. They list him as 'having been admitted on 18th November 1946 aged 25, having previously been at Trinity Hall, Cambridge.' I find this date extremely interesting as I was born eight months later!

His address is given as New Market Road, Onitsha, Nigeria and his father is listed as Julius Osakwe Anionwu, retired merchant. Lawrence was called to the bar on 26th January 1949.

Trinity Hall also holds correspondence about him studying for twelve months at the Imperial Defence College, now the Royal College of Defence Studies, in Belgrave Square, London – which he was expected to complete on 16th December 1960. A few months earlier, on 1st October, Nigeria had obtained its independence from Britain. I would have been thirteen years of age at the time and living with my grandmother in Wallasey.

Dad returned to Nigeria in 1949, two years after my birth, where he set up thriving law practices in the northern city of Jos and in Onitsha. In 1957 he was appointed a Senior Crown Counsel in the Eastern Nigeria Civil Service, and in 1958 the Federal Government appointed him Nigerianisation Officer in preparation for independence in 1960. On his return from studies in London he was appointed the first Nigerian Permanent Secretary to the Minister of External Affairs.

In 1963 he travelled to Rome to take up the post of Nigeria's first Ambassador to Italy. Here he lived with Regi and his children Emmanuel and Florence, both born to local women he had met when working as a lawyer in Jos. Years before, Aunty C became aware of their existence, travelled to the north of Nigeria and obtained permission from their mothers for the children to live with her at Onitsha. I never met my sister as she married an Italian and remained in the country, and while my stepmother Regi was in contact with her, she has never been traced despite the valiant efforts of my cousin Joy.

In 1966 my father was transferred to London to take up the post of High Commissioner. This did not happen for reasons that I had never understood, but which must have been related to the terrible events unfolding in Nigeria. This same year had witnessed deadly inter-ethnic military coups and the slaughter of thousands of Igbo civilians in the north.

On 30th May 1967 Colonel Emeka Ojukwu, the military governor of the Eastern Region of Nigeria, declared independence of the south-eastern region naming it the Republic of Biafra. Less than two months later saw the outbreak of the tragic Biafra or Civil War that lasted from 6th July 1967 to 15th January 1970.

I never asked him the question: 'What did you do in the war, Daddy?', but while writing this book I trawled the Internet to see whether there was any information, and came across two interesting items.

The first was that the UK National Archives held information entitled: *Activities of Mr. L O U* (sic) *Anionwu, 01/01/1967– 31/12/1967* which both excited and intrigued me greatly. Imagine my surprise to discover that the document was a copy of three typed A3 pages of a confidential 700-word note of a meeting my father had on the 14th June 1967 at the Foreign and Commonwealth Office (FCO). This was just a mere three weeks before the outbreak of the conflict. It is also weird to realise that I would not have been too far away, completing my second year of nursing studies in Paddington.

My father spoke with Sir Saville Gardner, Permanent Under-Secretary and Head of the Diplomatic Service. The confidential record of the meeting was written for his superior, Sir Morrice James, then Deputy Under-Secretary of State at the Commonwealth Office. It was also copied to the Minister of State (then George Thomas), Mr Norris (Sir Eric Norris, Assistant Under-Secretary for West, East & South Africa) and Sir David Hunt, recently appointed High Commissioner in Lagos. The latter, according to foreign policy author Mark Curtis[10] had written in a memo to London just two days before: 'only way… of preserving unity [sic] of Nigeria is to remove Ojukwu by force and that Ojukwu was committed to remaining the ruler of an independent state and that British interests lay in firmly supporting the FMG (Federal Military Government)'. Curtis argues that previously confidential papers reveal that Britain's true interest lay in protecting their oil interests.

Gardner's note of the meeting with my father starts by recalling that he had last entertained him:

> ... *when he was (as we thought at the time) about to become High Commissioner in London just over a year ago. He told me that when the London appointment fell through owing to Ogundipe coming here, he was offered the Embassy in Moscow and subsequently the Embassy in Brazil, but he had declined both of these.*

Many years later I acquired a copy of *West Africa* magazine dated 25th February 1967, where on page 289 there was an announcement that my father had been named Ambassador to Brazil.

Gardner continues:

> *I gathered that in fact he had remained technically on leave but in receipt of full pay and had returned to the Eastern Region. He explained that he was anxious to keep aloof from both sides in the dispute, since if he made contact with either he would be suspect to the other.*

Brigadier-General Babafemi Ogundipe had been Chief of Staff and de facto Vice-President of Nigeria following the military coup on 16th January 1966 by Major-General Johnson Aguiyi-Ironsi. Prior to this, Ogundipe had been the Nigerian military attaché in London. The period of Aguiyi-Ironsi's rule was extremely short due to his overthrow and assassination on 29th July 1966.

My father said that the purpose of his visit to London was to make alternative holiday arrangements for his two children at school in the UK. The plan had been for them to return to Nigeria for the summer vacation, but this was no longer possible in the current situation.

Gardner asked him about the conditions in Nigeria and he replied that any break up of Nigeria would be a tragedy, the view of most educated Nigerians including those in the Eastern Region. He thought that the ideal would be a 'loose federation'. My father commented that the

> *tragedy was the appalling massacre in the North last year and the dispossessing of so many Ibo families had caused a bitterness throughout the Eastern Region which it is impossible to ignore. There was no family which did not have some member who had been either killed or dispossessed.*

My father did not believe that Ojuwku was unreasonable or unduly ambitious:

> *... he was, on the contrary, a well-educated and moderate person who had everything to lose from the materialist point of view in a row with the Federal Government since he had a fortune of over £½ million in investments outside the Eastern Region.*

He argued that sanctions would never succeed in bringing Ojuwku to heel and that a resort to military force would be disastrous. My father was then asked how he thought a solution could be found. He replied that he saw no prospect of Gowon and Ojuwku coming together and could not identify anyone in Nigeria 'big enough to be able to influence a settlement on the right lines'. As a result he thought that some outside influence would have to be brought to bear. Gardner pointed out the difficulty of imposing a solution from outside, unless the person was acceptable to both sides.

My father recognised that 'it would not be desirable for the British to take any initiative and, indeed, thought it would be better for white faces not to be too prominent'. He felt that there might be a role for the Commonwealth Secretariat but wondered whether they had sufficient prestige. He suggested that they should associate with 'somebody with a reputation like Kenyatta to carry the necessary weight'.

The note of the meeting ended:

> *Mr. Anionwu concluded with, I thought, a rather forced optimism that, if only the present difficulties could be got over, there was a splendid future for Nigeria and no reason why the various Regions should not work together in what could still remain a Nigerian nation.*

The second item I found online concerned a US National Broadcasting Company (NBC) clip about a 'Biafra War Press Conference', which was never broadcast. It was filmed at London's Mayfair Hotel on 20th June 1967, six days after my father's meeting at the Foreign and Commonwealth Office. It describes the clip as a:

PRESS CONFERENCE WITH M T MBU; A MEMBER OF THE SECESSIONIST STATES EXECUTIVE COUNCIL & CHAIRMAN OF THE PUBLIC SERVICES COMMISSION; & LAWRENCE ANIONWU; FORMER PERMANENT SECRETARY OF THE NIGERIAN EXTERNAL AFFAIRS MINISTRY IN LAGOS. MBU COMMENTS ON THE PROBABILITY OF ENGLAND RECOGNIZING THE NEW STATE OF BIAFRA. ANIONWU COMMENTS ON THE

PROBLEM OF ISSUING PASSPORTS TO DIPLOMATS. ORDINARY CITIZENS CAN CONTINUE TO USE NIGERIAN PASSPORTS; HE SAYS.

The now deceased Chief Matthew Tawo Mbu was an eminent politician who had also been the first High Commissioner for Nigeria in the UK between 1955–1959. During the war he was appointed the Biafran Foreign Minister from 1967–1970.

Anionwu relatives later informed me that Dad had been in Biafra for the duration of the war. He had worked for the Republic of Biafra as a Permanent Secretary, firstly in the Ministry of Labour and then in the Ministry of Works. At one point he had been living and working in Aba when the town was the target of a major bombing raid on 21st December 1967. Fortunately he was at his office as the kitchen of his home received a direct hit. Regi was in the lounge with a guest, but neither was injured. Less fortunate that day were the many people killed in the market and at Onyejiaka Hospital, including the owner Dr. Augustine Onyejiaka.

After the war ended Dad retired from public office and settled in London with Regi.

- o – 0 – o -

So in June 1972, and two and a half years after the war ended, my father and I were to meet for the very first time. One of the photographs he gave me that day showed him greeting Pope Pius VI following his appointment as Nigeria's first ever Ambassador to Italy.

Meeting my father was an incredibly pleasant experience that was obviously full of emotions. Both he and his wife tried to make me feel at home, inviting me to come and visit again and whenever I wished. But it was not until three weeks later on Saturday 8th

July, six days after my birthday, that I saw them again – after my stepmother had called wondering why I had not been in touch since my first visit. It was all probably too much for me and in all honesty the easiest strategy was to hibernate.

On the second visit my father recognised my keen interest in politics. He seemed delighted at my wish to learn more about the history of Nigeria, particularly the Biafra War – so much so that for my birthday present he bought me a copy of journalist John de St. Jorre's newly-published book *The Nigerian Civil War*, inscribing it: 'Happy birthday and in remembrance of June 15th, Lawrence 1972.' A more recent publication that has also helped me to understand the background of this horrendous conflict is Chinua Achebe's *There Was A Country – A Personal History of Biafra* (2012).

It was at this second visit that I met my Uncle Sunday, my father's youngest brother. He was with his wife Joy and four young children and invited me later that day to come back with his family to their flat near Finsbury Park. It soon became a home from home for me as it was so welcoming and hospitable, and I loved the youngsters: Charlie, Jenny, Tony and baby John. Time spent there became a very important way of introducing me to Igbo food, culture and Nigerian family life. They invited me to birthday parties in their home and to community events such as weddings. This was a gradual introduction to both my wider family and the large Onitsha community in London. Anyone originating from Ogboli-Eke is viewed as being originally related, so much so that that they are forbidden to marry each other.

It was at this time that my father informed me that I had a 16-year-old half-brother called Emmanuel (or Emma) who was in a private school in Hampshire. He was clearly concerned about his son's poor progress in subjects such as English and needing to re-sit examinations. As my father was due to return to Nigeria he asked me to visit the school, talk to his teachers and let him know what they had to say. So off to Hampshire I went and met Emma for the first time. The visit must have been somewhat disconcerting for him, particularly when I fed back the negative comments from his tutor. He shrugged off my offer to help him when in London for his holidays, and wasn't too happy when I persevered and organised some additional tuition. We never became close friends but I kept in touch with him – more out of a sense of duty to my father than anything else. Emma was incredibly arrogant but at least he was happy with the records I gave him as presents after discovering his craze for songs by Barry White!

My father was impressed with how I responded to his request for help with Emma, and it seemed to further cement our relationship. Initially I was shy around my father and rarely offered my own opinions. But one day he made a remark that I totally disagreed with and, before knowing it, I responded quite vigorously with my own views. He was absolutely delighted, saying it was clear that I had been biting my tongue for some time and that it was enjoyable and enlightening for us to debate. We then started to converse more freely about a variety of matters, and he used to ask me questions about the current British political scene and other subjects. However, I never felt confident enough to ask about his relationship with my mother. He did reveal his efforts to try to contact her in Stafford in 1960 when he was studying in London, but he was unsuccessful as her family were no longer living at that address.

My mother was genuinely delighted to hear that all was going well, even though she was clearly shocked that I had found my father so quickly. By July 1973 I had once again moved, this time to West Ealing. Here I shared a spacious flat with three other women for four years, before eventually leaving the rented sector. My own bedsitting room was large enough to have both a bed and a sofa, so Dad stayed with me when he came to London. He slept in my bed whilst I used the sofa and although it was comfortable, sleep did not come easily as he snored loudly, just like me! During one of his trips the phone rang and it was my mother with a query about a medical clue in a crossword puzzle. I quietly asked her if she would like to speak to him and while surprised, she agreed. My Dad was also happy to talk to her so I left them alone to chat together. I never asked either of them about their one and only discussion, but was very pleased to have linked them up in this way.[11]

I wrote to my Great-Aunt Kate to tell her that I had met up with my father. She received my letter on 5th September 1972, which happened to be her 83rd birthday! Her reaction to my news was very moving:

> *It was an unexpected treat, like an extra birthday treat ... Meeting with your father and discovering that you liked him and were acceptable to him was quite an experience. I am happy for you. It is good to feel that you really belong, and I am sure you will enjoy a stay in Nigeria when the time comes. Although we do not have any physical contact, I never forget you. You always have a place in my prayers.*

It hadn't taken me long to decide that I did indeed want to visit Nigeria, and as soon as possible.

XII

First visit to Nigeria

I was determined to visit Nigeria, but despite not having much money, it never occurred to me to ask my father for help in purchasing the air ticket. The funds came in a rather unusual way following a scooter crash at a roundabout as I was nearing my workplace one Friday morning in September 1972. My father had been extremely worried about me and insisted that I recuperate at his home in Palmers Green. The subsequent award of £150 compensation paid for my EgyptAir flight to Nigeria in July of the following year.

Dad returned to live in Nigeria and wrote to let me know that he had arrived at Onitsha on 24th November. The destructive legacy of the war was still being felt. The main post office had been completely damaged and the smaller local one was not coping, so there were delays in receiving my letters, which did not always arrive in the order they were sent.

He went back to his legal practice and became active in village affairs. Relatives told me that in choosing not to take the Ozo title my father may have been following in the footsteps of one of his role models, Sir Louis Nwachukwu Mbanefo. He was a renowned lawyer, jurist and Chief Justice of the Eastern Region of Nigeria. Equally prominent was his friend Chief Atanda Fatayi Williams, a colleague at Trinity College and former Chief Justice of Nigeria.

In July 1973, a year after our first meeting, my father wrote: 'I am glad you have been to see your Mum and that she is happy about your proposed visit to Nigeria.' Then he thanked me for books that I had sent him via Regi, especially *The Man Died: Prison Notes of Wole Soyinka*, adding that he was better informed for having read it. Published in 1972 it recounted Soyinka's 27-month imprisonment without trial during the Biafra war and the searing mental trauma of solitary confinement.

So at the end of that July, I set off on my first trip to Nigeria – stopping off in Cairo to visit the pyramids and see the Tutankhamun exhibition again. Stepping off the plane in Lagos on 31st July, the sweltering heat wrapped itself around my body as though enveloping me with the warmth of my Nigerian family. The country was under military rule and led by General Yakubu Gowon, the same regime that had taken over after the July 1966 coup and assassination of Major-General Aguiyi-Ironsi. Gowon's image was visible on posters throughout the airport and armed soldiers were everywhere.

The trip was mind-blowing, enjoyable from start to finish but with a few unsettling and pleasant surprises in between! My father had written to let me know that he would meet the flight at Lagos, which was then the capital of Nigeria. The plan was that we would stay a few days with a very good friend of his, Mr George Nicol, a solicitor and businessman who lived in the smart Lagos neighbourhood of SW Ikoyi. We would then travel nearly 300 miles by car to Onitsha, via Benin City.

It was with great excitement that I looked around for my father in the airport's arrival lounge. In addition I eagerly absorbed the sounds, colours and smells that assailed me. He was nowhere to be seen and I waited and waited patiently while new arrivals came and went. I knew nobody and had no telephone number except my father's at Onitsha. An unexpected boost to my morale was that several members of staff immediately recognised the name of my father and took pity on my plight. Showing one of them his phone number I asked where the nearest phone box was so that I could call and see if the family could tell me where he was. They very gently laughed saying it was difficult enough to get through to Lagos telephone numbers never mind as far away as Onitsha.

When it became late they suggested that I should stay in a nearby hotel and that if my father turned up they would let him know where I was. They found a cab for me and warned the driver to take good care of me. Once in bed I just cried my eyes out for ages because this was not how I envisioned my first evening in Nigeria. Exhausted, I fell fast asleep before being awoken by the telephone ringing in my room. To my utter joy I heard my father's voice at the end of the phone apologising and saying that he was in the lobby downstairs. He asked me to pack my case and meet him in the foyer – I was dressed in a flash! It transpired that he had misunderstood the time of my arrival (a mix-up between 24-hour and 12-hour timing). Anyway, all was sorted out and I was extremely relieved as we drove off to his friend's house.

We stayed there for a few days and I was made truly welcome, but the experience proved to be a major culture shock. Mr Nicol was a rotund and jovial man, obviously quite well off and had a servant called Friday. I was starting to realise that people can be called by the days of the week as I had an Uncle Sunday, so another day didn't surprise me. What did though was the way in which Mr Nicol would bark his orders out for Friday, who was a middle-aged man. In response he would come running in shouting 'Sah!', and sometimes his boss would just want him to turn the television on or get him a drink. This seemed crazy and quite upsetting but when I discussed it with my father he said this is a different way of life although not everyone acted like that.

The other aspects of my stay were enjoyable as everyone was extremely friendly and very keen to show me parts of Lagos life that I wanted to see, such as the market. Cloth was bought for me, which was used at Onitsha to make my first traditional wrapper and blouse.

The only downside was the mosquitoes as they took such a liking to me that I was soon covered in bites. I took anti-malarial medication religiously, nets usually covered my bed and a green mosquito repelling incense coil was lit at night. I also learnt the importance of wearing clothes that covered my arms and legs in the evening when mosquitoes came out in force. Fortunately these precautions succeeded as in all my trips to Nigeria I never fell ill with malaria.

It was wonderful to have time with my father during that long drive from Lagos, and en route he pointed out landmarks and the different types of tropical vegetation. He laughed at some of the rather naive comments I made on the journey. As an example, I couldn't see anything similar to the yellow AA boxes in Britain that you would call from should you have a breakdown. He said: 'No, there's no such thing, you just make sure your car is serviced very well before you set out on your journey.' He added that if you did break down there are mechanics galore and one would emerge from the bush onto the main road.

The scenery was incredible and the vegetation was so lush that I just sat back and thoroughly enjoyed the drive. Hawkers on the road would wave baskets of fruit and other food, and my father would occasionally pull over and quickly haggle the price down. We stopped off at Benin in the mid-west and I still can recall those red dusty roads. We stayed with my cousin Vicky and her family and she took some time off work at the university to take us to the local sights, including the palace of the Oba of Benin.

We then continued our journey along the very straight road to Asaba. My father merely told me that we were going to visit a friend's house in Asaba; he could be a man of few words. While he had a great sense of humour I realised that he would only tell you things when he was ready. It was clear that some motorists thought they were competing in a Grand Prix race – never a relaxed passenger at the best of times, that particular stretch of road from Benin resulted in a sudden increase in my heart rate due to the audacity of some of the drivers.

As we drove into the compound I saw people dancing with what looked like sticks with black feathers on them. They were waving them around and as we got nearer the house the sound of drumming became louder and I could see people holding a photograph of a man. I turned to my father in the car and asked: 'What's happening, is it a wedding?' to which he replied: 'No, it's a funeral.' My shocked face said it all.

- o – 0 – o -

When we got out of the car my father was greeted by a huge number of people. He introduced me as his daughter, and it was quite amusing to watch the reaction. It was clear that although a few were already aware, most weren't – but while surprised, their unanimous reaction was huge smiles followed by a warm embrace. At some point he introduced me to a cousin and asked her to look after me. She took me into a room where women in black dresses were sitting around a four-poster bed. Lo and behold, there was a dead man dressed in a suit, and lying in state on the bed! I couldn't believe it. There was a big fan hanging from the ceiling whirring away and people were also waving traditional fans to keep cool.

As a nurse I was obviously used to seeing dead bodies, but I had never seen one laid out in a house. Later on we went out into the compound where suddenly I saw a group of people running while carrying a coffin, and every so often throwing it up into the air. To say I was flabbergasted would be an understatement. My cousin explained that it was a ritual that symbolised the soul of the deceased person's struggle in leaving the body.

The next scene was when the coffin was being lowered into the grave. There was a huge crowd paying homage to this well-known personality. One contrast with a British funeral was the level of noise. There was a lot of weeping, wailing and shouting, and to my horror, one particular woman seemed to be about to leap into the grave. My father, seeing my amazement, tapped my arm and whispered into my ear: 'Don't worry, many of those that scream the loudest loved the person the least.' It certainly relaxed me and in fact I had to bite my tongue to avoid laughing. It was comments like this that made me realise we had a very similar sense of humour!

After the funeral we crossed over the splendid Niger Bridge into Onitsha. It had been built in 1965 to replace the ferry crossing. Akunne Abadom, an Onitsha elder, recently recounted how as a young boy in 1949, he and others went down to the ferry to welcome my father home from his studies in the UK. Unfortunately they waited in vain as he had returned via Enugu. On all future visits I would continue to be impressed by the stunning view of the Niger Bridge as it signalled the approach to Onitsha.

The family had decided that it would be best if I stayed with my Aunty Cecilia (or Aunty C as she liked to be called) in New Market Road, Onitsha. I later discovered that this was because there were severe tensions between my father and his wife Regi and also between her and my father's relatives.

We went to the house where I was given the most incredible welcome. I'll never forget it. My Aunty hugged me and generally fussed over me before showing me off to a host of visitors. I was introduced to her eldest daughter Nkiru who took charge of all my needs when her mother was out of the house. Everybody called me Lizzy (even though I never used this name) and as an elder daughter from Ogboli Eke I was also addressed as 'Abii' as well as 'Ada'.

Aunty C immediately decided that I had to have an Igbo middle name. At that point I had my Catholic names of Elizabeth Mary and my surname was still Furlong. My Aunty sat me down with other relatives and had a family discussion, something that was to happen very frequently during my stay. I didn't understand a thing, as it was all in Igbo, but occasionally some of it would be translated. There was no sense of feeling left out and it proved a useful way of picking up a few Igbo words here and there. It was decided that my new middle name would be Nneka, the Igbo name of Aunty C. I was extremely touched as it means 'My mother is supreme'. My Nigerian family were always asking about my mother and seemed to recognise how much she had done to bring me up.

It was also quite hilarious to see the reaction of people when I was introduced as 'nwa L.O.V., the daughter of L.O.V.' (a familiar way of referring to him). Some people actually realised before they were told. I couldn't believe how many people described me as 'Little Lawrence' or 'Little L.O.V.' There were also constant observations concerning how much we resembled each other.

I slept like a log that first night at Onitsha, tucked up in a bed covered with a mosquito net. In the morning, three distinct noises woke me up – cocks crowing and the sound of high-life music from a nearby shop (both of which I would always enjoy hearing), and what seemed to be several people whispering, either just outside or actually in my bedroom. I peered through the netting with one eye only to see a group of women sitting around my bed quietly talking to each other. What on earth was going on? I was quite shocked that my private space had been invaded. One of the women saw that I was awake and suddenly ripped back the net and told me they were relatives who wanted to greet me. Shouts and exclamations of 'Chukwu Dalo!' (Thanks be to God) and 'Ewo!' (Oh no!) together with the greetings of 'Nno' (Welcome) and 'Kedu' (How are you?) were heard from all and sundry. This was also accompanied with lots of hugs, kisses and comments on how much I looked like my father.

Then my aunt shooed them all out and showed me where I would do my ablutions before having breakfast. In the bath was a large bucket that had been filled with warm water and I showered using the large plastic mug nearby. It was very refreshing and back in England I still use this method whenever the electric shower is not working.

My favourite of all the numerous memories of this first trip was being forced to learn a few Igbo words by Ike, a cheeky and sweet eight-year-old. His grandmother Aunty C (whom he called Mamma) was caring for him. He was the son of my cousin Nnamdi who was affected by sickle cell anaemia and living in England. Aunty C had apparently asked Ike to teach me some Igbo and he took on this duty with great gusto. He was also responsible for preparing my breakfast and he wouldn't let me have a bite of it until I spoke a few words to him in Igbo. This worked like a charm and I quickly learnt 'biko' (please) and 'dalo' (thank you), along with many other words, to ensure having some food together with that first cup of tea of the day! Now living in England, his lovely son is footballer Carl Ikeme, the goalkeeper for Wolverhampton Wanderers F.C.

A slightly more painful souvenir was when it was decided I should have my ears pierced. My aunty and others took me to the compound of a nearby house where I was asked to sit on a stool. Amid lots of joking and encouraging noises, a woman proceeded to clean and then rub each ear lobe, pierce them with a sharp instrument and then insert a piece of black thread through the hole. Fortunately it was all done very quickly and there were no problems apart from the sting that occurred when women came up from behind and pulled the thread back and forth to keep the hole open. It was all worth it when my father presented me with a lovely set of gold earrings – and I no longer felt out of place as the only woman without pierced ears!

- o – 0 – o -

It was wonderful to explore Onitsha. First on the agenda was a visit to Uncle Chike who was living in the family house in Anionwu Street. In my travels I noticed that there was still evidence of war-damaged property. In the few quiet periods I was able to read books purchased at one of the many stalls at Onitsha market or on the road. So it was that I discovered the works of eminent Igbo authors such Flora Nwapa's *Efuru* (1966) and *Things Fall Apart (1958)* and *A Man of the People (*1966) by Chinua Achebe.

While feeling accepted and welcomed in Onitsha it also became quickly apparent to me that I certainly stood out as a non-local. It wasn't just that my skin was a lighter brown colour, as this isn't that uncommon. It was more my general behaviour, accent and inability to speak Igbo. This frequently led to being referred to as 'Oyinbo' which is a Yoruba word that (while open to debate) is often used to indicate white or fair skinned foreigners. Children in the market would say it to me in a slightly cheeky and humorous way, but it can sometimes be viewed as a derogatory comment.

I was able to attend a lot of events such as Ozo Titles, weddings and yet more funerals. There would always be drumming, dancing by different Age-Grades (people born between a certain period) who would all be wearing the same costumes. There was plenty of food and drink such as palm wine. My camera was kept busy capturing images of beautifully dressed people, many in traditional robes. There were various rituals such as breaking of the kola nut by the most senior titled person at the event. It would then be handed out and although I really tried, it was much too bitter for me to eat. Then there would be libations with the pouring of Schnapps spirits on to the ground accompanied by prayers to the ancestors and numerous deities.

My father continued to introduce me to family and friends at Onitsha and elsewhere. The hospitality was overwhelming as it was clear that he was well and truly respected and loved by so many people. He also told me how pleased he was that I was comfortable with meeting so many of them. One day we drove nearly 70 miles to Enugu (meaning 'the top of the hill'), the former capital of the Eastern Region and initially for the Federal Republic of Biafra. We visited so many people that I started to lose count. At every home we were constantly offered drinks followed by a choice of food such as plain or jollof rice, pounded yam, eba (cassava) with fish, chicken, meat, okra or egusi stew. Bloated after the third meal and being driven to the next destination, I told my Dad that it would be impossible to eat any more. He explained that it would be necessary to just have a smaller portion, as it would be very disrespectful to refuse. It proved to be a very useful lesson for the future!

At Onitsha I met a very good friend of my father for the first time. He was Mr Albert Osakwe, a former Nigerian Ambassador and someone I would often visit in London. My Dad said 'Spot on!' when I later remarked that they seemed like young lads having a tremendous time, whether at the Onitsha sports club or on their trips abroad attending Rotary Conventions. Sadly, in 2003, his own security guard murdered Mr Osakwe at his home in Onitsha.

Throughout my stay, remarks were made at how pleased people were that I was willing to learn as much as possible, taste new foods and even try to speak a few words of Igbo. The time I had spent in London with my Dad and Uncle Sunday and his family were proving very useful, as I had at least tasted some of the traditional foods that were provided at various meals. Many a time I was regaled with stories of children, and even some adults, arriving from Britain who insisted on only eating cornflakes and whatever tinned food they had brought with them in their suitcase!

In between all these visits with my father, the younger generation of relatives took great delight in taking me to parties and clubs. This helped me to relax further as there was no question of being allowed to just sit down and watch others dance. Weddings were another opportunity to eat, dance and be merry. The range of music I was introduced to was fantastic, from modern to high-life and the more traditional Igbo sounds. High-life was my absolute favourite, although some tracks could last 15 minutes or more, so tough luck if you were not too enamoured with your dancing partner!

Although looking forward to returning home, it was with some sadness that, on 29th August 1973, I boarded the plane. Back in London I soon discovered Sterns record shop, that for many years was located behind Warren Street Station. It had the most incredible collection of West African and other world music. Over the years I was able to buy lots of records including many high-life classics. Favourites included *Joromi* by Sir Victor Uwaifo, *Salawe* by Chief Rex Lawson and *Ije Awele* by Chief Osita Steven Osadebe. Whenever they were played at the parties I attended with my cousins in London, memories would come flooding back of my incredible first trip to Nigeria.

For the first time in my life I now felt completely accepted and was absolutely thrilled with how I was embraced by so many relatives. Many years later my cousin Joy revealed that on meeting me, her mum, my beloved Aunty C 'was the happiest person ever. Your presence validated a lot of things for her and the whole family. She said that you are the blue print of your father and that says a lot.'

It was really heartening that my presence did not engender feelings of stigma due to illegitimacy or the colour of my skin. My father's letter to me dated 8th October 1973 sums this up and was an utter joy to read:

I am delighted that at least you enjoyed your brief stay at home. One result it has undoubtedly accomplished is your introduction to the family and by that I mean those who really mattered. They too are really happy. Left to them you should just start to work here.

XIII

From Furlong to Anionwu

The next few years were marked by a deepening relationship with both my parents. While I was never to feel any warmth towards Ken, and there were times when I couldn't understand why my mother stayed with him, fortunately on getting older I gradually came to realise what she must have gone through in trying to make a home for me. The change in my feelings was helped by the fact that, after I qualified as a nurse and health visitor, she started to open up to me. We would discuss some of her difficulties either in letters or over the phone, and I also started to make more frequent visits to see her in person. I would go on a Sunday, deliberately arriving when Ken was likely to be at the pub, stay about three or four hours, and then drive back to London.

I was also in regular correspondence with her, and with my father. The contents of the letters reveal sharp differences in their social and economic status and also in their everyday preoccupations. In November 1973 my father mentions returning to Jos to negotiate a new 5-year tenancy agreement. At the top of his notepaper which was headed 'Anionwu & Co, Legal Practitioners & Notaries Public', he addressed me as 'My dear Nneka' and signed off 'Lots of love,

Dad'. In preparing to re-establish his practice he requested that I obtain new legal stationery for him headed: 'LOV Anionwu, M.A., LL.B. (Cantab). i.d.c. Barrister-at-Law, Lincoln's Inn'.

Both my parents were extremely proud of how my career was progressing, and with news of my admission to the Community Nurse Tutor course. In addition, I had been awarded a Hospital Savings Association (HSA) Scholarship to cover the fees and I remember a congratulatory phone call from Mum. Dad wrote: 'I shall pass on the good news to the rest of the family. You know how happy they will be.'

In March 1974 he wrote to say how sorry he was to hear what Mum had been through as a result of the economic situation. He also apologised that the promised air ticket for a summer trip to Nigeria was not possible at the moment, due to cash flow problems as a result of over investing. Selling some of his land in Lagos, he continued, should ease this. By the following March he had moved into his new house in Awka Road, just within the boundaries of Ogboli Eke village. As armed robbers were still about, there was now an Alsatian dog for increased security.

In the meantime, Mum had clearly been experiencing severe financial hardship. Back in February 1974 she apologised about being unable to attend my HSA scholarship award ceremony at Kensington Town Hall, due to lack of funds. It caused me sadness and annoyance, as I would have sent money for the rail fare if I had been aware of her difficulties. In the same letter she recounted Ken's drink problem. Two years previously he had fought with a neighbour and spent a week in the eye infirmary. His unreasonable behaviour continued and he was making unfounded accusations about her. One day he had got blind drunk and everyone had walked out, staying overnight at the home of a friend's family. Mum wrote that she had planned to apply for a separation order but didn't, because Ken had said he would be different in the future. My anger, concern and frustration knew no bounds, maybe as it also highlighted the widely different social circumstances of my parents.

Both parents updated me with news of the family, be that in Wolverhampton or Onitsha, and were equally keen that I kept in touch. In November 1973 my father described preparations for the second burial of his Uncle Simon, head of the Anionwu/ Uyanwa family. This Igbo ritual ensures that the deceased person transitions successfully from a state of torment ('ita okazi') to one of peace and serenity.

By September 1975 Dad reports the family being overjoyed that Uncle Sunday had now returned to Onitsha after 18 years' absence. In August 1975 Mum was delighted when Marion and Pam came to stay with me for a holiday in London and, in thanking me for arranging the weekend visit, added that she couldn't afford to get their photos printed yet.

Each parent wrote about their worries and saw me as someone from whom they were comfortable to seek advice. In the first quarter of 1974 my father apologised in two separate letters for writing so much about his worries concerning Emma, who was now in the Upper Sixth and doing two 'A' level subjects. He complained: 'I have no idea whether he succeeded in the 'O' level exams. Please find out for me what it is all about.' By October he sounded a little more hopeful as Emma told him of my visit to his school in Surrey and our outings on Saturday and Sunday. 'Emma sounds more and more enthusiastic but I would very much like to see this enthusiasm put into action.'

A totally different anxiety for my father erupted with the onset of a major dispute concerning the famous Onitsha Market. On 10th June 1974 he wrote explaining that the market had burnt down and 'how the allocation of stalls grievously offended the entire Onitsha people and they are resolved to fight it. I am the Chairman of the Committee appointed for that purpose.' A full history of the whole affair, entitled *Onitsha Market Crisis* was written and published in January 1976 by Chief Nnamdi Azikiwe, the Owelle of Onitsha, former President of Nigeria and a close friend of my father.

On page 24 there is an account of my father being held in detention in November 1974:

> *Just before the motion to grant an interim injunction to restrain the first Defendant from opening the Onitsha Main Market, was argued, the Police invited Mr. L. O. V. Anionwu, leading Counsel of the Plaintiffs, to visit Enugu for a tête-à-tête. Of his own volition, he travelled the sixty-seven miles from Onitsha to Enugu in his personal car and, on arrival there, he was detained without trial. Mr Anionwu was formerly Senior State Counsel., sometime Permanent Secretary in the Federal Ministry of External Affairs and Commonwealth Relations, and one-time Ambassador of Nigeria to Rome. He was detained for three days and no reason has been given for this executive act.*

My father never wrote about or discussed this incident with me, although I still have a copy of the front page of a national Nigerian newspaper, *The Daily Times*, dated 29th November 1974. The headline of the article reads 'EX-ENVOY ANIONWU DETAINED IN ENUGU'.

On 6th March 1975 Dad sent me money to purchase books for his research on the history of Onitsha and the market. One that I was able to obtain was *Crowther – Gospel on the Banks of the Niger* by missionaries Samuel Crowther and John Christopher Taylor, originally published in 1859.

In November 1975 Mum starts a very long letter to me with: 'I would be glad of your opinion as … ' She then goes on to describe Ken's chronic bronchitis and asthma that will require him to retire due to ill health, and explains that 'he wants me to leave work regardless of reducing the family to living on Social Security. He thinks that it is my duty to put him first and accept this standard of living if necessary rather than go on working.' In explaining her resentment she continues:

What makes me really sick about the prospect of having to resign myself to that sort of existence is the fact that up to now I have been doing extremely well with the advanced shorthand course that I told you about, and I am within reaching distance of getting the job I have always wanted, doing verbatim reporting as an official shorthand writer. I've had to wait over twenty years for the children to grow up before I could go to classes and take the requisite exams, and now this has to happen.

Health problems were gradually starting to affect my parents. In October 1974 Mum had had an 8-hour spell of amnesia due to high blood pressure. Given all her worries this did not come as much of a surprise. In September 1975 Dad informed me that he had just been discharged from Iyi-Enu hospital, five miles outside Onitsha. He had been a patient there for seven days due to pneumonia and high blood pressure, and requested that I obtain some good medicine for the latter and give them to his friend Mr Osakwe.

In 1977 Dad stayed with me for a few days in the flat I was sharing. At some point during his visit he asked why I hadn't bought my own place instead of wasting money on renting. My immediate reply was that while my salary was sufficient for the monthly mortgage repayments, I did not have the money for a deposit. He gave me useful advice about always saving a percentage of my monthly earnings. Then, to my pleasant surprise, he offered to give me the deposit on a flat as well as paying the legal fees. The only requirement was that the property should be accessible from Heathrow airport.

- o – 0 – o -

Throughout this period my thirst for travel never abated, helped enormously by the introduction of much lower airfares through so-called 'bucket shops' and Freddie Laker's cheap transatlantic flights. I visited several countries for the first time, including Morocco. In the summer of 1976 I stayed at the Nigerian Embassy in Rabat with my diplomat uncle Akudo and his young family. He helped towards the cost of the air ticket as a present for having chauffeured him around London the previous year.

I made a repeat trip to the USA in August 1977, this time spending a holiday in Los Angeles with my cousin Obiageli, her husband and their first baby. By now I had become very interested in sickle cell disease and with this in mind made two further trips in the late 70s. There was also a tour of the Caribbean to view sickle cell services, courtesy of a travel bursary from the Commission for Racial Equality.

By January 1979 I had visited Nigeria three times, my second trip being in December 1975 for a holiday over Christmas and New Year. This time the relationship between my father and stepmother must have improved as I stayed with them in their new house on the Awka Road. Regi was pleasant and I had an enjoyable time. I was still pleased though that the house was within walking distance of Aunty C, so I could often go to see her and members of the Anionwu clan.

In London I had been spending a great deal of time with Onitsha people, and some of them had also returned for the festive season. Dad let me have the use of a car, giving me a great deal of independence and the means to go out on jaunts with relatives and friends. The traditional male masqueraders were out in force, running and dancing through the streets trying to frighten everyone. Women and girls were not supposed to look at them or know who they were, but occasionally rules were ignored for Oyinbos like me! This was a time of year when many people from far and wide came to take the Ozo title and they were incredible ceremonies. I thoroughly enjoyed them, even though I was often unsure of the significance of many of the rituals. Anyone could turn up, and of course there would be dancing, food and drink.

Six months following this trip I would formally change my surname to Anionwu. I had thought long and hard about the pros and cons of continuing to use my mother's maiden name versus switching to my father's surname. One decisive factor was the visit to Nigeria as well as socialising with the Igbo community in London. When I was in Onitsha, Anionwu rather than Furlong was used – for example, when relatives purchased my internal airline tickets. One cousin joked that I was a typical Oyinbo to worry about whether officials would notice the different name on my passport.

It amused me that in England there may well have been deep discussions to enable a decision, whereas in Nigeria it seemed ridiculous to even raise the subject. 'You are the daughter of Anionwu, what is the problem?' Well, I had spent 29 years of my life known to the world as Furlong! How would my mother and members of my maternal family react when I informed them about this change in name? What of all those people I knew professionally and socially? There was also the rigmarole of having to change all my official records and inform so many agencies, which at times appeared quite daunting. My mind was eventually made up though, and so on 12th July 1976 I changed my surname to Anionwu by Deed Poll.

The impact was quite interesting, because I had switched to a name that many people found much more difficult to pronounce, including me. My anglicised phonetic version, 'Annie-On-Woo', was not exactly as Igbo people would say it, but better than the experience of being called Elizabeth Onion! This was an introduction to the difficulties I would face in the future. When I was on the phone and told people my surname, there was sometimes a noticeable difference in reactions. Before, having a non-foreign sounding name and a very English accent, people were totally unaware of my skin colour. Occasionally, there would even be attempts to encourage me to collude with their racist comments. No longer, thank goodness, due to my now decidedly 'alien' sounding name.

- o – 0 – o -

The most significant impact of my visit to Nigeria was that I wanted to go and work there and was also starting to try and learn Igbo – a wish shared by my family in Onitsha, apart from my father. While he was pleased, he sounded a huge note of caution in pointing out that not having grown up in Nigeria I was unaware of the intricacies of life there and would be eaten alive. He explained that contacts were absolutely vital and that mine were few and far between. Therefore the best plan would be for me to wait until I could work in Nigeria at a very senior level.

At the time I thought my career was going reasonably well, having completed my nurse training, undertaken seven months' midwifery experience, lived in France for nine months and now qualified as a health visitor. I didn't have any further ambitions apart from doing a short course in tropical diseases at the London School of Tropical Hygiene and Medicine. This was completed successfully in early 1974, six months after returning from that first visit to Nigeria.

So my father sat me down one day and asked me how I could progress in my job – what advancement was possible? For the first time I focussed on the different pathways I could pursue, such as management, clinical or education. The last of the three appeared more appropriate for me. I loved teaching, whether in health promotion sessions with parents in the home and clinic or with pupils at the local secondary school. My father said, 'well how can you become a tutor, maybe you had better look into that?' My immediate reaction was that I was far too inexperienced, but lo and behold my application to do a one-year Community Nurse Teacher's course was successful! It was organised in collaboration with the Royal College of Nursing and the University of Surrey and started in the autumn of 1974. My fees were paid courtesy of the HSA scholarship, and after qualifying in 1975 my plan was still to work in Nigeria.

In the meantime I became a Community Nurse Tutor in Brent Health District, with an office in the School of Nursing at Central Middlesex Hospital. My role was to arrange in-service education for health visitors and district nurses, and teach student nurses about their work. It also included organising placements for the students, not only with community nurses, but also a day out with a public health inspector. Some students vowed never to eat in a restaurant again after witnessing cockroaches scurrying around the kitchens! Two friends who knew me from those days have recalled their impressions of me at the time.

Ursula:

I had recently started my training at Central Middlesex Hospital and you had given us a lecture about going out into the community. My first impression at this point was of this young black lady, with quite a huge Afro, but you appeared extremely English. You were so conservatively dressed and I thought, oh dear, you know she seems like one of those sort of strait-laced kind of black women. I didn't know you obviously, as I didn't know there was a radical side to you!

Suzette:

We first met at Central Middlesex Hospital in the 1970s when I was working in the outpatient clinic and you were one of the tutors in the School of Nursing. I was so taken aback because I had just finished my nurse training at Charing Cross and West London Hospital and now seeing someone black at the School of Nursing was very, very unusual. It was inspirational for me. You were so enthusiastic and I was really so surprised to see a black woman in that position. What I observed is that you were sort of very English when you were at the School of Nursing, then as you went on to do the Sickle Cell and the Mary Seacole work, something changed. It was in your dress and in your approach to people and getting involved in something within the black community. When you were in that School of Nursing, it's like, you're a part of that white establishment. Yeah, but that all changed eventually.

It was during this time that I first met Dr Milica Brozović, a Consultant Haematologist who had recently arrived at the hospital. We started to work informally with issues relating to families affected by sickle cell disease.

- o – 0 – o -

My social life had by now changed dramatically, as I was frequently socialising with Nigerian relatives and their friends. I had become particularly close to my cousin Joy, and there are great memories of us meeting up with her friends on Friday evenings in north London. The phone would be busy as they checked out where the weekend parties would be held, usually in flats of students around London. It always surprised me how many people could cram into them, staying way into the early hours of the morning. Money seemed to flow; it was, after all, the time of the Nigerian oil boom. Naturally there was food and drink aplenty and in between the dancing it was possible to catch up with all the gossip. Whoever was the DJ would always play a mix of records including soul, R & B, reggae and Motown together with modern Nigerian music. Often, at about 2am, there would be dancing to the sounds of traditional Igbo music and I would love watching Joy's moves! I started going out with Nigerian boyfriends and photos of the period show me slim and wearing much more fashionable attire.

It was at one such party late in 1973 where I met Beje, and I would go out with him for about two years. We had great fun together and visited many friends around the country as well as going off to Paris for a holiday. He was a member of the Itsekiri ethnic group from the Delta State of Nigeria, and was studying for a Masters degree in engineering. In April 1974 Dad wrote asking about him and thanking me for the photo of the two of us. He also queried whether I had written to Aunty C about him. While on a trip to Nigeria in September 1974, Beje and his brother travelled to Onitsha and had lunch with Regi and Dad. They stayed three hours and he met with Dad's approval: 'I find him very intelligent and interested in current affairs. I like him.'

Soon after, Beje came to Wolverhampton to meet Mum and on 3rd October 1974 she wrote: 'Hope Beje is well. It was nice meeting him and we all hope he can come again when possible.' In January 1975 I was pleasantly surprised to receive a letter from his father, a Chief from Sapele in Nigeria. 'I have heard about you going out with my son for some time. I am writing to your father today and will go to Onitsha to see him sometime this year. Extend greetings to your mother & I will write to her sometime if God permits.' My father wrote to tell me that he did indeed receive the letter and was looking forward to meeting him. We became engaged, but unfortunately this seemed to give him a licence to date other women. Consequently my relationship with him rapidly deteriorated and by the end of 1975 I had given him the heave-ho.

On 18th August 1976, I obtained a new passport in the name of Anionwu. By now I had also realised the need to study for a degree in order to progress to an even more senior level. It was therefore with delight that I obtained a place on a two-year Masters Degree in Tropical Health at the Liverpool School of Tropical Medicine, due to start in the autumn of 1976. I was also awarded, for two years, the very first King's Fund scholarship that had been established to assist senior nurses to obtain a higher degree and undertake research. All was going swimmingly well until the 1976 programme in Liverpool was suddenly cancelled, and consequently I was unable to take up the scholarship. Bitterly disappointed, I looked around for a different course and in 1977 accepted an offer from the Department of Nursing at Manchester University. The plan was to complete a two-year programme – firstly the Advanced Diploma, followed by an MSc in in Nursing Studies. Fortunately the King's Fund again agreed to give me the scholarship and one of my key supporters was Robert J Maxwell, their Secretary and Chief Executive.

The first year of study in Manchester put me off the idea of continuing to complete the Masters degree. The overall philosophy appeared to be narrowly focused on the Nursing Process, a theory of nursing practice very fashionable at the time. It was too hospital-centred for my liking and not flexible enough to even incorporate a community-based placement. Nor was there much enthusiasm for my wish to do a dissertation on sickle cell disease, which I had now become very interested in. The local Clinical Genetics Unit were friendly, but admitted that they rarely received referrals to provide genetic counselling for affected families. Apart from the odd general practitioner, there was no alternative provision within the community, as I discovered through my links with black community groups in Manchester.

An idea came to me as to how I could adapt the Nursing Process in order to incorporate a more home-based perspective. I organised a placement on the children's infectious diseases ward at Wythenshawe hospital, assuming that most of the patients would have a short admission. This turned out to be the case and I was able to obtain consent from parents to visit them both in the ward and at home. My interviews with the parents explored the impact of the in-patient experience and the transition home following the child's discharge from hospital.

My frustration with the nursing course was balanced with an exciting time in Manchester and making friends with students on other courses when I joined the University's Pan-African Student Association. There I met two wonderful women – Duduzile Lethlaku from the former Bophuthatswana (now part of South Africa), and Olive Morris, the now deceased Brixton-based community activist.[12]

We three 'Amazonians' gave some of the more misogynistic men a run for their money! Moves to exclude women from positions of influence and decision-making processes were firmly blocked. After that, all went smoothly and it was a truly informative and lively experience all-round. Life became much more interesting with time also spent volunteering at the Black Women's Co-operative in Moss Side. We also used to travel regularly down to London in my mini for meetings of the newly formed OWAAD (Organisation of Women of African & Asian Descent).

In July 1978 I returned to London with the hope of finding an MSc degree in Health Education. The person I spoke to at the Health Education Council pointed out that even if I obtained a place at this late stage, there still remained the challenge of meeting the course fees. He was quite taken aback with the news of my remaining year of the King's Fund scholarship, and then suggested contacting the health education guru, Alan Beattie. When I met Alan he had recently been appointed Director of the MSc in Health Education programme at Chelsea College, University of London: 'You immediately struck me as vigorous, energetic, animated, passionate, showing a real professional and practical concern about the issue of sickle cell disease, and from what you told me the situation for families was rather horrifying.'

After a long discussion it was felt that the ideal plan would be for me to undertake a research-based MPhil degree rather than the 2-year part-time taught Masters course. The problem was that, even with my recent Manchester qualification, I did not meet the academic requirements to register for a University of London postgraduate degree. Alan worked incredibly hard on my behalf, together with his Head of Department and university administrators. It was agreed that I could register, with the requirement that I sit (as qualifying examinations) the most pertinent papers from the MSc in Health Education – epidemiology and research methods.

So over the next two years I sat in on relevant sections of the course in preparation for the exams. At the same time, following my return to London, Dr Brozović had appointed me as Research Fellow in her Haematology Department. By now I had become more interested in putting my energies into developing services for families affected by sickle cell disease in the UK. While still enjoying trips to Nigeria, the vision of working there had started to fade.

My father was interested and supportive of these developments, and extremely proud of the progress I was making with postgraduate studies. But tragically, after finding my father in such a dramatic fashion in 1972, I was to know him for a mere eight years.

XIV

Losing my father

1980 was to be a very shocking year, although it started off well with a couple of cheerful letters from my father. On 9th January he wrote of his plans to come to London for ten days following a visit to see Emma and Obiageli in Los Angeles. I received his second letter on 23rd January informing me that he was now in LA.

Dad seemed fine when he arrived to stay with me in February. But on my return from a few days away, Dad greeted me in the hall and started to apologise for having broken a glass and for spilling water on the carpet. I quickly saw that all was not well with him physically. He seemed to have had a stroke – his speech was slightly slurred, and his face was drooping on one side. I asked him how he was feeling and whether he had any weakness down one side of the body, and he said yes, looking at me in a very scared manner. I immediately drove him to the Accident & Emergency Unit of Central Middlesex Hospital. It did indeed turn out that he had had a mild stroke, which was a great shock to everyone. He was advised to lose weight, cut down on smoking and flying, and was prescribed medication to reduce his blood pressure. It was very reassuring that he was in a hospital where I knew so many nurses and doctors.

Dad, ever the diplomat, proved to be an extremely popular patient. So much so that he managed to persuade a nurse to buy him chocolate, which he was thoroughly enjoying one day when I visited him. The nurse in question said that it was impossible to refuse, as he was such a polite, charming and humorous patient! When my father joked and said he wasn't feeling ill, it dawned on me that he did not appreciate the serious nature of his illness. I explained the dangers of another stroke, and he asked me whether it could kill him. It hurt me so much to reply in the affirmative and observe the look of shock on his face.

When he was well enough Dad returned to Nigeria, and the plan was that I would visit him in the summer. A month later he wrote to give me an update on his health. Dated 15th April, his letter informed me that his blood pressure was well down and his weight had also been decreasing (it was now steady at 14½ stone).

Nonetheless it was a surprise to receive a phone call in June from my father and hear that he was now in the USA! He had felt well enough to travel to Chicago to attend the International Rotary Convention, accompanied by his good friend Mr Albert Osakwe. He had also seen Emma graduate from his university in Los Angeles and was about to come and spend a few days with me in London, then return to Nigeria. I was quite anxious about the impact of all this international travel so soon after his stroke.

When my father arrived at Heathrow Airport on Monday 2nd June 1980 he telephoned to let me know that he would come by tube to the flat. His voice sounded so tired that I said, 'Look Dad just wait and I'll come and meet you at the airport.' My fears about his health were confirmed when I saw the look of utter exhaustion on his face as he pushed his luggage trolley towards me. I suggested that he rest as much as possible for the next few days prior to his flight back to Nigeria. He agreed to do this but asked if I could arrange an appointment with a solicitor and requested that I come with him. He wished to discuss the property in Palmers Green, as he and Regi were now on such bad terms that he was considering a divorce.

We went to the solicitors on the Tuesday. When he was called in I remained seated, but he turned and beckoned for me to come with him. As a result I heard his anxieties about the marriage and his wish for the house to be transferred from joint ownership to his name alone. On the final night of his stay we had a meal together and then both retired to bed early. He was due to fly out to Nigeria the next morning and I was going to drive him to the airport.

On waking that morning of Thursday 12th June 1980 I could hear a slight grunting noise from the bathroom. There was no reply when I knocked on the door, so I opened it and to my absolute horror found my father unconscious in the bath. I called an ambulance and he was taken once more to Central Middlesex Hospital. It was clear that his condition was extremely serious. The doctors prepared me for the worst. I sat by his bed for most of that day, intermittently making phone calls to inform relatives and friends. A few were able to come and visit him and they gave me tremendous support, as did the hospital staff. One of the nurses I knew even arranged for me to have a quick shower. My father was deeply unconscious and at one point a young female doctor told me that he was rapidly deteriorating. I kissed him goodbye and very soon after that he was pronounced dead.

- o – 0 – o -

It was all such a huge shock. Mr Osakwe, who had so recently been in Chicago with my father, fainted when his son phoned him in Nigeria to tell him the news. At some point later, it struck me that two days prior to my father's death had marked the 8th anniversary of our first meeting on 10th June 1972.

His death certificate stated his age as 59. Whether this was his actual age, or whether he was in fact 62 (as suggested by his old Cambridge college records that I tracked down in 2013), he was still young when he died.

My world seemed to come crashing down around me. Fortunately, friends, family and associates of my father provided me with constant support. My mother wrote: 'I was very sorry to hear about your Dad. I can well imagine how upset you must be. Try not to grieve too much. It's the last thing he would wish.'

The only fly in the ointment was Emma, who was due to stay with me on his return from Los Angeles. My keenness to help him at our time of bereavement came to an abrupt halt due to his arrogant and selfish behaviour. He had hardly set foot in the hallway when he demanded papers for the flat, assuming it was now in his possession (in 1982, during the period when Regi and Emma were still at loggerheads about Dad's estate, she wrote to me: 'For your amusement, your flat belongs to Emmanuel too!!').

Tired and stressed out with all that had happened, I lost my temper with Emma and rang my cousins to share what had transpired. They immediately came to collect him and gave him a unique Nigerian dressing down. This flash of greed was to be a mere taste of what I would come to experience, not only from him, but also ultimately from my stepmother.

At around this time I was revising for an imminent exam at the Institute of Education that would enable me to register for an MPhil degree (this would ultimately progress to a PhD, which was pretty unusual for somebody who had left school at 16). Interventions were made on my behalf and I was allowed to delay the exam until I had returned home from my father's funeral, which was to be held in Nigeria.

The whole period of organising for his body to be taken back to Nigeria was hazy, as is a lot of the period leading up to the burial. The Nigerian Government, their officials in London and my father's friends saw to everything. Due to his previous roles as the first Permanent Secretary of the Ministry of External Affairs, then Nigerian Ambassador to Italy, officialdom stepped in and everything was fast-tracked.

When our family landed in Lagos on 18th June we were met on the tarmac and driven off at speed with a police escort all the way to Onitsha. This, his last journey home, was in stark contrast to that first car trip together in 1973.

During the ten days before the funeral, rumours abounded about the possible causes of his death, including poisoning. Emma stated that Dad's enemies had invoked evil spirits to kill him, as during the night he'd heard three cocks crowing on the roof of the house. Being the last person to see him alive I was bombarded with questions and conspiracy theories until members of the family intervened on my behalf. One day I was in the sitting room with family members receiving condolences from visitors. A wailing sound was suddenly heard and got louder and louder until a distressed woman made a dramatic entrance. Approaching me, she prostrated herself on the floor sobbing something in Igbo. A relative informed me that she was the mother of three children, the half-siblings my father had introduced me to on a previous visit. All this sounds both gloomy and frightening, but it was tempered with overwhelming comfort from a wide range of people – and while at Onitsha I came to realise that Nigerian wakes are very similar to those of the Irish! Stories were recalled about my father and many jokes were told about him, which I found incredibly therapeutic.

Many obituary notices appeared in the Nigerian media posted by family and friends as well as one in the *Daily Star* on 26th June 1980 from the Onitsha Branch of the Nigerian Bar Association, of which my father was Chairman. *West Africa* magazine also included an obituary to him.

The burial service took place at All Saints' Cathedral, Onitsha on Saturday, 28th June 1980 and photos taken at the service show me looking absolutely distraught. My father's peers from the local Branch of the Nigerian Bar Association, all wearing their legal robes and wigs, carried the coffin into the cathedral. They also processed with the coffin to the burial plot within the grounds of his house in his beloved village of Ogboli Eke.

An unsuccessful search for my father's will commenced in London, Lagos and Onitsha. The latter produced a moment of dark humour as I accompanied a group of people hunting through papers at his office. Mr Osakwe pulled me to one side and asked me to distract an elder, as they had come across the gentleman's last will and testament!

On my return to Heathrow Airport a great friend of my father, Chief Rex Edijana Akpofure (now also deceased), met me on the tarmac. He had been the first African Principal of Dad's alma mater, King's College, Lagos. I stayed with his family and he then accompanied me to the Institute of Education and into a vast empty hall, bar one invigilator. Alan Beattie recalled: 'You sat (your exams) after everybody else but under rigorous examination conditions, policed and invigilated to boot, which you did and which you duly passed.' A few days later on 2nd July, (my 33rd birthday), a photo of me at the Akpofure home shows me smiling and looking much more relaxed.

- o – 0 – o -

The next few years were to prove extremely difficult, particularly in terms of the relationship with my stepmother Regi and my brother Emma. It soon transpired that my father, although a barrister, had not left a will and therefore died intestate. The wrangling about his estate would carry on for decades, although after a few years I dropped out of the whole vicious affair. It is still painful to recall the spiteful intensity with which certain parties looked after their own interests while colluding to exclude others, including myself.

And there was no love lost between Regi and Emma as they battled their counter claims out in the courts. Regi wrote me frequent letters asking for my signature on various documents and constantly complaining about Emma's behaviour. This included how, with a forged letter, he had closed his father's bank account in Los Angeles after withdrawing all the funds. These, she continued in a letter dated 13th January 1982, were spent on a car that was later sold, and flights around America and Italy: 'Really he cannot be, is not a <u>Son</u> of your Dad.'

Originally my stepmother promised in writing that she would ensure my inclusion as a beneficiary but then reneged, and I was ultimately left out. Advised to seek legal redress, for a few years I hired an Onitsha-based lawyer recommended by the family. As the years passed it struck me that I was wasting what little money was in my bank account. Emma had now sided with my stepmother and I eventually decided not to pursue any further action.

I realised that the only important thing was the joy of having known my father for eight years, and that we had got on extremely well. I was really lucky to have had the good fortune to find him so quickly, in contrast to those who had failed in their efforts to trace their biological parent/s. I had been introduced to many positive aspects of Nigerian family life and culture. My father had advised me so well about my career and had also given me funds to secure a mortgage. I reflected, though, that property and money weren't everything if you didn't also have a decent family life and a wonderful network of friends.

While Dad would have been horrified at this turn of events, he would also have been so proud of my future achievements in spite of everything. Having done an Internet search for 'Anionwu', my daughter discovered that my name dominated the results – commenting that my negative experiences reminded her of Bob Marley's rejection by certain members of his family, as set out in the lyrics of his 1969 song *Corner Stone*!

After my father's funeral, members of the Anionwu family pleaded with me to come back soon, as they were afraid I would never return. As a result, my next trip was just seven months later in December 1980. I stayed with my father's friends the Mbanefo family, due to the severe tensions with Regi concerning the estate. Once back in London I realised I wasn't sure when I would return, as it would never be the same without Dad.

There was no doubt that I fell in love with Nigeria from my very first visit in 1973. Like a pendulum, my cultural loyalties shifted so much so that I initially wanted to emigrate. Those rose-tinted glasses did eventually fade a little and while never settling there, I was to make many more trips in the future. I still feel a huge affection for and interest in the affairs of the country, and take great pride in my paternal origins. So many relatives keep an eye out for me, and I love being in their company.

Meeting my father rounded off my whole being, and filled those many gaps concerning identity. It also increased my self-confidence, evidenced by taking on his surname while retaining pride in my mother's heritage. Taking this decision had been unexpectedly liberating, as I had at last defined myself. This was in defiance of having an identity externally foisted on me by those wishing to label me by the colour of my skin – with all the associated negative assumptions. As Elizabeth Nneka Anionwu, I would go into the next phase of life helped by names that reflected my entire roots.

XV

Becoming a mother

Another spin off from meeting your Dad was to start moving in different circles. You met the man who was to become Azuka's dad at a Nigerian wedding in this country – how lucky was that!

My friend Sue is talking here about the marriage of my Nigerian friend Kezi that I attended in January 1981. The man in question was Nick. He was the best friend of the groom and was studying for a PhD in chemistry at a Yorkshire university. While born in northern Nigeria, he was an Igbo from a village near Onitsha. As a teenager his father had been killed during the massacres of Igbos in the north that led to the Biafran War.

Nick and I hit it off straightaway and were on the dance floor together for most of the night. Over the next three months we met up a lot and enjoyed each other's company. Everything seemed on track for us to have a future together. So we were happy that both felt it was the right time for us to have a child. My father's death, nine months earlier, had triggered an instinctive desire to start my own family. It is a huge sadness that he never survived long enough to become the loving grandfather that he would have been. Another influencing factor was my body clock as I was approaching 34 years of age; Nick was a month younger than me.

I thought, a little naively, that even if we split up it would be possible for me to cope with being a single mother. I had a flat, a job and a great network of close friends. Delores was a child-minder who I became friends with during my days as a health visitor. She always said that she would look after any children I might have, and that's exactly what happened!

It was a very pleasant surprise when I became pregnant so quickly. It was also an eye-opener to witness the reaction of family, friends and colleagues. Some thought I was too bookish and work-driven to ever imagine that a child would feature in my life. Others were amazed, as I had never spoken to them about my private life, leading them to presume that men did not feature in it. The most interesting response was the manner in which a few people from Onitsha probed the identity of the soon-to-be-father. They smiled and uttered a satisfied 'Eh-he!' whenever they were pleased with my response during the following interrogation:

'Is he black?' 'Yes.'
'West Indian?' 'No.'
'Nigerian?' Yes.'
'Igbo?' 'Yes.'

The excitement was mounting.

'Is he from Onitsha?' 'No'.

They looked quite disappointed until one of them said, 'Oh well, you tried!' to which they all agreed while beaming at me. Motherhood was an important rite of passage in their eyes so, regardless of my single status, they were genuinely thrilled with the news.

It is interesting that I cannot recall the moment I told my mother, or her reaction, but she never expressed any signs of shock or disapproval.

A few months into my pregnancy I embarked on a nine-week Churchill Travel Fellowship to look at sickle cell services in the USA and Jamaica. My first stop was in Washington, D.C. where I stayed with Sarah, my friend from Paris days. In her wonderfully forthright way she insisted that I must not drink any coffee or alcohol for the rest of the pregnancy. And so it was, but pretty soon after the baby was born I asked for a very strong coffee! In contrast I never missed alcohol and it wasn't until the christening that I supped some champagne. The taste was so awful that I became teetotal.

There was never a hint of morning sickness in those early months, which was fortunate in view of the amount of air travel involved in touring five US cities and then on to Kingston. The test confirming my pregnancy was actually carried out at a laboratory in Jamaica. Apart from severe heartburn in the later stages, pregnancy was wonderful. My weight did balloon though due to a craving for buttered toast and milk. On the plus side my skin tone improved and my hair became even curlier.

My friend Janet asked me to call her as soon as regular contractions started, as she wanted to be with me for the delivery. It happened to be one of the coldest months in years when my labour kicked off, and snow was heavy on the ground as she drove me to the hospital. I was supposed to have a 'trial of labour', which meant that a Caesarean section would be performed if no progress was made within a short period of time. This was because my hips were assessed as bordering on being too narrow which might result in the baby getting stuck. That's exactly what happened, and after many hours there were signs that my unborn baby was in distress. It was all quite frightening, made worse on over-hearing that the anaesthetist could not be found. Hours elapsed and the pain was becoming unbearable. The agony wasn't due to contractions but horrendous pain in my right lower back, later pinpointed to the sacroiliac joint. An epidural eventually relieved the agony, but labour lasted for a total of 22 hours! All this time Janet had been wonderful but she needed to go home to her own children. Fortunately Cynthia took over and I really valued such fantastic friends. She was also pregnant and I worried about the impact this complicated labour might have on her. A decision was eventually taken to deliver the baby by Kielland's forceps. It was now evening and by this stage I was convinced that the baby could not possibly survive and was resigned to the worst.

All was well though, and my healthy baby at last came screaming into the world. I immediately burst into tears of relief. There was also intense happiness when I was informed that this bundle of joy was a little girl! She had a huge mop of black hair and looked absolutely gorgeous. In January 1982 Regi wrote thanking me for the photo I sent saying: 'Azuka looks a bit like your Daddy and very hairy for a baby.' Pleased that she noted the resemblance, the other comment seemed a bit harsh! Not as shocking though as the black woman who visited me in hospital, peered at the baby and said: 'She's really pretty but what a shame about her flat nose. Just put a nose peg on it or pinch it everyday to straighten it out.' On hearing this when she was much older, Azuka said how pleased she was to have a sense of humour, probably from her Furlong Irish heritage. I agreed, but added that her Anionwu grandfather was also incredibly witty!

Nick took the train to London the next morning and was overcome with delight when he saw his daughter and first child. We agreed that her first name would be Azuka – it means 'Family support is more valued than money'. This was his Igbo name, one that can be given to both girls and boys. Her second name was Elizabeth.

For a variety of reasons our relationship eventually broke up, mainly because it turned out that he was married, even though planning to get a divorce. It was a dreadful period but one I could not discuss with my mother, probably because she had been through a much more difficult time. Whatever the reason, it was impossible to open up to her.

My stepmother Regi responded to the news with a very interesting comment in a letter dated 21st September 1982:

It has __not__ come to me as a shock to hear that Nick is a married man. This is typical of Nigerian men – those of them coming from Nigeria to do a higher degree in Britain or abroad.

Music became a refuge. One of the songs I kept playing in the front room at night was *Tell Me* by The Rolling Stones – maybe listen to the lyrics and see why. It's also, in my humble opinion, a great tune sung brilliantly by Mick Jagger and still one of my favourite tracks!

- o – 0 – o -

Nick and I were to remain on reasonably friendly terms for over 12 years. He occasionally saw Azuka in England prior to his departure for Nigeria in 1983 where he resumed academic activities at his university and ultimately became a professor. I would visit Nigeria with Azuka every year or two years up until her teens, when she would stay with him. Later there was a half-brother and half-sister. As she got older, the relationship with her father became less close. In 2014 Azuka's sister informed her of his death in Nigeria whilst he was staying at a hotel on academic business. Azuka and I were both 33 years old when our fathers had died.

My friend Sue had often wondered how I would manage with less sleep should a baby ever arrive. She remembered from our student nursing days that, after an exhausting shift, I could retreat to bed and be out for the count for 24 hours at a time. As it happened, there was one occasion when a feed was missed in the night due to sheer exhaustion. My painful swollen breasts woke me up with a start and I dashed into Azuka's room. There I saw a sleeping baby sucking away at nothing – the guilt was horrendous. So I sat next to the cot and the minute I saw a movement immediately picked her up and put her onto my breast. She literally lunged at it, not taking a break for ages. I never realised a baby could go so long without a proper breath. Anyway, we were both very relieved!

Life with a small child could at times be much tougher than I had expected, but Azuka was very placid and sweet and the support of friends and my previous health visiting experience all helped enormously. Even though I had continued working until just a few days before her delivery, there was still pressure for me to return as early as possible. Against my deepest wishes I reluctantly went back when Azuka was only nine weeks of age and it upset me for a long time. Fortunately it was possible to continue giving her a morning and evening breast feed until she was six months old.

My friend Juliet recalled: 'I know it was a difficult period, a single mother at the time and that you had to go back to work.'

I wished my Mum could have visited and given me much needed support. For whatever reason that never happened, as she only stayed once for a few days at the time of Azuka's christening. This was the only occasion that Azuka, Nick, Mum and I were to be gathered together. My sister Marion remembers a similar experience. Although they lived in the same town, Mum never came to see Marion at the hospital following the birth of her first child. We can never know what psychological issues were causing her to react in this way to the birth of her grandchildren.

It meant regular drives to Wolverhampton in order that Azuka saw her grandmother and the family – for which Azuka is grateful:

You always made an effort to keep in touch with her so that I would know her and that side of the family. You loved her and were very devoted to her, and worked hard to keep in contact with her. Neither of you were that tactile, unlike how you've been with me. She was quiet and always surrounded by a lot of books. As I was also shy we never seemed to be able speak to each other at great length. She loved animals and sometimes I sensed she liked them more than people.

Azuka's observations on Ken were interesting:

He was always very tactile, playful and friendly towards me. But as I got older I sensed there were some bad vibes and a history there between you two. I remember one occasion, it was either Christmas or Easter, and he got a bit drunk and started talking about the past. I could sense your body change and you got very tense, which is something that I'd rarely seen you do. The expression on your face changed and we left soon after.

Ken definitely went out of his way to be charming to both Azuka and myself during these day trips to Wolverhampton. Prior to my departure for London he would check the oil and water and repeatedly go over the directions to the motorway. My sister Marion recalled that as a teenager, even she knew the route off by heart!

Azuka did remember however:

As a kid I liked to suck my thumb and stroke my eyebrow. You have lovely eyebrows that I always wanted to stroke, but when I stroked your left eyebrow you'd wince in pain. When I was a bit older you explained that Ken used to beat you and had once hit you so hard that you fell into the fireplace and cut your eyebrow. It is a pain that has never really gone away. If you touch there it hurts. But also I wonder if it's an emotional scar as well.

When I reluctantly returned to work it was Dolores who came to my rescue, as she became Azuka's child-minder for the first two years of her life. She also acted as a mother figure to me and provided much needed guidance, support, humour and friendship.

The first separation Azuka experienced was at the age of two when I attended a one-week sickle cell conference in Toronto, Canada. During this period she lived with Dolores and her family while I stayed with friends and their young family in Toronto. They totally understood how much I missed her, and my feelings of guilt. I will never forget their kindness when they insisted that I use their phone, without charge, to make daily international calls to chat to her. It was always wonderful to hear Azuka's high-pitched chatter. On my return she came running towards me so fast that our heads nearly collided as I knelt to give her a kiss and a hug.

Life became easier for the next few years, thanks to her attending an excellent local nursery. Similar to many other parents, I had quite a shock when she left the nursery to start full time education, and I struggled to find appropriate childcare after school and during the holidays. We would both look forward to our annual week's holiday by the sea in Bournemouth!

Our visits to Nigeria started when Azuka was about 3½ years of age. I was determined that she would visit the country, her father and the Anionwu family from as early in childhood as possible. She says:

I always think of Nigeria like the Wizard of Oz, when Dorothy is in Kansas and it's black and white and cold and stoic. Then it goes to Oz and it's colourful and warm. That's what Nigeria reminds me of. So the Irish white side of your family is a bit like Kansas, black and white and a bit cold. Having said that, I always got on well with my cousins in Wolverhampton but I needed to be there for a bit before feeling relaxed enough to chat and play with them. Then going to Nigeria and it's just a burst of colour and energy and friendliness and love and feelings. I think Nigerians and Africans as a whole have a good way of making people feel at home and part of their family. That always struck me instantly. I felt a sense of belonging, which I'm sure you felt when you first went there.

Azuka loved Nigerian food such as the large snails, okra soup and meat stews. She copied others in chewing down to the very last bit of the bone. As well as spending time with her father in Port Harcourt, we also travelled to Onitsha where the Anionwu family made a tremendous fuss over her. One day we went to a traditional ceremony at Onitsha and Azuka quickly appreciated the importance of sitting quietly during the libations. She was particularly fascinated with the sight of coral bead necklaces and bracelets worn by so many people. At one point she nudged me and pointed to a titled elder woman sitting next to her and I saw that she had 'Azuka' tattooed on her arm. It was the first time my daughter had seen someone with the same name as herself. At this same event Azuka was observed taking a few sips of palm wine from a nearby cup and becoming slightly tipsy. She couldn't understand why I made her drink lots of water!

We also stayed with my cousin Joy and her family in Lagos where Azuka had a wonderful time with her little cousins. I was quite the anxious mother as this was her first trip abroad. Joy quickly sorted me out by telling me to get some well-earned rest during my stay. She also told me to get used to the fact that, from now on, Azuka would be busy playing with her cousins. It was just the right type of parenting lesson that I needed! At the end of our wonderful trip she cried her little heart out on the day of our departure for England. Not quite four, she plaintively asked me who she was going to play with back home.

In fact she also loved our visits to friends who were a great source of company for her and support for me. These included Janet and Sue as well as Ann and Steve. They all regularly welcomed us into their homes and Azuka grew up enjoying being able to play with their children. For many years the eminent haematologist Professor Lucio Luzzatto and his wife Paola lived close by and encouraged me to drop in on Saturday mornings. Here I would enjoy a wonderful cup of Italian coffee and a chat while Azuka played nearby. My academic supervisor Alan and his wife Kay were fantastic friends. They regularly invited us for a holiday at their home in Morecambe and their children became firm friends with Azuka.

My MPhil degree had now been converted to a PhD, and by late 1986 I had completed the research for the thesis. The problem was being able to afford a computer at home to type it all up, so I went into work to do it at the weekend. I would drive Azuka to stay overnight with my friend Ursula, where she loved being in the company of her children. Even so I was wracked with guilt at these frequent short separations and promised her that when it was all finished we would make a trip to Disneyland in Los Angeles. So it was, that having at last been awarded my PhD, we spent Christmas of 1988 in America. Here I was able to watch my seven-year-old daughter have one of the best holidays of her life.

- o – 0 – o -

Elaine, my cousin-in-law in Manchester, noticed Azuka's demeanour in childhood:

Azuka looked like a very shy child to me. She was very quiet. She wouldn't come forward like her mum. After meeting her, you could sit with her and you'd see that she was very attentive. It's only after she became accustomed to you and spoke to you that it became apparent that she was a very observant child.

As a young child Azuka once told me that she was a TV worm whilst I was a bookworm! She continues to be enthralled by the world of films, documentaries, theatre and musicals. By about nine years of age she had become determined to be an actress, and around the same time was identified as being dyslexic.

Azuka and I have a mutual interest in history, but as she points out, we have learnt about issues such as apartheid in South Africa, civil rights in the USA and Ireland's struggle for independence in very different ways:

I've always been aware of history and politics and I remember as a kid being very conscious of the apartheid struggle. When I was in the supermarket, I tried to put some oranges in the basket and the minute they touched the basket you threw them out because they had a Cape Town sticker on! I remember watching documentaries with you as a kid and films like Biko and Malcolm X and stuff like that whereas friends my age were watching EastEnders with their parents. I was always very aware and remember listening to Irish folk music and African music. I grew up with a black and white poster in the front room that was in memory of Olive Morris, your late friend and community activist.

I always got the sense that you were very proud of your blackness, maybe more so growing up in London where there's lots of mixed race people. You had natural hair and for most of my childhood I remember you in a kaftan. I grew up in a time where people used the word 'half-caste' a lot and I remember using it and you going 'No' and explaining why.

As Azuka became older it was interesting to hear her reflections concerning identity. When very young she had once described herself as half English, half Irish and half Nigerian!

As a child I didn't know the difference between black and white. I think that was because parts of the family that I knew as a kid were white so I just didn't know there was a difference. It wasn't until I was five and went to school that I learnt about race. As a kid I used to embrace my Irish side a lot more than my Nigerian. I've grown into my pride at being an African and my name, but I used to hate my name and wished I were a Katie or a Tracy. Africans give their kids names that they can grow into.

The most difficult period for us both was during her adolescence. Like many parents it was incomprehensible and painful to witness a seemingly overnight change in the relationship with your previously loving and sweet child. It certainly wasn't helped by our obstinate personalities. Azuka felt very lonely coming home after school to an empty flat. I constantly encouraged her to attend some of the varied extra-curricular activities but without success. So we had the typical shouting, door-slamming and ultimatums and I wouldn't wish the experience on anybody. After one row, Azuka started blasting out the sounds of Tupac, the late US rapper. This particular song,

Hit em up, is probably one of the best-known 'diss' songs. There was a bitter on-going East Coast/West Coast rivalry and the lyrics were targeted at his enemies, Notorious B.I.G. (aka Biggie) and J.R. Mafia. Suffice to say it was done to provoke a reaction from me, as it is riddled with profane language. It worked. I snapped and threatened to remove all her Tupac tapes if she didn't turn it off immediately. That also worked! At some point in the future she explained that some of his lyrics resonated with her own feelings of adolescent angst and solitude. Later on she introduced me to his incredibly tender song *Dear Mama*, with words relevant to our own previously rocky relationship: 'You are appreciated, When I was young, me and my mama had beef...'

There were just the two of us living in the flat, and nobody that either of us could immediately turn to when tensions arose. Once again it never crossed my mind to pick up the phone and speak to my mother. And there were no relatives living close enough to us who could provide an immediate refuge for Azuka when she felt lonely and overwhelmed, or when a crisis loomed. Fortunately on one such occasion it was half term and Azuka travelled to stay with my sister and her children in Wolverhampton – thank you Marion, as it provided the breathing space the pair of us so badly needed!

I did not grow up with the opportunity to pick up hints about parenting at close quarters. Friends like Ursula realised that this might be part of the problem:

What was great was the way you would explain things to Azuka. I didn't think you were too strict, you hardly ever lost your temper with her and you seemed to prefer giving an explanation. But I came from a family with so many of us and I think you were sometimes wary of setting stricter boundaries. I don't think it was anything major; it was just that I think you only had one child and hadn't got that experience of dealing with challenges and temper tantrums. I'd think, God almighty child, just leave me alone kind of thing (laughter)! You know, there were times when I would have just taken charge of Azuka and dealt with her but I didn't want to interfere. So I think not having had that experience and being on your own, it came out sometimes in your parenting.

During these turbulent teenage years I was working at the Institute of Child Health and discovered that a colleague was going through a similar experience. We formed a mutual self-help group and found it very cathartic to discuss our latest adolescent outbursts and run-ins.

Drama and musical theatre were to provide a sanctuary for Azuka and a wonderful English teacher recognised her abilities and acted as a mentor. Good times were had when friends attended a variety of productions and marvelled at her talent. After secondary school, Azuka had a spell at the BRIT School for Performing Arts and Technology and was also accepted into the National Youth Theatre. Following three years at drama school she realized her dreams to become an actress. She appeared in plays at the Birmingham Rep and the Liverpool Everyman and gained brilliant reviews in the national media. Azuka entered into a relationship with one of the actors and became pregnant with her daughter Rhianne, who was born seven months following my retirement – well planned! A couple of years later she auditioned successfully for the regular role of Louise, the receptionist then nurse in *Casualty*, the BBC weekly television series.

As Juliet observed: 'Now you are absolutely joyful being with your little granddaughter!' Mia, a very longstanding friend, summed it up for me:

It's been a blessing for you, being a mother. You've clearly enjoyed the role and it's gone so quick. It doesn't seem that long ago when we were on the phone gossiping. You said to me that you were expecting a baby and I became very animated and excited. Now your daughter's on TV and you're a grandmother.

Charles, Prince of Wales at my CBE Investiture, Buckingham Palace, July 2001
(Charles Green)

Mary Seacole Centre for Nursing
Practice, Thames Valley University –
now University of West London, 2000
(Joanne O'Brien)

Mary Seacole Memorial Statue, London's
St Thomas' Hospital on
day of unveiling 30th June 2016
(Philip Chambers)

With Dorothy Boswell CEO and Lonzie L Jones, Exec Director of
USA National Association for Sickle Cell Disease, 1977 (Guy Crowder)

Brent Sickle Cell Centre, 1980

Sickle Cell fundraising Gala 1984 – organised by England and Spurs footballer Garth Crooks (Centre)

With Nick, 1981

Photo I took of Nick and our daughter Azuka, 1982

With Azuka aged 3 (Andrew Pothecary)

Actress Azuka, aged 28 (John Clarke)

Professor Marcus Pembrey, Anne, Princess Royal and me, 1991
(Institute of Child Health)

FROM SICKLE TO SEACOLE

XVI

Why sickle cell disease?

I have already touched on some of the factors that gradually triggered my desire to improve services for families affected by sickle cell disease. Before returning to them, it might be helpful to give a brief overview of the condition.

Sickle cell disease is an inherited anaemia affecting the haemoglobin inside the red blood cells. It originated in those parts of the tropics where falciparum malaria is prevalent – and children under two years with sickle cell trait have partial protection against the worst effects of this severe malaria. Sickle cell trait is found in 1 in 4 Nigerians and 1 in 10 of the African-Caribbean population. It also affects other groups in the UK with origins in South Asia, the Mediterranean and the Middle East – so it has an impact on a wide range of people (and is not confined to members of the black community, as many people still believe). Blue-eyed, fair haired, white individuals can also inherit the condition or the trait.

Sickle cell trait, or the carrier state, can be detected by a simple and cheap blood test at any time during a person's life. Although they don't have the illness, if they have a child with someone who also has the trait, there is a 25% chance that each of their children will inherit sickle cell disease. There is also a 75% chance that each child is healthy, either through inheriting sickle cell trait (50% chance) or the usual haemoglobin type (25% chance).

There are several types of sickle cell disease, the commonest being sickle cell anaemia (Hb SS). The others are sickle beta° thalassaemia (which is usually as severe as Hb SS), Hb SC disease and sickle beta+ thalassaemia. These last two are generally milder but this is not always the case. Sickling of the red blood cells can cause them to change shape to one resembling a farmer's sickle or a banana. This then blocks the flow of blood, creating mild to life-threatening complications.

The condition can be extremely varied and very unpredictable. Painful crises are the commonest problem. They can be mild or so excruciating that hospital admission is required for treatment with drugs such as morphine. Severe infections are common, requiring a daily preventative dose of antibiotics during early childhood. Complications of sickling can affect many parts of the body such as the lungs, kidneys, eyes, hips and shoulders. It can also cause strokes from childhood onwards. While survival is improving, the illness can still result in early deaths. US authors Claster and Vichinsky noted in a November 2003 *British Medical Journal* article that the average life span of 17 years in 1973 had, thirty years later, increased to 50.

It is estimated that there are between 12,500 and 15,000 people with sickle cell disease in Britain. In comparison, the Cystic Fibrosis (CF) Trust states that there are over 10,000 people with CF, an inherited illness affecting the lungs and digestive system. CF mainly affects white Northern Europeans and less frequently black and minority ethnic groups. The figures for sickle cell disease have not been updated for many years and John James, the Chief Executive Officer of the UK Sickle Cell Society, thinks there are probably nearer 20,000 cases. Around 1 in 2,000 babies in England are born each year with sickle cell disease and the figure for CF is 1 in 2,500.

From the early 1980s it became possible to detect whether an unborn baby has sickle cell anaemia, although the procedure carries a risk of miscarriage. The couple then have to make the complex decision of whether to terminate or continue the pregnancy.

There were three main triggers that got me involved with sickle cell disease. Firstly, when working as a health visitor, I began to come across children with the condition. This revealed my appalling ignorance about it, and my inability to be of much help to the devastated parents. My search for a support group came to nothing. Secondly, and at around the same time, I met up with Peter Moses and became a volunteer at his Supplementary Saturday school for young black children. He died in 1972 from leukaemia, which was incorrectly perceived by some to be sickle cell anaemia. Finally, the late Jessica Huntley, co-founder of the black publishing company Bogle L'Ouverture Publications, challenged my own lack of knowledge. She was rightly concerned that if I, as a black health visitor, didn't have the information, who else would?

These encounters were to play on my mind constantly, and it all came to a head in late 1976 at Central Middlesex Hospital where I was working as a Community Nurse Tutor. Here I met up with Dr Milica Brozović, who a year before had taken up duties as the Consultant Haematologist. Known as Misha, she delivered two lunchtime talks about sickle cell disease and I made sure to attend both. They were inspiring and informative but also made me angry that I had never been taught about the condition during my nursing or health visiting courses – both of which had taken place when London already had a significant African and Caribbean population. I was not alone in wondering whether the illness was so neglected because it mainly affects marginalised black communities.

I remember asking Misha a lot of questions at each session. She came up to me at the end of the second talk and commented that I seemed very interested. We had a discussion and she was delighted to learn of my strong community links, both as a specialist nurse tutor and through my involvement with black voluntary groups. We seemed to hit it off straightaway and soon recognised our combined strengths, be that in medical, nursing, teaching or community development. Our ambition was to raise the profile of the illness in order to improve care for patients, both within and outside of hospital. And that is how our working relationship started! It was one of mutual respect and recognition that, together, we could be a formidable team.

By now, I also had a personal interest in the condition. I had been introduced to a cousin called Nnamdi who informed me that he had sickle cell anaemia. Joy's only living brother, he lived in Birmingham and was to survive into his 60s. There had been a younger sibling who had died in Nigeria, and while never diagnosed with the illness, he had had a history of symptoms very similar to Nnamdi's.

Soon after her arrival at the hospital Misha had been struck by how many patients were being admitted with excruciatingly painful sickle cell crises. What concerned her was the lack of knowledge about the illness among the patients, their families and the health professionals caring for them. In addition, the poor management of pain horrified her. I will never forget how she described the scenes between some of the patients and staff as 'a battlefield'.

At a 1988 conference in Hackney Misha recalled:

Twelve years ago when I arrived at my present hospital, the Central Middlesex Hospital in Harlesden, I had never seen a patient with sickle cell disease. On my first day I was called: 'Dr B., could you come to ward D3 to deal with Francis?' 'Who is Francis?' 'Oh he is a sickler.' 'What is wrong?' 'He is rolling on the floor, screaming on top of his voice and using really unspeakable words.' 'Why is he doing it?' 'Oh, he is demanding pethidine.' 'Why is he demanding pethidine?' 'Because the nurses won't give him any more.'

Misha also observed that patients and the parents of children with sickle cell seemed very isolated and anxious. This reminded me of my health visiting days and the positive outcomes of bringing lonely mothers together. I offered to set up a support group with two interested local community nurses who had strong links with the hospital. Shirleen was a paediatric liaison health visitor and Cynthia a district nurse. Both were of Caribbean origin and extremely keen.

With this in mind Misha asked if I would be willing to see a young adult on the male medical ward, as she was extremely worried about him. Yes, it was Francis. He was curled up in bed, facing the wall and hidden under a blanket. I introduced myself and explained my interest in sickle cell disease and that Dr Brozovi had asked me to visit him. After some time he turned over, pulled his blanket down and stared at me for what seemed an age. It was only when I mentioned the plans to set up a support group that he became animated and interested saying: 'I thought that I was the only person in Brent with sickle cell!'

I then went to the children's ward to see a brother and sister who were constantly being admitted. Their mother was there and was delighted to hear about the proposed group. During a subsequent visit one of them told me about a very young girl who had been admitted earlier that day. They were concerned that the nurses did not appear to be taking any notice of her. She was under the bedclothes quietly sobbing her little heart out and had been in severe pain for many hours. Immediately calling a nurse I made it clear that I would not leave until she administered an analgesic. The child's mother arrived and told me that unless she made a fuss, no-one seemed to keep an eye on her daughter. And she was incredulous that some nurses claimed patients wanted medication to feed a drug addiction – even applying this argument in the case of a young child. It was an accusation that I was to hear time and time again, and from so many people. The mother was angry and frightened, but expressed delight when I offered to visit her at home. There it became apparent that she had received minimal information about the illness, and she eagerly soaked up what little I was able to provide.

Looking back, my refusal to be restricted by hospital and community boundaries was to be a key factor in breaking down barriers encountered by families. I was a guest in their homes and it was often here that they revealed their fears, concerns and hopes for the future, and the stigma they were subjected to. I had taken the same approach at Manchester University to ensure that my project incorporated family experiences in both the ward and at home.

The hospital nursing staff appreciated my growing knowledge of the illness and positive rapport with patients, some of whom they viewed as 'difficult'. Possible reasons for the latter are to be found in the excellent 1972 publication *The Unpopular Patient* by nurse researcher Dr Felicity Stockwell.

A few years later, and now a sickle cell nurse counsellor at Willesden hospital, I took a call from a children's nurse at Central Middlesex Hospital. She asked me to come and see this same patient who had been due for discharge but was 'acting funny' and had wet herself. It was a very hot day and I observed that the child had extremely dry and cracked lips – not a good sign for somebody with sickle cell anaemia. It was an indication of dehydration, and such a lack of fluid in the body can trigger sickling. Her fluid intake chart had not been completed since the previous evening, which was a serious omission. She told me she felt very tired and I noticed a slurring of her speech and weakness down one side of her body. It quickly became clear that she had had a stroke. Fortunately she was to make a near complete recovery.

Back to 1977, Misha and I took a two-pronged approach to address the key issues of educating health professionals as well as providing support for patients and families. The first was to organise a sickle cell seminar in February that was attended by over 200 hospital and community health staff. During the planning stages I came across a brief reference in the *General Practitioner* journal about the launch in May 1976 of OSCAR, the Organisation for Sickle Cell Anaemia Research. We invited Neville Clare, a co-founder who had SC disease, to give a talk.

Secondly, and a month later, the support group held their inaugural meeting and my community links were to prove helpful. We obtained, free of charge, a room at the Learie Constantine Community Centre which was a venue often used by local Caribbean groups. Contacts within the black media also resulted in welcome publicity, including a radio interview on Alex Pascall's pioneering BBC Radio *Black Londoners* programme. The *West Indian World* newspaper also included a free advert about the event. As a result 16 people attended as well as Shirleen, Cynthia and myself, and we were all very heartened by the enthusiasm.

Misha encouraged me to write up the outcome and this became my first ever publication about sickle cell disease. Called 'Self-Help in Sickle Cell Anaemia', it was published on 21st September 1977 in *World Medicine* magazine. Nowadays support groups are common for many health conditions, but re-reading the article reminded me how unique it was back then, certainly for sickle cell disease.

The people attending ranged from a mother with her three children (she had lost a 16 year old daughter last year following a cerebrovascular accident during a crisis) to a cheerful 20 year old who arrived by motorbike – and contrasted sharply with a 26 year old man who was ill and depressed having entered hospital six times during the past year. It was the first opportunity for almost all of them to meet anyone else with the same condition. The effect was dramatic: one could feel the sense of relief they experienced; and the surprise to find they were not alone was clear on their faces.

The group was originally called Brent OSCAR and remained as such for two years. It met regularly and raised funds to produce education materials and buy a film projector, essential for the frequent talks and film shows now being organised. Previously stigmatised individuals and families were becoming more confident about speaking to journalists and opening up about the impact of the illness. As a result the group gained significant publicity and an increased profile, soon becoming better known than the national group. This caused so many tensions that eventually the local group decided unanimously to break away.

Group members from outside Brent insisted that the new association should become national, so in 1979 it transformed into the Sickle Cell Society. Membership grew at a rapid rate and celebrity Patrons were appointed such as comedian (now Sir) Lenny Henry and children's television presenter (now Baroness) Floella Benjamin.

Funds were raised for national dissemination of information, a welfare fund, scholarships and an annual children's holiday. The Society also supported local health services – purchasing a computer for the Brent Centre and laboratory equipment to screen newborn babies at Central Middlesex Hospital. Screening began in November 1981, only a few weeks before my daughter was born, and was one of the main reasons I was urged to come back to work a mere nine weeks after her birth.

I also acted as a voluntary Information Officer for the Society until stepping down from the committee in 1987. At the time the official estimate was that at least 3,000 people in Britain were affected by sickle cell – disputed by the charity as a gross underestimate, as was later proved correct. Campaigning became a critical part of our work, with one of the best examples being the October 1981 report *Sickle Cell Disease – The Need for Improved Services.* This highlighted the difficulties faced by families up and down the country, using information gleaned from letters and phone calls to the Society as well as input at public meetings.

The report contained 24 recommendations for improving services, balanced equally between comprehensive care and screening. These included the need for a national policy to screen babies, collection of statistics about incidence and death rates, guidelines for casualty and in-patient care together with follow-up at specialist clinics.

All this activity generated even greater interest from the media. In June 1984 the Channel 4 television programme *Black on Black,* produced by Trevor Phillips, featured weekly items over a 3-week period.

Celebrities were also filmed donating blood. A direct result of this was a phone call from someone introducing himself as Garth Crooks, a football player for Tottenham Hotspur (Spurs) and England. He had been disappointed that an overseas match had made it impossible for him to take part in the TV programme – but he now wanted to organise an annual Gala Dinner and Dance so that he and his famous friends could help raise funds for sickle cell.

Garth invited me to become a member of his planning committee, which was meeting the following week. I enquired where and Garth replied 'White Hart Lane'. I asked 'What number?' After a short silence he burst out laughing, saying it was clear that I didn't follow the game, and that it was the home of Spurs football stadium – oops!

- o – 0 – o -

My increasing involvement with sickle cell made me investigate where I could learn more about the condition, as well as how to develop appropriate services. It didn't take me long to realise that the USA was the best place to visit in view of the developments that had occurred there since 1972. So in August 1977 I decided to go on holiday to Los Angeles, staying with my cousin Obiageli and her family. While there I could also undertake a sickle cell fact-finding mission. The cost of the trip was reasonable, as that very year Laker Airways had started operating cheaper flights from London to Los Angeles.

In addition, I discovered that the National Association for Sickle Cell Disease (now the Sickle Cell Disease Association of America) and a local group were located in this very city! Both generously donated leaflets, posters and films to take back to London. They advised me to return in September of the following year, during National Sickle Cell Awareness Month. They also invited me to speak at their Annual General Meeting and conference in Minneapolis.

So I was back in 1978 for five weeks, and at the conference met delegates from all over the country. Many thought I was an African-American, probably due to my huge Afro hairstyle, and they were always pleasantly surprised to hear my English accent. For example my British pronunciation of the word capillary was quite different from the US version. They were also astonished to hear about the significant black and minority ethnic presence in the UK, and that sickle cell disease was an issue.

During my visit the national organisation generously arranged for me to attend an intensive haemoglobinopathy counselling course at the Oakland's Children's Hospital Medical Center of Northern California. It covered sickle cell and thalassaemia, the latter being a severe inherited anaemia requiring monthly blood transfusions. The course provided me with a wonderful opportunity to get to know the delegates, mainly African-American nurses. Their generosity was overwhelming. We all got on incredibly well and they virtually adopted me for the week!

In the USA, nationally funded comprehensive sickle cell centres were created through funds generated following the 1972 Sickle Cell Control Act. This legislation arose from a mixture of lobbying by sickle cell groups, health specialists, the Black Panther Party and the media. A significant amount of credit is also given to Colby King, a black research fellow at the Department of Health, Education and Welfare (HEW).

In the autumn of 1970, King was assigned to prepare a report about the response of the National Institutes of Health (NIH) to sickle cell. The project had been prompted by a letter from the mother of an affected child writing to the department asking for help. King demonstrated NIH's low priority and minimal resources allocated to sickle cell in comparison to funds approved for conditions of equal or lesser prevalence. He also identified the lack of equitable representation on NIH advisory boards, with only one black member out of 113.

His report was submitted to Robert Patricelli, a deputy undersecretary at HEW at a time when officials were preparing options for President Nixon's Health Message. Patricelli also discussed the report with his father Leonard who was president of WITC, a Connecticut television station. The latter decided that his station would run a campaign 'to do something about sickle cell anemia'.

He kept his word, as November 1970 saw the launch of the first detailed and influential TV and radio series on SCD. By April 1971 they raised nearly $34,000 to establish the first comprehensive paediatric sickle cell centre at Washington's Howard University. This was prior to the national government funds released following the rapidly-written and enacted 1972 National Sickle Cell Control Act. There would be some parallels in England 30 years later with the last-minute inclusion of a funded screening programme for sickle and thalassaemia in the ten year NHS Plan, launched in 2000.

All of these US activities coincided with the aftermath of the Civil Rights movement. The title of the Act highlights the apparently contentious objective of reducing the number of cases through screening populations for sickle cell trait. There was a huge outcry, as this was perceived to be a eugenic measure against predominantly black at-risk communities. So there was a major effort to clarify that funding was for comprehensive centres to deliver care and undertake research, as well as screening and genetic counselling. By 1976 there were 15 such centres. I visited the San Francisco centre, where I spent time with Sylvia Lee, an African-American Paediatric Nurse Practitioner who had seven years' experience in sickle cell disease. Her philosophy of care influenced me immensely, and gave me the opportunity to see a black nurse working in this way. What a role model! It gave me the idea that once back in Brent, I too could develop a similar service.

In my report of this mind-blowing trip I observed:

It is apparent that great strides have been achieved in the United States in the last seven years or so, but that this is perhaps just the start of a realisation that Sickle Cell Disease must now be treated as a major health problem for some foreseeable time. There are many lessons to be learnt from the American experience for the situation that exists in Britain as it is in a similar position the USA found itself during the period of the late 60s and early 70s. That is Sickle Cell Disease is a low health priority with no health education material, very little awareness amongst both the professional and lay community, and virtually no specialized support for affected individuals and families.

I was fortunate to also be awarded two travel fellowships to study sickle cell services, one from the Commission for Racial Equality (CRE) in 1979 and the other from the Winston Churchill Memorial Trust in 1981. The first enabled me to visit the Caribbean countries of Jamaica, Guyana, Barbados, Trinidad & Tobago and St Lucia. The second funded a tour of five cities in the USA and a one-month visit to Jamaica.

These fantastic opportunities provided me with so many insights that were to be of great help in developing services in Brent. In the US I absorbed a great deal about strategies to establish services for marginalised communities. In the Caribbean I learnt about various cultures, including attitudes and health beliefs towards sickle cell disorders. Both trips included some unexpected incidents that will stay with me forever.

During my stay in Guyana in July 1979 I reconnected with my old friend Walter Rodney, who I'd first met through his publisher, Jessica Huntley of Bogle L'Ouverture publishers. He was still a major political activist and not at all popular with the government in power. Our meeting was organised in great secrecy due to the many death threats he had received. A car arrived to take me to his current address – he moved homes frequently – and a few minutes into the journey I was taken aback to hear Walter's voice: he was hidden under a blanket in the back of the car! He told me all about the current political tensions and the numerous street demonstrations that he had spoken at.

I told him about my own experience the previous day when arrested in the street for taking photographs in the capital of Georgetown. The policeman informed me that my camera had been aimed at the headquarters of the People's National Congress (PNC), the political party that was in power. He refused to believe that I was actually taking a photo of a beautiful Hindu temple. A crowd gathered and soon elicited that I was from London and that my trip was concerned with sickle cell. They all rounded on the policeman and formed a barrier between us, at which point somebody gave me a lift back to where I was staying. As in 1970 in Paris, my hobby of photography had once again got me into trouble! Sadly, this would be the last time I would see Walter as he was assassinated in Guyana the following year, on 13th June 1980, and just one day after my father's death.

During the Churchill Fellowship tour I stayed in Washington, D.C. with Sarah, my friend from Paris days. On 30th March 1981, and just down the street from her house, there was an assassination attempt on President Ronald Reagan. While watching the endless replays on television, I suddenly heard a man calling my name from downstairs. Peering over the stairs and seeing guns pointed at me, I just froze in fear. As Sarah recounted: 'You had left the downstairs door ajar and I had called the police having recently had a robbery and also letting them know you were staying with me. The lights weren't on, and it was dusk. All you could see were two crouching male figures, with guns drawn!' Meanwhile back in south London, between 10th and 11th April, Brixton was aflame with an uprising.

By 11th May I was in Jamaica at the laboratories of the Medical Research Council Sickle Cell Unit. The radio was on and suddenly someone shouted that Bob Marley had died in Miami. Nine days later, courtesy of a nurse from the unit who had sweet-talked a policeman, we managed to jump the queue and see the singer lying-in-state at Kingston's National Arena.

All these trips were to make a great impression on me, as I told a conference in 1986:

When I kept coming back to Britain I would be so enthused by the American situation, don't forget it was just after the end of the Civil Rights era in the late 1970s when I was going, and I would come back to staid, stuffy old racist Britain and they would say 'You really have got a bee in your bonnet about sickle cell, it really isn't a great problem.'

- o – 0 – o -

By September 1979, Misha had obtained two rooms at Willesden Hospital. Here I ran the Brent Sickle Cell and Thalassaemia Information, Screening and Counselling Centre. It was the first such service in the UK and I would be the only nurse there for six years. I remained a member of the Haematology Department, as nursing management could not find a way of slotting me into their structure.

It was an uphill struggle to convince a range of local and national authorities about the significance of the condition – so imagine my surprise when in 1985 a letter arrived asking if I would accept an MBE in the forthcoming New Year's Honours list. After some consideration I wrote back thanking the powers that be for the recognition, but refusing it on the grounds that government support was needed to improve sickle cell services.

There would eventually be some secretarial support but it would take until 1985 to secure extra funding for the appointment of two health visitors to assist with the increased sickle cell work: Marvelle and Nina. Nina, who spoke Gujarati, also helped to develop awareness of thalassaemia within the local South Asian community.

From the outset, Misha and I decided that we needed to obtain resources to develop awareness programmes for lay and professional groups. The lack of knowledge concerning the true prevalence of sickle cell also needed to be addressed. It was clear from the patients we had met that there was an urgent requirement for specialist medical care, information and support. Moreover, a few years previously, I had come across this astonishing statement in a 1976 book entitled *Genetic Counselling* by Stevenson & Davison:

> *Sickle-cell anaemia is not of great consequence to us in the context of genetic counselling in the United Kingdom. The sickling trait and sickle cell anaemia appear to be confined to peoples of African and Eastern origin.*

This shocking ignorance was a key driver that led me to travel all the way to USA to access training in sickle cell and thalassaemia genetic counselling.

An open-door blood testing facility was vital to reduce the barriers for those wishing to know their haemoglobin type. Fortunately blood samples could be taken at the hospital. Misha arranged for people to access this service without the need for a referral from a family doctor. I was authorised to complete the relevant blood investigation request forms. This all seemed quite revolutionary in those days!

I ran the genetic counselling sessions and arranged family studies. Misha and I had previously visited our local regional clinical genetics centre to establish what services they provided. We were given a very warm reception but while there was genetic counselling for cystic fibrosis, there were no similar services for sickle cell and thalassaemia apart from the very occasional referral. There was an incorrect assumption that general practitioners, paediatricians and haematologists were addressing these needs.

No effort seemed to have been made to establish whether this was actually the case.

If there had ever been doubts about the need for a specialist service of this kind, the amazing response we had speaks for itself. By 1987 more than 3,000 people had attended screening and genetic counselling sessions, with over 50% being self-referrals. In 1979 I was in contact with 70 individuals with sickle cell disease and by 1988 this had risen to 382. Of these, 112 were under the age of 16 years.

- o – 0 – o -

Back in the autumn of 1978 Misha had appointed me as a Research Fellow, and my first project was to develop a register of local patients. Using hospital activity analysis data, all records were pulled that included the diagnostic code for sickle cell disease. I stayed on at work for many a long evening ploughing through hospital medical notes.

A total of 57 patients with sickle cell disease were identified and to my surprise, numerous errors were discovered in the other records. Blood results neatly pasted in the notes revealed these individuals to have sickle cell trait and *not* sickle cell disease. It was yet another illustration of the utter confusion there was between sickle cell trait and the illness itself. I also came across a lack of knowledge about the Caribbean, where many of the patients came from. This doctor exemplified it: 'I examined this pleasant Jamaican lady from Barbados...'

In January 1981 our article describing the characteristics of 70 patients was published in the prestigious *British Medical Journal*. Entitled 'Sickle-cell disease in a British urban community', the paper was produced by a team of us that included Misha, Dr Diana Walford, two haematologists, and a statistician, Dr Betty Kirkwood. It was the first paper of its kind in the UK and I was pleasantly surprised when Misha made me first author. It was so typical of the way she acknowledged my contribution, even though I was not a medical doctor and had only recently commenced work on my PhD degree. Later on in my academic career, I became aware that this was not always standard practice. Misha also taught me about the power of disseminating evidence through mainstream professional journals.

The pilot study for my PhD degree entailed interviewing five parents from outside Brent. The account of one mother formed the basis of an article in *Nursing Times* in July 1979. Called 'Learning to cope with sickle cell disease – a parent's experience' it was written in collaboration with my supervisor Alan Beattie. 'Miss J', as I called the mother, had been identified as having sickle cell trait during pregnancy but wasn't informed of this until just before she had her son.

Following his birth she asked two different doctors if her son would get the illness and each said no, he would be fine. His first admission to hospital at ten months of age lasted four weeks, and that was when he was diagnosed with sickle cell anaemia.

I don't know whether I was coming or going. I thought I would die, actually, because I was walking like I'm not walking at all. I think I was floating, and every time, every day I go up to see him, he looked like he finished.

My main study involved interviewing 22 parents of children with sickle cell disease who had been followed at Central Middlesex Hospital from 1962 onwards. My mother very kindly transcribed all the recorded interviews for which I was immensely grateful.

Many parents spoke about their dreadful experiences, mirroring those of Miss J. Only one woman had ever heard of sickle cell at the time of diagnosis (in a child who she and her husband had adopted). All of the mothers had been identified as carriers during pregnancy, but none had been informed of their result and no partners were offered screening. No baby was tested at birth even though it was possible to do so.

The relevant investigation, haemoglobin electrophoresis, had been developed during the 1950s and was not expensive. It amazed me that screening and clinical care for sickle cell disease had such a low priority given that it was one of the first conditions to be recognised as a molecular disease. Linus Pauling, the noted American physical chemist and Nobel Laureate, had established the molecular basis of sickle cell anaemia way back in 1949.

In 1982, Princess Diana and Prince Charles were expecting their first child, Prince William. I thought about the different approach that would have been taken if one or both had been found to be a carrier of an inherited genetic disorder. Every effort would have been made by the health professionals to establish and inform the couple if they were at risk of having an affected child. This is exactly what those parents interviewed by me had wanted.

In 1981 I had been pregnant with Azuka, and my own screening at Queen Charlotte's Hospital had been excellent. The Consultant Haematologist, Dr Elizabeth Letsky, was ahead of many of her peers in establishing routine sickle cell and thalassaemia screening and genetic counselling in pregnancy. This would prove to be an important experience for me. In March 1982, not long after my return to work, I started to offer genetic counselling to pregnant women with sickle cell or other carrier states. Having been so recently pregnant made it easier to empathise with fears of parents-to-be. Many of the midwives at Central Middlesex Hospital were from Caribbean, Irish and African origin and were a great bunch of people to work with. They made me extremely welcome in their world!

- o – 0 – o -

It soon became clear that my role would embrace everything 'from cradle to grave'. In the early 1980s up to three of our local patients died each year and there would be other losses among those I knew through the Sickle Cell Society. Dr Ade Olujohungbe was a Consultant Haematologist and Medical Advisor for the organisation. He had the illness and sadly died in 2013, weeks before his long awaited 50th birthday. He was so friendly, intelligent and extremely committed to improving the quality of treatment for the condition. His passing shocked so many people.

This was the worst aspect of my work and I would dread the call that somebody had died or was dangerously ill. They were always so young, and the shock and grief of their family and friends was utterly heart breaking. One would be dear Francis who had only just started to come to terms with his illness. I would often do a home visit to bereaved families. One was to a Nigerian diplomat whose very young daughter had recently died. He suddenly started to weep saying that fathers missed their children as much as their mothers. It was heartrending.

Sometimes Misha asked me to act as an intermediary for doctors finding it difficult to cope with different cultural expressions of grief. This could range from huge numbers of family and friends angrily demanding answers to some howling in utter anguish. One doctor opened up to me about his dread of dealing with these multiple displays of grief, as he had never come across it before he came to London. His own words were: 'My middle-class white background and my medical training have not prepared me for such powerful expressions of loss.'

After a few joint meetings with bereaved relatives we took some time to discuss his observations. His main reflections centred on how I listened with respect and did not interrupt, regardless of occasional accusations against the hospital of racism and/or negligent care. In fact I would make sure that the family knew where to make a complaint. Questions were answered immediately and where all the information was not available, a promise was made to investigate further. He noticed how at ease I seemed to be with various cultural attitudes to death and dying. Of interest to me was the way he pointed out how members of the group would often determine when it was time to stop talking and/or challenge those who they thought were being too brusque with me.

I said that it was important not to feel personally challenged. Time was required to ensure that possibly years of pent up emotions could be expressed at this time of utter shock and grief.

It was often young black individuals who had suddenly died. Our in-depth discussion allowed us both to avoid tiptoeing around certain issues. He revealed that he had never really understood why so many black relatives and friends came to the hospital, nor why some acted so aggressively. I asked him to consider whether he was actually scared of black people when they acted in such a raw, emotional and challenging manner.

Looking back, the 1980s proved to be a hive of activity with looking after my daughter, running the Brent Centre, and involvement with the Sickle Cell Society. It seemed that I was only happy when operating with one foot in the community and one in the health service. I was also busy writing explanatory articles about sickle cell for nurses, health visitors and midwives.

Our pioneering service in Brent created huge interest in the NHS and the media. There were interviews and numerous talks given at public meetings, and money was raised to produce information. In 1983 the Sickle Cell Society obtained funding from Thames Television Telethon for a long-overdue publication *A Handbook on Sickle Cell Disease: a guide for families* that I wrote with June Hall, a teacher and Trustee of the charity. It was illustrated by Bryan Jones who was a young artist affected by sickle cell anaemia and who sadly died a few years later.

An immensely gratifying venture was the regular specialist one-week courses that Misha and I organised. These were partially driven by my own experience of having to travel all the way to the USA to study, but were also in response to numerous requests for training from health professionals and voluntary groups up and down the country. An example comes from Alison, a former Clinical Scientist Laboratory Director in Cardiff:

> *I phoned up Brent Sickle Cell Centre out of desperation to find information for somebody in the community venturing into doing something to fill the gap in services. That person had watched a programme on Black on Black. We were absolutely dependent on the generosity of people like yourself and Nina in Brent and being part of that growing national network of nurse counsellors and community initiatives.*

Another is from Carol, a retired consultant haematologist.

> *I always remember meeting you when you came to speak to the Trinidadian society at Reading; I was already interested in sickle because of working at St. Thomas', so, in my case you were preaching to the converted! It was thanks to you that we got the funding for Miggie to be a counsellor, which was superb!*

There was no doubt that working and lobbying for sickle cell consumed a lot of my time. As Nina, a friend and former colleague said: 'What I admire about you the most is how focused you are. Though I have at times said under my breath, enough about sickle!'

- o – 0 – o -

When I was actively involved with sickle cell issues, I was determined that Azuka would come with me to as many events as possible, both at home and abroad.

With your sickle cell stuff, I went around with you a lot. When I was younger I could see you as a campaigner and I remember once when I wished I had sickle cell. Also I remember playing with the dolls in the nursery and a vivid memory is giving one particular doll a blood transfusion!

We travelled far afield to countries such as Jamaica, Bermuda, the French Caribbean isles of Guadeloupe and Martinique, Nigeria and Holland. While in Amsterdam, Azuka wanted to visit the house where Anne Frank and her family had tried to hide from the Nazis. Later she insisted on watching the video purchased at the museum, the 1959 film *The Diary of Anne Frank* starring Shelley Winters. It wasn't a good idea as she became incredibly distressed and started to weep inconsolably.

Alone at a Dutch colleague's flat I desperately looked through her videos and was delighted to see *The Sound of Music*, one of Azuka's favourite musicals of all times. Thankfully a smile appeared on her face just a few bars into the notes of the opening song: *The hills are alive...* She commented years later how the film was covering the period of the Nazis' invasion of Austria but in a much less searing manner than the Anne Frank story.

My ability to speak French resulted in requests to run sickle courses in Martinique and Guadeloupe. In 1990 a comprehensive sickle cell centre was opened in Guadeloupe's capital of Point-à-Pitre. There was intense local pride that it was the first such French centre, and ahead of 'la Métropole' i.e. the European territory of France.

Azuka attended a local school where none of the children spoke English, although some of the teachers did. She was the centre of attention and still remembers the friends she made, regardless of language barriers. Her other abiding memory was of the tasty and nutritious food that she ate at the school, including guavas! My memories were of the amazing hospitality, discussions, sea-bathing and dancing to Zouk and Biguine music.

- o – 0 – o -

All seemed to be going swimmingly well in Brent until an unexpected and unwelcome sea change occurred around 1987. Misha appointed a new consultant, which resulted in two significant developments. The first was welcome, as by 1988 it heralded an expansion of newborn screening throughout the North-West Thames Region. The funding obtained enabled the appointment of more health visiting and administrative staff.

The second, and much less pleasant, was the change in culture due to a different management style. In contrast to Misha's inclusive style I gradually sensed one of harassment, bullying, criticism and control. There was now a hierarchal atmosphere with a clawing back of semi-autonomous working practices. There was micromanagement, memos galore and checks on everything. I can laugh now, but sometimes it felt as though I needed permission to even go to the toilet! On a more depressing note, nothing I did seemed to be right. Weirdly, this took me back to how my stepfather had made me feel, a dark place indeed.

What particularly saddened and confused me was how my relationship with Misha suffered, as she appeared to step back from it all. It would only recover after my departure. At around the same time I went to Nigeria to co-run Professor Akinyanju's Lagos-based annual sickle course. At some point he took me aside and urged me take six months off work, as this would be essential if I was to ever complete my PhD thesis.

My subsequent request for paid study leave was turned down flat, which made me extremely angry. I decided to take the six months off with three months' paid sick leave to have an overdue hysterectomy for fibroids, followed by three months' unpaid leave. I just survived financially due to the King's Fund coming to my rescue again with a £1,000 grant and by signing on for benefits.

Coming round from surgery, I saw the wonderful Professor Luzzatto was peering down at me and asking how I felt. He was in charge of the Haematology Department at the hospital and I suddenly felt very safe! The next day my friend brought seven-year-old Azuka to visit me and I could see my daughter's anxious glance at the intravenous drip in my arm. On the positive side I made a rapid recovery and was soon home. It was wonderful to at last be able to take Azuka to and from school as well as successfully complete my thesis!

Worsening tensions, that also affected Nina, marred my return to work and I don't think the award of a PhD improved the atmosphere that much. It was probably one of the most stressful periods of my working life and Nina recalls us once both crying in the Human Resources (HR) Department.

We decided to seek advice and support from our union, which led to us taking out a grievance. This shook a member of the HR staff who said they had never had to deal with one taken out against anyone so senior. Well, I thought bitterly, this is a chance for you to gain some experience!

To be fair, top management at the hospital tried frantically to resolve the issues by suggesting alternative management structures and work location. They genuinely seemed to value our lengthy involvement in developing highly acclaimed services. In the midst of all of this I experienced severe headaches and took myself off to the Occupational Health Service.

High blood pressure was detected and I immediately made a decision to leave the job and as early as possible, even before I had obtained another post. Azuka was still young and my family history of strokes was such that I determined no job was worth the risk. At least I had my health visiting qualification and would be very happy to return to that career.

There was, of course, a tremendous sadness at the thought of leaving the world of sickle cell and all the families I knew so well. It was made even more difficult when a group of them asked me to reconsider my decision. A friend commented: 'I think for you it was a good move but it was a big loss for the Brent Centre.'

Ursula, a friend and a mother of a daughter with sickle cell anaemia reflected:

It was quite sad because it was almost as if, despite the fact that you are doing all this good work, you had no right to be so noticeable. It seemed as though you needed to know your place, so for me as a user of these services I felt a little bit ill at ease with those same people of authority. And also in terms of people of authority, it kind of saddened me that that was the case because who else was better placed to represent us, parents of children with sickle cell, the black community, the cause that you were fighting for? So I couldn't understand sometimes why it all had to be so unpleasant.

Happily for me, it turned out that the well-known quote from Alexander Graham Bell really did happen: 'When one door closes another opens.' In fact, many, many doors were to open up for me during the next phase of my career. The good news was that this included the opportunity to remain involved with sickle cell disease. It would be through research, writing, lecturing, being a member of policy advisory committees and ultimately becoming a Patron of the Sickle Cell Society!

XVII

Rescued again

Having made up my mind to leave and look for a post as a health visitor, I received a phone call that was to change everything and totally lift my spirits. Life can be very sweet! It was from Professor Marcus Pembrey, Consultant Clinical Geneticist at the University of London's Institute of Child Health and Great Ormond Street Hospital for Children.

He wanted to apologise about being away on the day I was due to come and talk to his MSc in Clinical Genetics students. There must have been something in the way I spoke that alerted him to my dejected state of mind. It didn't take him long to discover my plans to quit and, to my eternal joy, he asked if I would consider working at the Institute! Marcus was aware of my ambition to establish a course on multi-ethnic aspects of screening and genetic counselling. As he later reflected: 'The lesson from that quite simply is you never know when you're having a conversation, what effect it might have, you just do what you think is the right thing to do.'

He went on to say:

Haemoglobinopathies screening was an important part of genetic services and a significant issue that we weren't covering at the Institute. When I arrived here we were isolated from the community. A sort of ivory tower, both clinically and in research and it was important to try and break that down. I had a considerable background in haemoglobinopathies.

Firstly, it happened that I carried beta thalassaemia, even though I apparently don't come from the right ethnic group. So this showed I was beginning to think that things are not always the way they seem. You can't pigeonhole people. Having beta thalassaemia in the family encouraged me to study the subject when I was a student and that got me into haemoglobinopathies research.

Then I was out in Saudi Arabia showing that they didn't suffer as badly from sickle cell disease, due to their raised fetal haemoglobin. I had already done a public health education film there, before even appointing you here. So it was entirely obvious that I wanted to go on and do something similar here but nobody seemed to be doing it.

You raised the ethnicity issues. There was a part of me that felt, why should haemoglobinopathies be nothing to do with clinical genetics? So I think you were helping me with a political agenda. It proves to people that clinical geneticists can get involved in haemoglobinopathies screening.

These views were music to my ears and in contrast to reactions previously described.

Marcus continued:

I was pretty clear about the sort of person I wanted to have teaching on our programmes and was vaguely on the lookout. It didn't take me long to realise that we were thinking alike.

So you were a breath of fresh air and a dream come true! As the Mothercare Professor of Genetics and very soon after the Vice-Dean, I was in a position to do something.

One of the people with whom I had previously discussed the idea of setting up a course was Dr Sheila Adam, then Director of Public Health at North-West Thames Regional Health Authority. She used to work in Brent and was a keen advocate of the pioneering sickle cell services that Misha and I had developed. As a result Sheila encouraged me to pursue my plans and offered to partially fund my salary for three years. Marcus then managed to obtain the remaining amount from Sheila's counterpart in the North-East Thames Region.

In the autumn of 1990 I attended a formal selection interview in front of an impressive panel of academics at the Institute of Child Health. It included Professor Roland Levinsky[13] who was the Dean and an internationally recognised expert on immunodeficiency disease. I was initially quite anxious in front of this literally towering intellectual, but my responses to the varied questions about plans for teaching, research and publishing must have been satisfactory as I was appointed Lecturer in Community Genetic Counselling.

Following my appointment it was decided that I would hold a joint Lectureship between the Departments of a) Clinical Genetics & Fetal Medicine and b) Epidemiology, the latter led by Professor Catherine Peckham. Those seven years at the Institute of Child Health would prove to be incredibly happy and productive ones. Having said that, the memory of my first morning was one of initially feeling an absolute nervous wreck. I vividly recall sitting alone at a desk to start designing the first course that would be held just a few months later in January 1991. Looking at the blank pad of paper I wondered to myself: 'What on earth have you got yourself into?!' Then I picked up the phone to book various speakers, received enthusiastic responses and immediately felt better. It also helped that secretarial support was arranged and that Paula would provide it so well throughout those years.

Marcus's management style suited me down to the ground. As he commented, it was characterised by putting all his effort into attracting the right people and then 'not really managing anybody.' A couple of examples come to mind. Firstly, his response when I hesitantly mentioned an invitation I had recently received to visit Guadeloupe. It was for two weeks in October 1990 and not long after starting work at the Institute! Marcus was delighted to hear that not only would I be a guest of honour at the opening of the Sickle Cell Centre but also that I would jointly run a course.

The second example of Marcus's refreshing management style was when I asked for an annual leave card to book time off for Azuka's half-term holiday and discovered their non-existence in the department! 'One of the first things I did was to abolish holiday forms because the senior staff didn't have to fill them in. It seemed wrong, and it actually achieved nothing because my main problem was getting people to take their holidays.' Both illustrated a seismic and heartening shift away from the work culture that I had recently left.

There was also a keen respect for nurses and one influence soon became apparent. During a meeting we were talking about some aspect of the profession and Marcus kept referring to somebody called Sue. It took some time for the penny to drop. When I asked if he was talking about Sue Pembrey, he said 'Yes, you do realise that she is my sister?' What a small world!

Sue was an iconic figure in nursing due to her research on the role of the ward sister. She had also set up and run the famous Oxford Nursing Development Unit at the Radcliffe Infirmary. My first contact with her had been as far back as July 1971 when she

spoke at a conference on Private Practice. Organised by the Young
Socialist Medical Association and reported in *Needle* magazine, Sue
had spoken on Agency Nursing. She argued that the attraction for
nurses was more the flexible hours rather than money, and should
be a lesson for the NHS.

I titled the two-week course *Genetic Counselling for the
Community – A Multi-Ethnic Approach*. It would focus on the
similarities and differences faced by couples at risk of genetic
disorders such as sickle cell disease, thalassaemia, cystic fibrosis
and Tay-Sachs disease. The latter progressively destroys nerve cells
in the brain and spinal cord resulting in death at about the age of
five years. There is a significantly higher incidence of the illness in
people of eastern European Ashkenazi Jewish descent, although it
is also found in other populations.

This is exactly what had always fascinated me about these
inherited conditions. It is generally well recognised that all have
a higher incidence in certain ethnic groups. Those at increased
risk of the various thalassaemia syndromes include populations
originating from the Mediterranean, the Middle and Far East as
well as South Asia. Cystic fibrosis is most commonly found in
people of white Northern European origin.

Many health professionals thought that only certain groups
were at risk of a particular genetic disorder. The classic misunder-
standing is that cystic fibrosis was only seen in white people, thalassaemia in Greek and Turkish-Cypriots, Tay-Sachs in Ashkenazi
Jews and sickle cell in the black community. Less well known was
that all of these conditions are also seen in other groups, although
usually to a lesser extent. Between them, all these genetic disorders
impact on most communities in this country.

Twenty courses would be held between 1991 and 1997. A total
of 296 people attended who were mainly midwives, haemoglobinopathy counsellors and genetic nurses. There were also doctors,

family planning nurses and health visitors. Most came from the UK, with the majority from the North Thames Region of London, and there was at least one overseas participant on each course.

On completing the course they were keen to retain contact with the Institute in order to share their news as well as hear about key developments. It was therefore encouraging to obtain a grant from the King's Fund to produce a newsletter that we called *Linkage*. It met the desired objectives as well as enabling past students to keep in touch with each other, wherever they were in the world.

The professional diversity of the participants was a welcome surprise. I had thought that most would be midwives and haemo-globinopathy nurse counsellors, but I had not expected generic genetic counsellors to attend – I assumed they would think the course had too narrow a focus. All appreciated the emphasis on clear explanations of genetic inheritance through a varied use of educational tools (some of which proved to be more stressful for participants than others!). This was illustrated in a review in *Linkage* by four doctors undertaking the MSc in Clinical Genetics and who had attended the course:

> *The teaching aids, videos and dice game were useful and we all felt it would help us in explaining autosomal recessive inherit-ance to patients. None of us appeared to enjoy watching our videos, but the insight we gained from viewing the role-play will help us in our clinical practice.*

I quickly became aware of the many sensitive issues that could affect students due to their own experiences or belief systems. These included the ethics surrounding perceptions of disability and the option of prenatal diagnosis and termination for an affected unborn baby.

During the first course I realised that midwives were constantly comparing their varied experiences with the recently introduced 'Bart's Test'. I had never heard of it so asked them to explain further and, oh boy, they did just that! It turned out to be a new way of identifying pregnant women with a possible increased risk of having a baby with Down's Syndrome. Many thought it had been introduced too quickly and felt unprepared for their role in informing the women about the exact details of this test compared to other forms of screening. As a result, they were very anxious and strongly urged me to include a session about it in future courses. The whole topic of screening for the condition was taken on board and the programme included a speaker from the Down's Syndrome Association.

Another speaker was Dr Elizabeth Dormandy, who also decided to attend one of the courses:

We first met in the mid-90s when I spoke on your course and had been working with Professor Nick Wald and his team running the Down's Syndrome Screening Programme. My responsibility was education and training across 30-odd hospitals in North Thames. I could see that you were aiming to equip people to offer support, help and counselling to women and their families from a broad range of backgrounds and perspectives. I found that incredibly exciting.

I had studied within a bio-medical model and previously worked in the laboratories where everything was clear-cut, yes or no. Your course enabled people to think about screening from the perspective of people being offered it.

We knew the uptake of Down's Syndrome Screening varied hugely from 30% in some areas to 90% in other areas. This variation occurred year on year and it was obvious there was something going on other than women's decisions.

I realised how important it was that you got parents and people with the condition to come and talk to course participants. As a white liberal I was sort of aware of different people's perspectives on ethnicity, but also a bit scared of it. I was able to see the similarities and appreciate the differences and it gave me confidence to talk about it. I learnt that we all come with different prejudices – some we are aware of and some we are not, but we need to work through it.

One of the most vivid examples that came to light on the course was an account from a midwife. One morning she had collected a large quantity of notes in preparation for a busy antenatal clinic. Seeing that the first one had an Indian name she put it lower down the pile to avoid having to immediately address 'language and cultural problems'. When the woman's turn eventually came the midwife was mortified to discover that she was an Oxford graduate and medically qualified. This incident shocked the midwife, exposing as it did her stereotypical and negative assumptions. It spurred her on to realise that she needed to seek the advice, resources and challenges the course could offer.

As there were always participants from varied ethnic backgrounds I was really pleased when they felt encouraged to speak openly, although it could get quite fiery at times. There was a determination and confidence on my part to incorporate these lively discussions throughout the course. This sense of ease to open up contentious discourses probably arose from my mixed heritage and having lived in different parts of the UK and abroad.

One favourite souvenir was a thank-you present from the June 1995 cohort. It was a small, colourful plate designed by Charlotte

Firmin that had a circle of children from diverse backgrounds forming a ring around the edge of it. The students had gone to the trouble of commissioning it, and several decades on I still treasure this beautiful and thoughtful item.

A month or so after the end of each two-week programme, participants returned for a follow-up session to discuss whether it had had any impact on their work. Their managers were also invited, as was a representative from the Department of Health. Marcus recalled:

> *The other thing that I remember was the innovative way that you sent them away saying: 'Right, you've learned something, now put it into practice'. I never thought of that, you introduced it, a brilliant idea. They were great classes as they were brought back to make a short presentation and be put on the spot about what they learned. I would try never to miss one of those because of what you learned from those was the barriers to introducing good practice.*

> *Some would say they went away to look at this and were listened to. As a result there's now a special nurse or midwife leading on this type of screening and counselling. In contrast, others would say that their recommendations were blocked and you learned politically about what the issues were. The person from the Department of Health found it so illuminating.*

About 50% of participants were able to get their manager to come along with them to the sessions, which were often an eye-opener for all of us.

There began to be a waiting list for the courses as well as many requests to speak about them – more than I could fulfil – from far and wide. Marcus and I were involved with running the first of several similar courses in Sestri Levante in Italy. Entitled *Genetic*

Counselling in Practice, they were held under the auspices of the European School of Medical Genetics.

In order to disseminate the philosophy of the course more widely I obtained a grant from the Department of Health to produce a 23-minute video and leaflet. Completed in 1993 it was called *From Chance to Choice* and described as 'a multi-ethnic approach to community genetics: the role of the primary health care team'. It featured Marcus, myself and several course contributors including Professors Bernadette and Michael Modell. Bernadette was a biologist and paediatrician who was internationally recognised for pioneering comprehensive treatment and screening services for thalassaemia, both in the UK and overseas. She was also a leading light in the developing specialty of community genetics. Her husband Michael was a Professor in General Practice with a particular interest in community screening for cystic fibrosis.

Baroness Cumberlege, then Junior Health Minister, launched the film in January 1994 at the Institute of Child Health. There was a huge turnout of over 200 ethnically diverse people from varied health backgrounds and voluntary organisations. The Institute had never seen anything like it! Marcus smiled at the recollection of it all:

Suddenly vast numbers of people were arriving at the Institute and Roland, the Dean was saying, 'What the hell is going on?' I said, 'I don't know, Elizabeth's organised it!' It obviously made an impact. The Dean, whom you never saw often, was suddenly in a photo opportunity with Baroness Cumberlege and she seemed a bit nervous.

- o – 0 – o -

Another exciting and enjoyable opportunity that arose for me during this period was involvement in policy issues and debates surrounding the ethics of genetics and reproductive choices. I became a member of the Gene Therapy Advisory Committee (GTAC) in 1993 and the newly formed Human Genetics Commission in 1999. The latter was known as the HGC and was steered by two incredibly eminent and charismatic Scots – the Glaswegian Baroness Helen Kennedy, QC (who was the chair) and her deputy, Alexander McCall Smith, Professor of Medical Law at the University of Edinburgh. He was also a bestselling author of works that included *The No. 1 Ladies' Detective Agency* series, set in Botswana. I still cherish the signed copy of *Morality for Beautiful Girls* that Sandy gave me in 2001.

Marcus wryly commented on my involvement with the HGC:

I was only too delighted to have a reversal [of roles] involving my study in Bristol, the Avon Longitudinal Study of parents and children. The Human Genetics Commission came down for two days to look into the situation, and there you were and sort of inspecting me!

Other committees that I belonged to during this period included the Department of Health's Antenatal Subgroup of the National Screening Group and the Nuffield Council on Bioethics Working Party on Genetic Screening. This was maybe why, in 1994, I was one of those invited to take part in the first episode of the *Hypotheticals* BBC2 TV series. It dealt with issues of reproduction and was moderated by Charles Nesson, a US Professor of Law at Harvard Law School.

Ruth Chadwick, Professor of Moral Philosophy at the University of Central Lancashire, reviewed the three programmes in the *British Medical Journal*. She sets the scene by explaining that 'in *Hypotheticals* health care professionals, ethicists, lawyers and police were taken through situations of increasing complexity by a moderator, with a view to establishing (a) what decisions they would take and (b) what principles, if any, these decisions are based on'.

Commenting on the first episode, she noted that a slightly unsatisfactory feature of this particular programme was the time allocated to different participants:

> *It would have been good to hear what Elizabeth Anionwu had to say about the disclosure to parents of genetic information about their aborted fetus found to have cystic fibrosis. Her point about racism and the choice between a black and a white egg was also passed over rather too quickly. The reason why egg donors are allowed to have a say in whether they donate to menopausal women, but not in matters of race, raises all sorts of ethical issues which were only gestured at.*

While at the Institute, it was also fantastic to continue with my sickle cell interests, and in many different ways. I was able to resume genetic counselling by providing local support to colleagues in Islington and Camden. These sessions took place at the Sickle Cell and Thalassaemia Centre, the paediatric and antenatal clinics at the Whittington Hospital and the prenatal diagnosis unit at University College Hospital, London. In 1991 I was invited to become a member of the Department of Health's Standing Medical Advisory Committee (SMAC) Working Party on Sickle Cell, Thalassaemia and other Haemoglobinopathies. The report was published in 1993 containing 62 recommendations but the only one that received funding was the production of a national haemoglobinopathy result card. However, the publication did raise the profile of the issues of concern to patients, families and professionals. This would assist in the conditions eventually having a much greater priority on the NHS agenda.

One media opportunity was to create some amusement! The BBC Radio 4 programme *Today* contacted me at an unearthly hour one morning to come into the studio to comment on some development in genetics and sickle cell disease. I said that unfortunately it would be impossible because of childcare issues. There was a slightly surprised response of 'Oh, really?' followed by an offer to interview me over the phone at work. I agreed, and some time after it was over told Marcus the story. He burst out laughing saying: 'Elizabeth, you don't seem to realise, there'd be people here who'd kill to get to the studio to be on that programme.'

The world of collaborating in research projects opened up for me in a way that I had not really envisaged. My room at the Institute was at the end of a corridor and the walk to the kitchen for a coffee enabled me to bump into staff from so many disciplines. This included public health, statistics, epidemiology and genetics. Suitable calls for research bids would be mentioned and meetings arranged to consider putting in a joint application. The discussions were intellectually stimulating and provided an opportunity to input ideas drawn from my NHS and community sickle cell and thalassaemia experience.

It was also immensely enjoyable, and gave me increased confidence to develop research and publication skills. This turned out to be an extremely productive period due to being a member of several research teams. Bids for various projects were awarded a total of nearly £1 million from the NHS and the Department of Health. One example of a successful outcome was the NHS Health and Technology Assessment (HTA) *Review and Economic Analysis into Screening for Haemoglobinopathies in the UK*.

I was also promoted in 1994, which I had good reason to be delighted about. As Marcus pointed out: 'Well, it's not easy to get a promotion to a senior lecturer here.' Those seven happy and fulfilling years at the Institute were to transform me and restore my self-confidence – so much so that thoughts turned to advancing my career, this time closer to home.

- o – 0 – o -

Azuka was now a teenager and I realised the need to secure a more local position. Marcus supported my ambition: 'It worked very well for you at the Institute. You were clearly destined to lead your own Unit, that's the philosophy here, and that's why you were to join Roland Levinsky's line as a Dean.'

He was referring to my appointment in the autumn of 1997 as Dean of the School of Adult Nursing at Thames Valley University (TVU), now the University of West London. At the time there were campus sites in Ealing, Reading and Slough. For two years I would manage 53 nurse tutors and immerse myself in the world of nursing and higher education. It would prove to be quite a culture shock, but I ultimately settled happily into a post that brought me back to my preferred calling.

After six months in post, I was awarded a Chair in Nursing. The positive impact of this appointment on others was quite an eye-opener, as some of my colleagues remember:

Ramesh, a senior nurse lecturer:

You were the first black person to be in such a high position at TVU and were very genuine. You came in with ideas and encouraged us enormously to stretch ourselves clinically and academically and that was what people wanted. I wanted to publish and sought your advice, and you immediately said yes, come and see me. For the first time I felt supported and after just two sessions with you I managed to complete the paper which was published in 1998.

Felicia, a Director of Nursing:

One big wow factor for me was that you're a Professor, a black Professor of Nursing!

Baba, a consultant haematologist:

It helped a lot of people be they doctors, nurses or others who saw you as a role model, even though they had never met you. I and other people felt very proud that you had progressed to the level of a Professor and a major nursing role, as well as making such an impact in sickle cell in the UK. You actually wanted to be associated with this person and I loved the name, which was a Nigerian name, Anionwu! It gave me hope that we can make it as well.

Although up to my eyes with management matters, I was determined to continue with my sickle cell interests. These included teaching, research and community activities as well as securing a fortnightly clinical link on a haematology ward in a west London hospital. I declined the offer of a sister's uniform from the Director of Nursing, instead requesting one for a staff nurse. It's good to know one's limitations! He told me later that he couldn't quite get over the shock of seeing a Professor of Nursing working on a ward. It was a great experience and also set an example to students and the few nurse tutors who had been reluctant to have their own clinical link.

Retaining my involvement with community and policy aspects of sickle cell was of particular importance. This was achieved through collaborating with Karl Atkin, Professor of Sociology at the University of York. We also shared a keen interest in the historical milestones that had led to sickle cell and thalassaemia gradually coming in from the cold and onto the NHS agenda. The best example was the inclusion of universal newborn and antenatal screening in the government's NHS Plan in 2000.

Within a few years all babies in England, and regardless of ethnic origin, were being screened for sickle cell disease – an incredible feat achieved through the dynamic leadership of Archbishop John

Sentamu who chaired the advisory committee and Dr Allison Streetly, Director of the programme.

We wrote about these developments in a book called *The Politics of Sickle Cell and Thalassaemia* that was published by the Open University Press in 2001.

In addition we had a mutual interest in working with the voluntary sector. Back in 1990, I had been extremely concerned about losing this contact after leaving Brent, but thankfully this never happened.

Karl recollects:

You were always such a good chair at those community meetings. This was a highly politicised world where you really had to have credibility with that audience.

Karl also pointed out that at dissemination meetings with doctors and policy makers, the top table would be predominantly white while the audience was predominantly black – and that even in the sickle cell world, some people had difficulty with the idea of an articulate and educated black woman:

You broke that mould and I think that was incredibly important ... [but] from seeing you in the many meetings over the years I could see that it was a struggle ... people looking to undermine you, and that's wearing over years and years. But in some ways you could use that to your advantage as well, because you gave credibility to the communities. It also meant you were slightly on the outside, which is not a bad thing.

XVIII

Mary Seacole

As with sickle cell disease, Mary Seacole had not been included in my nursing course in Paddington, which is quite ironic given she was buried a mere half-mile away! Soon after I started work as Dean of the School of Adult Nursing at TVU, it became clear that nothing much had changed. I was talking with groups of student nurses, as it was crucial to hear directly from them about how the course was going and to obtain feedback about their clinical placement experiences. One student talked about being unfairly treated and wanted advice. I mentioned how Mary Seacole, the Victorian Jamaican/Scottish nurse, had overcome rejection when her offer to go and care for British soldiers in the Crimean War had been turned down. A sea of blank faces looked back at me and it was obvious that not one of the twenty students had heard of her!

I systematically quizzed all future groups only to find that, apart from a handful of students, there was a widespread lack of knowledge. With a few exceptions this was also the case for many of their tutors (as well as senior nurses elsewhere), as their comments attest:

Ramesh, a senior nurse lecturer: 'I had never heard of Mary Seacole until you came on board. You not only raised my awareness but also that of the whole nursing faculty.'

Joan, a nurse consultant: 'I used to see you at conferences and the first time I heard about Mary Seacole was when you spoke about her in 2004, amazing because I'd been a nurse for 21 years!'

Elaine, a retired Head of a Nursing School: 'I had never heard of Mary Seacole throughout my entire nursing career. I taught student nurses and since I had never heard of her, the entire school never heard of her.'

So what was it that I found so compelling about Mary Jane Grant Seacole, and why is she still relevant for so many of us today? Certain aspects of her story continue to have a particular resonance for me.

To start with, there is Mary's pride in her Jamaican and Scottish heritage, her condemnation of the evils of slavery and the way she refused to accept discrimination. Finally, there is the manner in which she overcame any obstacle that might stop her from delivering compassionate and skilful nursing care.

I first learnt about Mary in 1984, at the launch of a new edition of her 1857 autobiography, *Wonderful Adventures of Mrs Seacole in Many Lands*. The editors were Ziggi Alexander (then a Brent librarian) and Audrey Dewjee, who had worked for Ealing Community Relations Council. Once home with my copy, it was fascinating to pore through the Victorian prose and follow Mary's fast-paced narrative. This covered her early years in Jamaica before travelling as a 'doctress'/nurse and entrepreneur to places such as Panama, the Crimea and London.

There were some frustrating gaps in her account, including the identity of her parents and her date of birth. All Mary coyly reveals in the opening paragraph is:

I was born in the town of Kingston, in the island of Jamaica, sometime in the present century. As a female, and a widow, I may be well excused giving the precise date of this important event. But I do not mind confessing that the century and myself were both young together and that we have grown side by side into age and consequence.

We simply learn that Mary Jane Grant's father was a soldier 'of an old Scotch family' and that her mother kept a boarding house in Kingston. She 'was like many of the Creole women, an admirable doctress … It was very natural that I should inherit her tastes; and so I had from early youth a yearning for medical knowledge and practice that never deserted me.'

Alexander and Dewjee explain that Mary's mother was one of many women who were notable doctresses and whose expertise was recognised throughout Jamaica. They cite Cuba Cornwallis, who in 1780 nursed Horatio Nelson at Port Royal through a bout of fever from which he was not expected to recover. Doctresses were 'familiar with the prognosis and treatment of tropical diseases, general ailments and wounds'. The Creole medicine they used 'evolved on the plantations, and was based on knowledge of herbal medicine and midwifery brought from Africa'.

Following two trips to England Mary returned to her mother's house. Here she made herself useful in a variety of ways and in the process learnt 'a great deal of Creole medical art'. On 10th November 1836 she wed an Englishman, Edwin Horatio Hamilton Seacole, but their marriage was to last a mere eight years. Her husband was delicate and Mary nursed him until his death in 1844. In her will she refers to him as the godson of Lord Horatio Nelson. Oral history recounted through the ages by the Seacole family suggests that he might have been the son of Admiral Nelson and Emma, Lady Hamilton.

Mary suffered another loss with the demise of her mother, but struggled on as a widow by taking on diverse business ventures (with varying degrees of success). Her boarding house was even burnt down but she soon rebuilt it, and by chapter two proudly tells us 'I had gained a reputation as a skilled nurse and doctress, and my house was always full of invalid officers …' It is worth pointing out to those who argue that Seacole was not a nurse that the first recognised UK nurse training school was only established in 1860 by Florence Nightingale at St Thomas' Hospital. This was four years *after* the end of the Crimean War!

The bulk of Mary's autobiography is an account of voyages to Panama and the Crimea to combine entrepreneurial activities with that of being a doctress and nurse. It reveals her feisty nature and determination to overcome whatever barriers she came across. What I find particularly appealing is Mary's refusal to be viewed as an inferior person on the basis of her skin colour. She displayed powerful networking skills, and was not afraid to seek help from those she knew at the highest echelons of medicine and the military. As a nurse I also admire the empathetic nursing care she provided, whether to victims of cholera in Central America or to sick and wounded soldiers in the Crimea.

Before the war, Mary had travelled to Panama to visit her brother and engage in business ventures that included running a boarding house. While there, she recounts this appalling incident:

> *A young American woman, whose character can be best described by the word 'vicious' fell ill at Gorgona, and was left behind by her companions under the charge of a young negro, her slave, whom she treated most inhumanly, as was evinced by the poor girl's frequent screams when under the lash. One night her screams were so distressing, that Gorgona could stand it no longer, but broke into the house and found the chattel bound hand and foot, naked, and being severely lashed.*

The enslaved woman was set free by the local authorities, but in revenge the mistress threatened to torture the woman's young child. The latter lived in New Orleans and was still her property under USA slavery legislation.

The poor girl trembled and covered her face with her hands, as though to shut out some fearful sight, and, I think, had we not persuaded her to the contrary, that she would have sacrificed her newly-won freedom for the child's sake … and at once (we) set afloat a subscription for the purchase of the child.

This account, together with Mary's numerous descriptions of discrimination, provides the context for her clear condemnation of racism and slavery.

My experience of travel had not failed to teach me that Americans (even from the Northern States) are always uncomfortable in the company of coloured people, and very often show this feeling in stronger ways than by sour looks and rude words. I have a few shades of deeper brown upon my skin which shows me related – and I am proud of the relationship – to those poor mortals whom you once held enslaved, and whose bodies America still owns. And having this bond, and knowing what slavery is; having seen with my eyes and heard with my ears proof positive enough of its horrors – let others affect to doubt them if they will – is it surprising that I should be somewhat impatient of the airs of superiority which many Americans have endeavoured to assume over me?

In the gold-prospecting town of Cruces, Mary Seacole ended up single-handedly caring for victims of cholera. The death of a young child touched her deeply.

I sat before the flickering fire, with my last patient in my lap – a poor, little, brown-faced orphan, scarce a year old, was dying in

my arms, and I was powerless to save it. It may seem strange,
but it is a fact, that I thought more of that little child than I
did of the men who were struggling for their lives.

So affected was Mary by this death that she undertook 'her
first and last' post-mortem examination to try and discover more
about the dreaded cholera that had killed the child.

She had better luck when some Americans she had nursed
rewarded her with an invitation to their Independence Day dinner.
Here a toast was made in her honour and the man making it
praised Mary's nursing care. He then got carried away and very
unwisely waxed on:

I calculate, gentlemen, you're all as vexed as I am that she's
not wholly white; and I guess, if we could bleach her by any
means we would and thus make her acceptable in any company
as she deserves to be. Gentlemen, I give you Aunty Seacole!

Mary was now fuming, and there follows one of my favourite
passages in her autobiography. After a few words of thanks she
retorted:

But I must say that I don't altogether appreciate your friend's
kind wishes with respect to my complexion … and as to his offer
of bleaching me, I should, even if it were practicable, decline it
without any thanks. As to the society which the process might
gain me admission into, all I can say is, that judging from the
specimens I have met with here and elsewhere, I don't think that
I shall lose much by being excluded from it. So, gentlemen, I
drink to you and the general reformation of American manners.

What a woman!

- o – 0 – o -

By 1853, Mary was back in Jamaica and caring for victims of a yellow fever epidemic. The medical authorities invited her to supervise nursing services at Up-Park Camp, the British military headquarters in Kingston. There was another short trip to Panama before planning a visit to London in the autumn of 1854. This was to resolve concerns she had about outstanding mining claims, as well as possibly embarking upon a new speculation.

Mary then learnt about the Crimean War and read about the shocking maladministration and appalling nursing care. She was also aware of the involvement of her beloved soldiers whom she had known in Jamaica. She heard of the campaign to recruit nurses to work under Florence Nightingale at Scutari's Barrack Hospital in Turkey. It caused her to change the purpose of her London visit.

I made up my mind that if the army wanted nurses, they would be glad of me ... I decided that I would go to the Crimea; and go I did, as all the world knows.

Arriving at Southampton, Mary immediately set off for London but missed Florence Nightingale by a few days, as she was already on her way to Scutari with a group of 38 nurses. Seacole unsuccessfully sought sponsorship to travel to the Crimea and also applied to be part of the second group of nurses about to depart for Turkey.

Once again I tried, and had an interview this time with one of Miss Nightingale's companions. She gave me the same reply, and I read in her face the fact, that had there been a vacancy, I should not have been chosen to fill it.

What continues to impress me immensely is the manner in which Mary responded to the rejections of her offers of help. It stands as a useful example to others who find themselves in that situation today. Firstly, it illustrates the deep hurt that racism can cause an individual.

Was it possible that American prejudices against colour had some root here? Did these ladies shrink from accepting my aid because my blood flowed beneath a somewhat duskier skin than theirs? Tears streamed down my foolish cheeks as I stood in the fast thinning streets; tears of grief that any should doubt my motives – that Heaven should deny me the opportunity that I sought.

Secondly, it provides a case study of how one determined 49-year-old Victorian woman of colour overcame despair at the numerous attempts to thwart her ambitions. 'If the authorities had allowed me, I would willingly have given them my services as a nurse.' She seems to draw on some inner strength, bouncing back in order to attain her goal and in such an inspiring manner.

Let what might happen, to the Crimea I would go. If in no other way, then would I upon my own responsibility and at my own cost. There were those who had known me in Jamaica, who had been under my care; doctors who could vouch for my skill and willingness to aid them, and a general who had more than once helped me, and would do so still. Why not trust to their welcome and kindness and start at once?

Eventually by the spring of 1855 Mary had raised sufficient funds to travel to the Crimea, having teamed up with Mr Thomas Day, a relative of her late husband. They established the 'British

Hotel' very close to the war zone, where they set up a store and canteen. Mary also ran a morning dispensary before visiting sick and wounded soldiers in their huts or on the battlefield.

War Correspondent Sir W.H. Russell described her efforts in *The Times* newspaper:

> *I have seen her go down, under fire, with her little store of creature comforts for our wounded men; and a more tender or skilful hand about a wound or broken limb could not be found among our best surgeons. I saw her at the assault on the Redan, at the Tchernay, at the fall of Sebastopol, laden, not with plunder, good old soul! but with wine, bandages, and food for the wounded or the prisoners.*

After the war suddenly ended in 1856, Mary returned to London where she was declared bankrupt. Key figures in the military and the media, together with members of the Royal Family, rallied round to ensure she was not destitute. One stunning example was the 4-day 'Seacole Fund Grand Military Gala' held in July 1857. The venue was the magnificent Royal Surrey Gardens located on the banks of the River Thames (in 1862 St Thomas' Hospital moved to this site temporarily for nine years). A total of 80,000 people attended the Gala and it was widely reported in the Victorian media.

Mary Seacole died aged 76 in London on 14th May 1881, as a result of 'apoplexy' or a stroke. Nearly a century later she was virtually lost to history, even to the extent of it not being known whether she was buried in London or Jamaica. There is a wonderful article written in 1975 by Miss J. Elise Gordon, former editor of the *Nursing Mirror*, which reveals how she eventually solved this mystery.

In the early 1970s she purchased a first edition of Mrs. Seacole's autobiography in a London bookshop. Inside was a slip of paper with details that enabled Gordon to locate Mary's burial place in St Mary's Catholic Cemetery in Kensal Green, north-west London. The derelict grave was restored with a new head-stone and re-consecrated on 20th November 1973, courtesy of many organisations. These included the British Commonwealth Nurses' War Memorial Fund, the Lignum Vitae Club (a London based group of Jamaican women), and the UK Jamaican Nurses' Association.

In 1980 Ziggi Alexander and Audrey Dewjee undertook research for the Brent Library Services exhibition, *Roots in Britain: Black and Asian Citizens from Elizabeth I to Elizabeth II*. Audrey informed me that it was launched at the end of October 1980 and included a panel about Mary Seacole:

> *She was the person most people wrote about in the exhibition comments book, stating that they wanted more details. On 14th May 1981, the centenary of her death, Brent Library Service and Harmony* [a Mixed-Race organisation of which Audrey was a member] *jointly organized a commemorative service for Mary Seacole in the Kensal Green Cemetery chapel and a wreath-laying ceremony at her graveside. Various local mayors and other dignitaries attended. This was followed by speeches and refreshments at Kensal Rise Library.*

This has now become an annual event.

It was the demand for more information about Mary that led to Ziggi and Audrey being commissioned to produce the new edition of her autobiography in 1984. The opening words, written by W.H. Russell in 1857, may surprise present-day readers: 'I should have thought that no preface would have been required to introduce Mrs. Seacole to the British public.'

Clive Davis published a review of the new edition in the *New Statesman*, commenting that

A cottage industry is beginning to develop around the exploits of 'Mother Seacole', a Jamaican Creole who became a Victorian celebrity for her work as a nurse in the Crimean War and then sank into obscurity for the next hundred years or so.

From the mid-1980s onwards, places and buildings began to be called after Mary Seacole in areas such as Reading, Leicester, Liverpool and London.

- o – 0 – o -

My own involvement with Mary Seacole revolved around two areas. Firstly, in 1998, I established a centre that I named after her. Then came an invitation in 2003 to become a founder trustee of the Mary Seacole Memorial Statue Appeal.

Elaine: 'I think your pioneering spirit caused you to get involved with Mary Seacole. Perhaps you used your experience of starting the Sickle Cell Society and sickle cell services and decided to bring Mary Seacole to the forefront of society.'

As Dean I had set up the Mary Seacole Centre in order to host a series of lectures concerned with multi-ethnic aspects of nursing. I deliberately chose the name to raise awareness among those who had never heard of her! To launch it, senior staff from the university kindly helped me to organise a multicultural concert at Ealing Town Hall held on 16th July 1998. It seemed to strike a chord with the arrival of a huge crowd of over 400 people.

A year later there arose an unexpected opportunity to make the unit a full-time reality, as the management hierarchy of the College of Nursing was about to be restructured. My boss, Pro-Vice Chancellor Lois Crooke, stopped me one day by the stairs saying 'Look, I know, you're thinking of leaving.' This came as something of a surprise to me, although I realised that Lois

293

was aware of how frustrated I had become, due to horrendously time-consuming administrative responsibilities. She acknowledged that the promised opportunities to undertake research had never materialised and assured me that she wanted me to stay on, requesting that I write my own job description!

So it was that on 1st September 1999, the Mary Seacole Centre for Nursing Practice was established. The objectives were to 'enable the integration of a multi-ethnic philosophy into the process of nursing and midwifery recruitment, education, practice and research'. It appeared to me that there was a predominantly white Eurocentric focus in many of these areas. Examples included:

The paucity of information in the curriculum about conditions such as sickle cell disease

An under-representation, in comparison to the local populations of Slough and Ealing, of students of African-Caribbean and South Asian origin

The near absence of non-white images used in teaching. Tutors were aware of this, pointing out that they were virtually impossible to obtain from their local Medical Illustrations Department.

We had been discussing how students are taught to recognise pallor, bruising and certain rashes in 'non-pink' skin. Many years ago I had read a newspaper account of a coroner's inquest into the death of a very young South Asian child in the northeast of England. It had followed a severe bleed after a tonsillectomy. The nurse had claimed to be unable to recognise increasing paleness, due to the brown colour of the child's skin. Other indicators of deterioration in health were not identified, as the nurse had failed to undertake regular observations of the patient's pulse and respiration rates.

Over its eight-year lifetime, the Centre was awarded more than a quarter of a million pounds for various research, recruitment and educational projects. There were three major pieces of work and I gave all of them an acronym to explain their purpose: CANDLES, MELTING and DATING. Looking back, they all sound somewhat romantic! They stood for:

CANDLES: Campaign to Attract Nurses/midwives from Diverse Local Ethnic groups in Slough. This was a successful community-development project that began to redress the under-representation of certain ethnic groups. Funding was also obtained for a recruitment video to assist staff in attracting a wider range of local applicants. The first viewing was shown at the House of Commons in March 1999.

MELTING: Multi-Ethnic Learning and Teaching in Nursing. This entailed the development of a website to house an online educational resource developed for students and staff. It was launched in 2002 and we suddenly had a global presence. An interesting, if unexpected consequence was the demand for inclusion of more information about Mary Seacole (in addition to research, teaching and committee work, I was also frequently asked to give lectures and write articles about her. It quickly became apparent that she was becoming a significant role model for many. Felicia: 'The Mary Seacole story has been absolutely transformational, not just to us as black nurses but to the nation.')

DATING: Diversity, Attrition and Transition Into Nursing. This was a study to monitor the impact of key diversity variables on the progression and transition into practice of student nurses. These included gender, country of birth, ethnicity and age. The research examined the outcome of 1,808 students enrolled on pre-registration nursing courses between 1999 and 2001. Findings of the study were published in 2008 in the *Journal of Advanced Nursing*.

Karl observed:

I felt that you had always been perceived as a member of the black community, rather than a well qualified nurse, and very successful one. It would have been around the late 90s when the establishment woke up and started to celebrate that. The Royal College of Nursing also recognised you as someone who made a contribution to the profession.

He is referring to a couple of awards I had received unexpectedly. The first was a CBE (Commander of the British Empire[14]) in the 2001 Queen's Birthday Honours List for my services to nursing. This award came as a great shock and I still had reservations concerning the 'Empire' bit. On reflection, it was an important recognition for a black nurse, in view of the difficulties that many faced in the profession.

Azuka and cousin Elaine came to the Investiture at Buckingham Palace. My daughter wanted to know why Prince Charles had burst out laughing while he was pinning the medal on me. It had been due to the response I gave to his complimentary remarks about my colourful Nigerian gown: 'It has been said that I look pretty in pink!'

Then in 2004 I flew to Belfast to receive a Fellowship of the Royal College of Nursing, a great accolade from my peers. This honour was for the development of nurse-led sickle cell and thalassaemia counselling services and education and leadership in transcultural nursing.

My family and friends have made it clear how proud they are of these achievements. My pal Juliet beautifully encapsulated their sentiments:

I was very proud, and still am, that you are an expert in your field and that you are a woman of colour, a woman of colour! I can't overestimate the importance of that.

- o – 0 – o -

In the summer of 2007 I made the decision to retire. About to turn 60, I was now feeling the need to slow down a bit – after all, my working life had started at 16! I was also keen to have more control over my future activities. Moreover, Azuka had just given me the magnificent news that I would be a grandmother in the New Year. To top it all, the university awarded me the title of Emeritus Professor in Nursing.

So there was a huge amount to celebrate, and my friends Nina and Majorie helped organise the most fantastic party to do just that! Joan B: 'You've got a really good set of friends, colleagues and neighbours who came to the party. It was just a lot of fun and you were dancing and pulling up people saying "Come on, we've got to dance!" So we all ended up dancing and it was a great night.'

It has not turned out to be a quiet retirement, due to grand-parenting duties and my increased involvement with the Mary Seacole Memorial Statue Appeal (founded in November 2003 by the chairman, Lord Clive Soley, when he had been a Member of Parliament. A group of Caribbean women in his west London constituency had asked him to accompany them to Mary Seacole's grave. There they pointed out that this was her only memorial and wondered if he could help raise funds for a statue in her honour).

Around this time, general awareness about Mary began to improve for a variety of reasons.

In 2002 the BBC launched a television poll to determine the 100 Greatest Britons, and the overall winner was Sir Winston Churchill. It was quickly pointed out that no black British people had featured on the list. In response, Patrick Vernon organised an online vote in 2004 for the 100 Greatest Black Britons via his

Every Generation website. Mary Seacole was the winner, and the subsequent publicity helped to raise her profile – including an article in the *Guardian* on 14th February 2004 by Nightingale biographer Mark Bostridge, who agreed that her selection is more than justified. Acknowledging her nursing abilities he is however, like many of us, unhappy about Mary being referred to as the Black Nightingale:

> *But while there is every reason to commemorate her remarkable contribution to nursing, the comparison with Nightingale does justice to neither. There is no doubt that in terms of practical nursing expertise, Seacole far outdistanced Nightingale's experience. Her work included preparing medicines, diagnosis and minor surgery.*

The next round of media attention came in 2005, with the bicentenary of Mary's year of birth. It kicked off with the announcement that historian Helen Rappaport had identified a lost portrait of Mary Seacole, which is now on display at the National Portrait Gallery. Then came the first major Seacole biography, written by Jane Robinson, a social historian specialising in the lives of women.

There was also the monograph *A short history of Mary Seacole* that the Royal College of Nursing had commissioned me to write. It was designed to be a resource for nurses and students, and a copy was sent to the library of every College of Nursing and Midwifery in the UK.

An area that I was particularly keen to explore was the relationship between Florence and Mary during the Crimean War. In her autobiography, Seacole recalls seeing much of Nightingale – but there are few further details except for their first meeting at Scutari. Here Mary describes her impressions:

... standing thus in repose, and yet keenly observant – the greatest sign of impatience at any time a slight, perhaps unwitting motion of the right foot – was Florence Nightingale – that English woman whose name shall never die, but sound like music on the lips of British men until the hour of doom.

There appeared, though, to have been very little written about their relationship by other commentators. So I was excited to come across some observations in *A Culinary Campaign*, the 1857 memoirs of Alexis Soyer. He was a celebrated French chef who had settled in England and worked at the London Reform Club. He had heard about the appalling food being consumed by British soldiers in the Crimea and volunteered his services. He managed to transform the quality of nutrition cheaply through the invention of his 'Soyer Field Stove'.

It turns out that Soyer, like Russell of *The Times*, was a great admirer of both Nightingale and Seacole. He recalls that in the Crimea, Seacole recounted to him at least twenty times that Nightingale was very fond of her, having provided overnight accommodation for her at Scutari. When he visited the Land Transport Corps Hospital, Soyer passed on Mary's greetings to Florence, who said with a smile: 'I should like to see her before she leaves, as I hear that she has done a great deal of good for the poor soldiers.' Soyer replied:

She has indeed, I assure you, and with great disinterestedness. While I was there this morning, she was dressing a poor Land Transport Corps man, who had received a severe contusion on the head. In order to strengthen his courage for the process, as she said, she made him a good glass of strong brandy and water, and not charging him anything for it; and I hear that she has done this repeatedly.

Once again, Florence commented: 'I am sure she has done much good'.

However, further material has emerged that reveals Florence Nightingale to have been in two minds about Mary Seacole. Back in 1990 Ziggi Alexander cited 1870 correspondence between Nightingale and her brother-in-law, Sir Harry Verney MP. Interestingly, Florence made it clear that her views should not be made public, as the relevant page was headed 'Burn'.

She writes:

Mrs Seacole. I dare say that you know more about her than I do. She kept – I will not call it a 'bad house' but something not very unlike it in the Crimean War. She was very kind to the men &, what is more, to the Officers – & did some good – & made many drunk. (A shameful ignorant imposture was practised on the Queen who subscribed to the 'Seacole testimonial'). I had the greatest difficulty in repelling Mrs Seacole's advances, & in preventing association between her & my nurses (absolutely out of the question) when we established 2 hospitals nursed by us between Kadikoi & the 'Seacole Establishment' in the Crimea.

In 2004, Bostridge referred to undated documentation of conversations between Florence and her sister Parthenope, wife of Sir Harry. In researching her 2005 Seacole biography, Jane Robinson discovered previously unpublished material from this same source. Nightingale describes Mary as a 'woman of bad character' who did indeed keep 'a bad house' and who had to be discouraged from visiting a sick Florence in order to 'quack' her. This is what makes history so interesting! In my mind, nurses of today should know about both their contributions. *Nursing Standard* provided me with an opportunity to expand on the reasons for this in the 2011 *YouTube* video *What can Florence and Mary teach us about nursing today?*

- o – 0 – o -

In 2009, Martin Jennings was chosen as the artist to design the memorial statue for Mary Seacole. He is an internationally renowned sculptor whose body of work includes statues of poets Sir John Betjeman (at St Pancras International station) and Philip Larkin (in Hull). The site of the memorial statue is in the gardens of St Thomas' Hospital, London. Jennings explains that 'the sculpture represents her marching defiantly forward into an oncoming wind, as if confronting head-on some of the personal resistance she had constantly to battle ...'

In that same year, the second only known photograph of Mary Seacole was re-discovered, together with a rare signature. It was found by Dr. Geoffrey Day, then working as Fellows' and Eccles Librarian at Winchester College. The photo was in an elegant private Crimean War campaign scrapbook, compiled by former Coldstream Guards officer, Ely Duodecimus Wigram (1802–1869). In 1916, it was presented to the Library of Winchester College by the then Headmaster.

The scrapbook contained incredible Crimean War memorabilia including a collection of autographs and photographs. One of the signatures belongs to Queen Victoria and there is also a letter written by Florence Nightingale from Balaclava. There are ten photographs, all of senior military personnel (including Lord Raglan, commander of the British troops) except one – Mary Seacole. Permission was given by Winchester College for the image to be used to raise funds for Mary's memorial statue.

In addition to twelve trustees and eleven patrons, the Appeal selected over forty high profile Ambassadors from a wide variety of backgrounds. They included Dr Day, jazz musician Courtney Pine, together with past Children's Laureates Malorie Blackman and Michael Rosen. Also appointed were two Dutch Seacole researchers, Drs Corry Staring-Derks and Jeroen Staring. Spending hours in the British Library, they unearthed a vast source of previously unknown Victorian newspaper coverage about Mary Seacole. *Nursing Standard* became the Appeal's media partner and regularly included free one-page promotions about the charity.

Planning consent was obtained from Lambeth Council in 2012, in spite of vociferous and continued opposition from a dozen or so people who were against it being installed at St Thomas' Hospital. They frequently cite it as an example of political correctness because they do not consider Seacole to be a nurse or even black. It brings to mind Nobel prize-winning author Toni Morrison's comment to journalist Claudia Dreifus in 1994:

> *What I think the political correctness debate is really about is the power to be able to define. The definers want the power to name. And the defined are now taking that power away from them.*

They are also concerned that, unlike Florence Nightingale, Mary Seacole did not have any links to the hospital. The 2013 statement by Sir Hugh Taylor, Chairman of Guys & St Thomas' NHS Foundation Trust, is well worth a read:

> *Mary Seacole was a pathfinder for the generations of people from black and minority ethnic backgrounds who have served the NHS over the years and she remains a positive role model for the current generation. The Trust is proud to be hosting the statue, not least because it speaks to the diversity of our local population, our patients and the staff who work here.*

This view was admirably demonstrated countrywide in January 2013, when Michael Gove threatened to exclude Mary Seacole (and others) from the proposed national curriculum. In the space of a few weeks, over 36,000 people signed an online petition successfully demanding her inclusion. Organised by Operation Black Vote, the petition quickly went viral.

It seems to me that young children occasionally know more about Mary Seacole than some adults. Their understanding, though, has at times caused me to smile! A friend of mine informed me of the response of her six year-old daughter to a query about what she had learnt at school that day: 'We had a talk about two old dead nurses. One was Florence Nightingale and the other was Mary, umm, Mary Sequin.'

When my granddaughter was seven she informed me that she was being Mary Seacole as part of a class presentation on Victorians. Naturally I was absolutely delighted, although a bit taken aback when she asked if I had ever worked with her as a nurse!

Following my retirement I had the time to embark on a UK tour to talk about Mary Seacole and help raise urgently needed funds for her memorial statue. Fortunately, invitations to speak came from a wide variety of individuals and organisations including nurses, trade unions, black and minority associations and women's groups. They were wonderful sessions that demonstrated the appeal of Mary to so many people, and from such a wide range of backgrounds. This positive response refuted critics who dismissed the idea that 'Mother Seacole' could ever be considered as a role model.

The audiences well and truly understood that the statue campaign was not about undermining the achievements of Florence Nightingale – but they did want to hear about other historical nursing figures too, as articulated by Felicia, a Director of Nursing:

We were always brought up with Florence Nightingale. That's all we knew. We never had any Black, Asian or Chinese nursing figures that we could aspire to. I had never learnt about Mary Seacole, didn't have a clue before I met you.

I really wish that we could be taught about the achievements of other Crimean War nurses alongside Florence Nightingale and Mary Seacole. There were many, but examples include Betsi Cadwaladr from Wales, Eliza Mackenzie (a naval nurse) from Scotland, and the Irish Sisters of Mercy under Mother Francis Bridgeman. There was also the Russian nurse Darya Lavrentyevna Mikhailova, otherwise known as 'Dasha of Sevastopol'. It is equally important to discuss their strengths and weaknesses, and that includes Mary and Florence!

My talks about Mary Seacole continued for an extended period of time, as it took the charity over 12 long years to raise the original target of half a million pounds (which was quite depressing at times, but the encouragement of friends kept my spirits up – such as Joan B's wonderful comment: 'You follow through with everything, so for me the Mary Seacole statue will happen. You are Mary Seacole!'). Then came a last-minute additional and unexpected hefty charge from the construction company, to install the memorial. Happily the money was obtained in November 2015 from Her Majesty's Treasury, courtesy of funds allocated to charities from banking fines.

The Memorial Statue was unveiled by Baroness Floella Benjamin on 30th June 2016 in the gardens of St Thomas' hospital, overlooking the River Thames and the Houses of Parliament. Remarkably, it is the first one for a named black woman in the UK. The ceremony proved to be incredibly inspiring. While the previous few days had been cold and wet, the sun decided to shine for a few hours and provide some Jamaican weather for the near 400 invited guests! Media interest was intense. I had a very early start to do a pre-recorded interview with broadcaster Jenni Murray for transmission later that morning on BBC Radio 4 *Woman's Hour*.[15] After the unveiling ceremony people immediately came in their numbers to see the stunning monument and be photographed in front of it with their children and other family members.

Sir William Howard Russell would be delighted, having written this about Mary Seacole in 1857:

I trust that England will not forget one who nursed her sick, who sought out her wounded to aid and succour them, and who performed the last offices for some of her illustrious dead.

CONCLUSION

XIX

Mixed blessings

You've led the life that Mum should have also led.

Friends and family who became aware of my story have wanted to know more about my emotional reaction to the events in my life. In this final chapter I want to reflect on this question, and on the impact of my birth and upbringing for my parents.

Despite its rocky start, plus a few unpleasant episodes along the way, my life has been extremely fulfilling. Most importantly, it has been a vindication of all that my mother had to endure. Writing this book has been painful at times, particularly trying to make sense of why my birth created so much drama and anguish. There were unexpected revelations within the documents relating to my first nine years in care. It took until my mid-60s to discover their existence within the archives of the Father Hudson's Homes. I had only been seeking photographs!

Re-reading correspondence from my parents was poignant, reminding me of long-forgotten details. Attempting to uncover all those unknown facts about both sides of my family history has been time-consuming but fun – and it continues.

Many people have been surprised to hear about my early circumstances. A common reaction is to wonder why it never left me with severe psychological problems, exemplified by Nina's remark: 'I think it's amazing that you've come through all this and never stopped, had a bout of depression or taken tablets.'

People are delighted that I appear to have overcome various difficulties and achieved so much in my life. They are curious about the key influential factors, and there is a natural desire to know whether I have experienced any negative consequences.

It was impossible to answer these queries without recourse to others, and I also felt that it was important for me to take a step back. All the family and friends I approached kindly agreed to my request for help, and I was able to interview 30 of them. Their frank and detailed responses have filled in so many gaps and helped to clarify how others view me – and some who have known me prior to finding my father in 1972 are also in a position to comment on any changes they have observed.

Initially, I had wanted to call these memoirs *A Cambridge Union: Being neither white nor black*, the second half being a line from *Cross*, the poem by Langston Hughes. My great friend Elizabeth Dormandy, who has guided and supported me through the process of writing this book, appreciated the title but felt that it did not do justice to the numerous positive outcomes of my story. In trying to explain this further, she said: 'There are many people who have crossed your path who would see your birth as a blessing.' The words 'mixed blessings' immediately came to mind as a better way to represent the wide-ranging consequences of my arrival in 1947.

- o – 0 – o -

From the beginning of my life, I have been fortunate to benefit from many kindly forces. They have prevented my life, and this book, from ever becoming a 'misery memoir'. Having said that, my parents and I were to experience a range of ups and downs.

My mother was to be most affected and yet to me, emerges as the strongest, most intelligent and most determined of us all.

Before my birth, she told no-one else that her illegitimate baby would be brown-skinned – a development that created even bigger shockwaves than the pregnancy itself. Everyone was apprehensive about what the future might hold, and in order to provide a home for me, Mum sacrificed completing her studies at Cambridge, fore-going the glittering academic career that undoubtedly lay ahead. Today, a single mother can combine both of these options.

It must have been heartrending that despite all those efforts, her ambitions to care for me were never fully realised. She would endure years of horrendous poverty with few opportunities to employ her formidable intellectual abilities. And yet, my sister Marion and brother Frank have told me independently that Mum never saw herself as a victim. The one time she obviously cracked was after witnessing the harsh beating that was meted out to me by my stepfather.

Thank goodness that Mum would also be the recipient of kindness and joy. In spite of their estrangement, my grandparents responded to her cry for help. They rescued me from violence and took me to the safe haven of their home in Wallasey. This makes my brother Frank's recollection of one morning in February 1970 all the more poignant:

Mum answered the door to the postman who gave her a tele-gram. I saw her crying and asked why she was so upset. She said that Gran had died. I was a teenager and realised that I had never met her or Granddad.

Mum's greatest joy was to be with her children and she was loved by all of us. Frank's view was that 'Mum had inner strength and there wasn't an ounce of wrong in her'. We all remained in constant contact with her until her death in 2003. Mick, her eldest son, would die in 2015 aged 61, so she never suffered the anguish of losing him. Mum always wished she could have helped us more but we had in fact been supported by her in so many ways.

Examples included doing the bookkeeping for Frank's butcher's shop, transcribing interviews for my PhD study, child minding for Pam and others, and helping out with Marion's homework. Having passed the 11+, Marion went to Mum's old grammar school that was run by the nuns. 'Mum was the one I turned to and it was great. She helped me get through those years at the convent.' Most importantly, her presence was always there in the background, constantly loving and worrying about all five of her children.

Marion explained how Mum and I were so alike:

Mum thought the world of you; she loved us all the same. You are similar to her more than anything with your intelligence, but also your determination. Mum had quiet determination. You're a much more forceful character and you've been able to perhaps achieve all the things that she couldn't. You've led the life that Mum should have also led.

My mother's steely willpower has definitely been a very influential force. Nina:

I don't know where you get your strength from, but you are very resilient. You are mindful of whatever things are happening and you bounce back stronger. Maybe it's from your mother, because she's had to probably put up with much more than your father did.

Mum had met Ken in 1952 when I was five. They wed in 1953 and were married for a total of 41 years. He died in hospital aged 68 years on 11th August 1994, following a stroke. It is the only funeral where I have not felt any sense of grief for the deceased person and I shed absolutely no tears at the service. On a more positive note, it was wonderful that Mum, Mick, Frank, Marion, Pam and I were all together once more. It had been such a long time since this had happened.

Pam and her husband bought a house with a granny flat attached. This was such a kind and generous gesture as it provided Mum with security, close to her family and grandchildren. She was able to spend the remaining nine years of her life there, very content with all her activities. Aside from her family, she kept busy with reading, walking her dog, learning new languages and watching wildlife documentaries. In addition, she informed me that she

... joined Mensa in 1979, and found their activities (or such of their many and varied activities as I was able to take part in) very stimulating. I tried my hand at writing for some of their publications, and had a number of poems and short articles printed.

Religion also played an important role and Mum became involved with the Methodists. Writing to me on 8th April 1994, just four months before Ken's death, she had reflected: 'Looking back over the ups and downs, in my own small way I can say with the Psalmist "Thou hast brought me to great honour, and comforted me on every side." May He do the same in His goodness for all my children.' She eventually switched to the Church of England, where she could take the sacrament. As she explained:

No account of my life would be complete, however, without mentioning that during this period God led me to make a serious study of the Scriptures, and to turn to Him in prayer and meditation. Even from the first stirrings of this conversion experience, life seemed to become easier to cope with.

When Azuka and I saw Mum in September 2003, she seemed well, as shown by the last photos taken of her during our visit. However, she did tell me of being scared that she was going to die. Weeks later, Marion and Pam called me to say she was extremely unwell and hardly eating or drinking. It turned out to be the opportunity to nurse my mother in her final illness. In January 2004, this experience was described in a regular *Nursing Times* column that I used to write.

When she suddenly deteriorated I set off on the motorway from London with a heavy heart. I was shocked by how frail and bedridden she had become and, as the only nurse in the family, I was aware that my sisters were looking to me for guidance. I was somewhat taken aback that part of me wished that I did not have any nursing knowledge because it meant that I understood that she was extremely ill.

However, it was with great satisfaction that I was able to give her a bed bath, ably helped by my sisters. At this point I was delighted to be a nurse. The opportunity to make her feel more comfortable and assist her to take a small amount of fluids was both gratifying and extremely consoling. Her senses were still intact because, as soon as I had left, she told one of my sisters that my visit had turned out to be a busman's holiday.

A few days later, on 27th October, Mum died at home in the early hours of the morning, aged 77 years. Cause of death was bronchopneumonia, congestive cardiac failure, hypertension and chronic renal impairment.

The funeral demonstrated the love of all of her children, as Mick, Frank, Marion, Pam and I assembled to mourn her loss. We were the ones she had fought so hard to protect, and to ensure that we had a decent life. It was a very difficult ceremony for everyone. While crying for the suffering Mum had endured, I knew that she would have been happy that we were all together and celebrating her life. Also there were Uncle Michael and Aunty Pat, enabling Mick, Frank, Marion and Pam to get to know them at last. Unfortunately transport difficulties had made it impossible for Aunty Sheila to attend.

My paternal cousin-in-law Elaine recalled:

When I went to your mother's funeral in 2003, I did wonder how it would be for you. I had not seen that side of the family around you before, but they just took you in. I had the feeling that they thought they had to protect you a bit, you know the sadness, and Azuka was there with them.

- o – 0 – o -

In terms of my identity, the final piece of the jigsaw fell into place after finding my father. However, despite knowing Dad for eight years, I was never able to speak to him about his relationship with my mother. Then again, how many children would? It is embarrassing to interrogate parents about such intimate aspects of their life. Consequently there was so much that I never discovered. Here are just some of the questions I would have loved to ask:

How did you meet my mother?
What were your feelings towards her?
What was the nature of your liaison, and how long did it last?
How did you respond to the news of my mother's pregnancy?
How did you react when you first saw me in Father Hudson's Homes?
Why did your planned marriage not take place?
Once back in Nigeria, did you ever feel any guilt about the lack of contact until I met you just before my 25th birthday?

There was no doubt that I was incredibly happy to have met Dad so easily, and to have spent that relatively short period with him in London and Nigeria.

Sarah: 'When you finally learned more about your father, it seemed to me something in you relaxed, almost as if the puzzle pieces had begun falling into place. I was truly glad that you could now connect with your father, who embraced you wholly and introduced you to members of your Nigerian family.'

It was unbelievable how much we looked like each other as Elaine described in this incident at an Onitsha wedding in London. 'We were just sitting there when an elderly lady came up and asked you if you were the daughter of L.O.V. I couldn't believe it! She had never met you before but immediately saw the resemblance.'

Dad was able to develop an affectionate, humorous and caring relationship towards me. It was exactly what I needed. The guidance he gave me was immensely influential in enabling my career to progress so well. The financial support he provided paid for the deposit on the flat. I have lived there ever since and it is a constant reminder of him. Dad's sudden death was incredibly distressing, but I took solace from being able to be with him during those last moments of his life.

While loving Mum, I always felt concerned about her because of the difficulties she experienced. My friend Juliet picked up on this: 'I hear from you about your father and when you speak of him you smile and you laugh, I don't see that when you talk about your mother.'

According to Elaine, having a short fuse is another characteristic that we shared. 'The weaknesses I see in you is, as Nigerians say, "all fingers are not equal". We are not all brilliant; some are more flawed than others. That gets you intensely annoyed. You don't show it, but when someone is taking too long to understand what you're saying, you get very frazzled. You don't suffer fools gladly and that's from your father!'

It is clear that Dad was delighted I had tracked him down, and as well as showing me love, took great joy and pride in my achievements. I find it interesting that in 1973, a year after we met, and now back in Onitsha, he brought one of his nephews properly into the fold of the Anionwu family. There is no way I will know whether our own reunion had prompted this action. Many years later another cousin, living in North America, tracked me down via the Internet. He had contacted me in order to link up with his unknown Anionwu family.

My father appeared to have lived a more charmed life than my mother, and to a great extent this was true. There were, however, aspects of his family life that were to cause him considerable grief. Including me, Dad had seven children from five women, three of whom have died. He and his wife Regi lost their only child, a daughter, in infancy. Their marriage was turbulent at times and they would experience periods of separation. The two other deceased children were his son Emma and a younger daughter. An older daughter settled in Italy without trace. Of his two youngest children who live in Nigeria, a son followed in his footsteps and is a barrister and a daughter is married with children. It was really sad that Dad never lived to know his granddaughter Azuka; they would have loved each other so much.

It is ironic that although she had so much less to leave, Mum was more organised and left a will, and had already paid for her funeral expenses. There was £66.44 in her savings account. This was in stark contrast to my wealthier barrister father, who died intestate. He would have been distraught that the family descended into decades of wrangling over his estate and that in 2002 Emma was to die in his mid-forties, leaving behind two young children.

- o – 0 – o -

Looking back at my own life, there have certainly been many more ups than downs, for which I am extremely thankful. The key factor is that my mother never gave me up for adoption. During the period of her pregnancy, my grandparents had expressed their intention to look after me. After my birth, when this was no longer an option and adoption was discussed, the nuns informed them that 'there was no chance of finding adoptive parents for a coloured child' – which is just as well, because my mother would never have agreed to it.

I have never felt any sense of rejection. It was a pleasant surprise to discover that before my admission into the Father Hudson's Homes, Mum had looked after me from birth to six months (and not three months as I had always thought). A huge amount of bonding will have taken place during this period together in the Mother and Baby Home – and I look back at the joy I experienced myself when feeding and cuddling Azuka at that same age.

It must have been a heart-wrenching time for Mum when the cot suddenly became available for me at Father Hudson's Homes. Her commitment to make a home for both of us must have been well and truly reinforced at the time of this traumatic separation. So much so, that Mum refused the offer from Newnham College to return to her studies, against the keen desire of her parents and the Catholic clergy.

Many people have expressed their astonishment on hearing about my time in care.

Elaine: 'I was extremely surprised when I heard you lived in a Convent. But then the positive thing is that your mother never really left you.'

Ursula: 'When you used to give me stories, and I'd look at your face, as if, is she for real? Did that really happen? Would nuns really ask her to stand on a chair with a wet bed sheet over her? West Indians always have to say, are you sure? When I really learned your story, I was gobsmacked with the whole care picture. It really made me think, wow, this is a woman who's done much more with the cards she has been dealt.'

Joan B: 'There was this comedy of assumptions; I just thought you'd been privileged. It is not just how you speak, it's how you hold yourself, it's how you think, but again it is assumptions, never have assumptions! I thought you'd come from this really grand family. I first learnt your story when you spoke at one of my training sessions. You just started outlining your life, in really logical steps. It was not only captivating, but I was gobsmacked because I just didn't know.'

Hopefully, their reactions help to explain why I was motivated to write these memoirs – and are a reflection of the fact that I did not have the horrific experiences of some children growing up in Catholic orphanages, or of the child migrants they sent to former colonies such as Australia. Children caught up in this tragic nightmare have been referred to as the 'Lost Children of the Empire'. There are also so many narratives by those who valued the love of one or both adoptive parents, but still felt an immense sense of rejection by their biological ones. Several have deeply touched me. Apple co-founder Steve Jobs' biographer, Walter Isaacson, describes Jobs' adoption by a couple, who then changed their mind as they wanted a girl. Adored by his subsequent adopted parents, Jobs discovers as an adult that his biological parents eventually married and had a daughter. Another one, as discussed in Chapter 11, is Scottish/Nigerian poet Jackie Kay's autobiography *Red Dust Road*. In it she describes the weird first meeting in Lagos with her biological father, and his attempts to rid her of evil spirits through exorcism.

Although my experiences were more positive than these, it does seem odd that I am unable to remember the name of any nun or teacher that I was in touch with during my first 11 years. Neither do I have any recollection of stories about my early childhood, as none were handed down to me.

This came home forcibly when telling my own daughter and granddaughter tales of their younger days. Maybe this prompted me to discover as much of this information as possible, not only for myself, but also for my descendants – but I haven't been able to find the photographic records that I hoped for when I first set out on this search. As previously highlighted, I only had two photographs in early childhood that my mother gave me. The earliest is the one on the cover of this book, which shows me aged around nine months sitting on her lap in the grounds of St Teresa's nursery in Father Hudson's Homes. Unfortunately I managed to lose a small black and white photo of me as a toddler, inside a hall of some kind, riding on a tricycle. The next one in my collection is when I am aged 11 years and living with my grandparents in Wallasey. So that's been hard for somebody like me who loves images, photography and history.

- o – 0 – o -

My early life was one of repeated and unexpectedly sudden moves, a total of six before the age of 16. They were to a variety of geographical locations, institutions and homes that were in both working and middle class environments:

1. *Catholic Mother and Baby Home to the Father Hudson's Homes, Coleshill*
2. *Father Hudson's Homes to Nazareth House convent, Birmingham*
3. *Nazareth House to Mum in a council housing estate in Wolverhampton*

4. *To my grandparents in Wallasey*
5. *Back to my Mum in Wolverhampton*
6. *From Mum's to work in a residential school for delicate children on the borders of rural Shropshire*

Then came London, Scotland and Paris, before settling back in my beloved London! I like to think that this might provide the reason for Karl's comment: 'One of your greatest strengths is your adaptability.' As somebody who has known me for very many years, he noted, 'I think as time went on, you also seemed more at ease with your mixed heritage.'

The fact that my skin colour was different from all the other children's in the convent was obvious to me from an early age. I clearly did not want to stand out – demonstrated by my washing my face repeatedly to try and make it white like theirs. But apart from a few years, I have always been proud to keep my hair natural. Juliet: 'Your Afro suits you and it's an outward sign, I think, of your inner confidence.'

Here's how my friend Mia sees it, and in her own inimitable way:

I've seen you as a light skinned black person. It was only later on when you started talking about your memories of growing up that I realised you were mixed race. Identity has always been an issue that comes up in the community, particularly for mixed race people. It's very important for them that they talk about their identity. You don't ram it down people's throats.

Tangled Roots is a project funded by Arts Council England[16] which notes that '12% of UK households are mixed race'. As part of this project, Dr Katy Massey has edited two anthologies of over 50 life stories of mixed race people in Yorkshire (2014) and more widely within Britain (2015).

In 2014 I became aware of AMRI, the *Association of Mixed Race Irish*.[17] When meeting founder members Rosemary and Conrad, I unexpectedly had the impression of 'coming home'. They were born in Ireland, but with the exception of their accents, we discovered a range of shared experiences. I was also signposted to the following published narratives: *Back from the Brink* (the poignant 2007 autobiography of Irish/Nigerian footballer Paul McGrath); and *My Eyes Only Look Out* by Margaret McCarthy (2001), which includes twelve accounts of the '*experiences of Irish people of mixed race parentage*'.

While always describing my heritage as Irish and Nigerian, the fact is that I never grew up in either of these countries. There was, however, an important and early exposure to Irish culture, courtesy of the nuns at Nazareth House and my grandparents. This was in sharp contrast to reaching the age of 25 before eventually discovering my Nigerian roots.

'Where are you from?' My brown skin colour is a permanent feature, and one that many people have immediately noticed throughout the years. Regardless of external classification, I am ultimately and defiantly responsible for determining my own identity! It's best expressed in the lyrics of *I Am That I Am* wonderfully sung by Peter Tosh:

I'm not in this world to live up to your expectations. Neither are you here to live up to mine.

It has taken time, but like my role models of Mary Seacole and Barack Obama, I am now at ease with my dual ethnicity. Friends and family have observed this.

Felicia: 'When you have talked about your heritage, you're very proud of both sides.'

Elaine: 'I don't think you have any identity issues. I think that you are comfortable in all settings. I'm sure if I put you in the middle of China you would blend in!'

Joan B: 'What I see in you is somebody who has taken that duality of identity and used it to its best. You don't discard it, you don't disown it, you just say this is me and I want to understand the world better and other people better'.

Ursula: 'It was almost as if you had two lives. There was a really nice multi-culturalism about your parties and your social life. You had lots of white friends and lots of black friends and were able to identify with both. But you were still almost like a kind of a representative for black women.'

Negative attitudes towards mixed-race individuals may have lessened but they still exist. These are best exemplified by derisive comments aimed at Barack Obama ('he's not really American') and Mary Seacole ('she's not really black'). The constant challenges made against their reputations and achievements remind me of this extract from a 1975 speech made by Toni Morrison at Portland State Black Studies Center in Oregon, USA:

The function, the very serious function of racism is distraction. It keeps you from doing your work. It keeps you explaining, over and over again, your reason for being. Somebody says you have no language and you spend twenty years proving that you do. Somebody says your head isn't shaped properly so you have scientists working on the fact that it is. Somebody says you have no art, so you dredge that up. Somebody says you have no kingdoms, so you dredge that up. None of this is necessary. There will always be one more thing.

- o – 0 – o -

I am the first child of my parents and have younger maternal and paternal half-brothers and half-sisters. The ones I know best are on the maternal side and it was a proud moment when one of them said, 'I think you were what we all sort of hoped to be one day.'

It has been interesting for me to ponder the characteristics that I may have inherited from my parents. As the child of two very bright people, some of their genes have certainly helped me to succeed in exams and secure much needed scholarships for courses and travel.

A sense of humour is a trait that I would like to think they also passed down! While interviewing Felicia, she started to laugh, saying, 'you're so funny, you could do stand-up, Prof!' Mum and Dad were both known for their ability to make people laugh and I often observed my father's dry and quick-fire wit. Marion had more opportunity to witness this side of Mum: 'She had a fantastic wicked sense of humour, was always laughing and found humour in the daftest things. My happiest memories when I was a kid were listening to Mum joke and laugh.'

Were the seeds of my political and radical nature a throwback from the actions on both sides of the family? On the maternal side there is my Fabian and Irish Republican-supporting grandfather, Irish nationalist Great-Aunt Kate and a Kehoe great-great-grandfather risking his life in Wexford working as a hedgerow teacher. Then there is my father who was jailed without charge for three days when he was chairing the Defence Committee of Onitsha Market traders.

There are other aspects of my behaviour that have probably been influenced by my upbringing. In his autobiography *Dreams From My Father*, Barack Obama describes being put on the spot by Chicago activist Marty Kaufman, his future boss. Applying for a community-organising post, he challenges Obama: 'You must be angry about something. Well-adjusted people find more relaxing work.' My deep-seated anger about injustice and racism has perhaps been directed into campaigning for improved sickle cell services and the Memorial Statue for Mary Seacole.

Sudden bouts of aggressive behaviour towards me in childhood have possibly left me with a dread of the unexpected, such as loud noises or turbulence during a flight. I also have an abiding abhorrence of violence, war and prejudice. This is maybe why a favourite anti-war ballad is *The Green Fields of France*, particularly sung by The Fureys & Davey Arthur. Ronan McGreevy in *The Irish Times* (18th February 2015) reports on a radio interview with Eric Bogle, who wrote the song. The lyrics, Bogle says, are in response to the anti-Irish sentiment in Britain during the IRA bombing campaign of the 1970s.

Two books that have had great resonance for me have been *Philomena* by Martin Sixsmith and, mentioned above, Barack Obama's *Dreams From My Father*. While there are significant differences between their lives and mine, there have been some interesting parallels. Philomena Lee grew up in Ireland and became a single mother in 1951 at the age of 18. Like my mother, she looked after her son in a Catholic Mother and Baby Home, but for the much longer period of three years. Then the nuns arranged for him to be adopted by an American couple, without Philomena's consent. After searching for her son for 50 years, she sadly discovered that he had died. Did my skin colour, together with the 'respectable' status of my grandparents and my mother's determination, prevent us from experiencing such deception ourselves?

Obama's first journey to Kenya in 1988 has an interesting parallel with mine to Nigeria in 1973. I was 26 when I first visited Africa, and he was 27. We both returned with a possibly over-romantic view of our trips, but we both felt extremely welcomed, and had the sensation of coming home. There were also similar experiences at the airport (be that in Nairobi or Lagos). While waiting to be collected, we both spoke to somebody who imme-diately recognised the names of our fathers.

Obama's grandmother spoke Luo and no English and she was pained that he was unable to speak to her. He asked his half-sister to explain that 'it's hard to find time in the States. Tell her how busy I am.' Her translated reply was that she understood, but that 'a man can never be too busy to know his own people'. This completely resonated with my own experiences of being unable to speak Igbo.

While I appear to have coped well with a turbulent childhood, it certainly had some impact on my life. It is not hard to understand why it has been difficult for me to trust men and make long-term relationships. Looking back to my childhood, my grandfather was the only male figure that I related well to and admired. Sadly, I was to know him for only just over a year before his untimely death. Later on there was the great relationship with my Dad, but he was also clearly a bit of a ladies' man.

Ursula:

You have a no nonsense kind of attitude when it came to men. I could see very clearly that you weren't going to take any crap from them! I've seen that many times, you tick them off and your tut, tuts, and the expression on your face as if, you know, what's wrong with that idiot? That's not to say that you didn't admire them, because I remember many a time when we sort of got all excited about the guys we saw.

I have indeed met some great men! The late, great John Holt expressed it best in a line from *Till I'm Gone*, a beautiful reggae song that I love dancing to: 'Don't know why our love can't get together'.

Parenting skills were another area that I did not have too many opportunities to learn about while growing up. I lived with my mother for three periods that totalled just over two years: from birth to six months, from the age of nine for 20 months, and at the age of 16 for a few months at most.

There has also been an effect on my state of health. Azuka observed astutely,

> *As well as your asthma from childhood, I think that your stress and high blood pressure came out as you've got older, due to years of bottling things up. I've only seen you cry twice in my life. Once was during my fiery teenage years and the other was at Gran's funeral.*

The fact that none of this got out of hand is due to all the family members, individuals, friends and organisations who rescued and helped me. Their support has made such a difference to who I am today.

Music has always played a crucial role in calming me down when life gets far too stressful – and someone who has played an important role in this respect is my cousin-in-law Elaine. She has also been such a great source of support and friendship, together with her four wonderful children Ngozi, Ndidi, Ife and Nnamdi.

Elaine grew up in the Dutch West Indian island of Aruba and she introduced me to the sublime sounds of the late Dutch contralto, Aafje Heynis. Whenever I feel really tense, the track I turn to is her singing *Dank sei Dir, Herr* (*Thanks be to God*). As well as being incredibly relaxing and uplifting, it is absolutely glorious. It reminds me how much I appreciate everybody who has helped to make my life so rewarding and enjoyable.

Last but not least come my daughter Azuka and granddaughter Rhianne. My mother bore a terrible brunt in becoming a single mother back in 1947, in contrast to the more recent (and less stressful) experiences of Azuka and myself – although we have all benefited from her incredible determination. In the process we have become strong, independent mothers and successful women in our chosen careers. What will Rhianne make of this complex and diverse heritage?

Here's how Azuka has summed it all up:

I think you've got a great story and an unusual story, because you've overcome a lot. You're an open minded, peaceful, loving person. Some people go through all that stuff and can become bitter, angry, depressed, or use drugs. Just one of those experiences you went through could send someone over the edge. So I think it's an incredibly positive and unique story, and it's funny as well! A lot of people will relate to it, some aspects more than others. I was thinking about the film The Butler *as it reminded me of you a bit. You've lived through so many big changes in history. That Nelson Mandela quote sums you up: 'A good mind and a good heart can do great things.'*

Last photo with Mum, taken by
Azuka, September 2003

Chatting with Rhianne on day of the
unveiling of Mary Seacole Memorial
Statue, captured by Azuka

With Azuka and granddaughter Rhianne, March 2016

Footnotes

1. http://www.bbc.co.uk/programmes/p0342x00

2. https://archive.org/stream/chroniclesofcoun00grif/
chroniclesofcoun00grif_djvu.txt

3. http://www.killowenhistory.com/wordpress/?p=12

4. http://www.britainfromabove.org.uk Search for 'The Longbridge Motor
Works and Nazareth House, Longbridge, 1928'. Image reference: EPW024829

5. http://www.independent.co.uk/news/
nuns-abused-hundreds-of-children-1171988.html (1998) and
http://www.theguardian.com/world/2003/apr/12/religion.childprotection (2003)

6. http://nma.gov.au/blogs/inside/files/2011/04/Ray-Brand-3.pdf

7. www.huntleysonline.com

8. This was a far cry from the dreadful experience of adopted Scottish/
Nigerian writer Jackie Kay, as set out in *Red Dust Road* (2010). She
describes travelling to Nigeria to meet her Igbo father for the first time.
Now an evangelical preacher, he tries to transfer his guilt and shame on to
her in a series of bizarre attempts at exorcist-type preaching.

9. Know Onitsha Families. 3rd Edition. (1989) Eke-Prince P.O. Ekwerekwu.
Onitsha, Nigeria.

10. https://markcurtis.wordpress.com/2007/02/13/nigeriabiafra-1967-70/

11. It was interesting to read in Pauline Prescott's 2010 autobiography *Smile
Though Your Heart is Breaking* that her long lost son Paul, who had been
adopted, engineered the same action between his biological parents. He had
discovered that his father was living in the USA and it was the first time
that his mother and father had spoken together in 50 years.

12. https://rememberolivemorris.wordpress.com

13. Watching television on New Year's Day in 2007 I saw Professor Levinsky's image appear and was shocked to hear the news. Now Vice-Chancellor of the University of Plymouth, he had been electrocuted during a storm by a trailing live power cable.

14. Or 'Cool, Black and Exceptional' as suggested by a friend.

15. http://www.bbc.co.uk/programmes/b07h2vm1

16. www.tangledroots.eu

17. www.facebook.com/Mixed-Race-Irish

Acknowledgements

All of the following people have been extremely helpful to me during the process of producing these memoirs. Many kindly agreed to be interviewed and my thanks to Nalini Patel for transcribing the interviews and to all those who have provided assistance in numerous other ways. I am extremely grateful to you all and apologise for any omissions.

Dr Elizabeth Dormandy has been an incredibly supportive and critical friend to me throughout the entire writing of this book. Our regular meetings and lunches at Friends House in London made all the hard work that much more enjoyable!

Also, huge thanks to Catherine Gough of Fine Words for a wonderfully calm approach and for her expert and speedy editing.

Now to all my Furlong and Anionwu family members in the UK, Nigeria and the USA! You have really gone out of your way to help me and I have really appreciated all the support and enthusiasm from so many relatives. They include Aunts Pat Glass, Doreen Furlong and Nwachinemelu Joy Anionwu; sisters Marion and Pam, brother Frank; cousins Chinyelugo Osita Anionwu, Ugobueze Joy Ikeme Arah, Dave Glass, Anne Kearsley and Elaine Unegbu.

My appreciation to all my lovely friends for all the information and advice provided: Akunne Abadom and family, Akunnia Ejor

Abomile and family, Juliet Alexander, Suzette Alleyne, Professor Karl Atkin, Dr Carol Barton, Alan Beattie, Ann Clwyd MP, Dr Moira Dick, Sandra Edwards, Franca Egbuche, Rose Grant, Jean Gray, Dada Imarogbe, Dr Baba Inusa, Wendy Irwin, John James, Ursula Johnson, Mariama Kabba, Felicia Kwaku, Marvlyn Le Fleurier, Sarah Massengale-Gregg, Dr Alison May, Mia Morris, Joan Myers OBE, Freddie Onyechi, Nina Patel, Professor Marcus Pembrey, Michelle Pickard, Sue Rees, Joan Saddler OBE, Paelo Saddler, Ramesh Seewoodhary, Janet Shea-Simonds, Megan Thomas, Jackie Wetherill and Alison Winter.

A special thank you to the late John Roberts CBE, QC for finding my father. Also to Siobhán Clemons, Team Leader – Origins Service, Father Hudson's Care for her sensitive and helpful manner in responding to my enquiries.

Ben Galley, publishing consultant, ShelfHelp is greatly appreciated for all his helpful advice.

My thanks also to professional genealogists Megan Owens and Records Ireland, Irish Family History Research Service together with Wolverhampton Archives and Local Studies.

I am also very grateful to Malorie Blackman OBE, writer and former Children's Laureate for her wonderful Foreword.

Professor Jane Cummings, Chief Nursing Officer for England and Conrad Bryan, co-founder Association of Mixed Race Irish, kindly set aside time to read my memoirs and provided extremely positive feedback – their quotes have been hugely appreciated!

Finally, a very special word of thanks to my daughter Azuka and granddaughter Rhianne for their constant love and encouragement.

Acknowledgements

Every effort has been made to trace copyright holders and to obtain their permission for the use of copyright material. The author apologizes for any errors or omissions and would be grateful if notified of any corrections that should be incorporated in future reprints or editions of this book.

Lightning Source UK Ltd.
Milton Keynes UK
UKOW01f0216300917
310150UK00006B/267/P